Improving school effectiveness

Edited by
John MacBeath and Peter Mortimore

Open University Press
Buckingham · Philadelphia

Open University Press
Celtic Court
22 Ballmoor
Buckingham
MK18 1XW

email: enquiries@openup.co.uk
world wide web: www.openup.co.uk

and
325 Chestnut Street
Philadelphia, PA 19106, USA

First Published 2001

A catalogue record of this book is available from the British Library

ISBN   0 335 20687 5 (pb)   0 335 20688 3 (hb)

Library of Congress Cataloging-in-Publication-Data
Improving school effectiveness/edited by John MacBeath and Peter Mortimore.
        p. cm.
    Includes bibliographical references and index.
    ISBN 0-335-20688-3 – 0-335-20687-5 (pbk.)
        1. School improvement programs–Scotland–Case studies.   I. MacBeath,
    John E. C.   II. Mortimore, Peter.

    LB2822.84.G7 I67 2001
    371.2'009411–dc21

                                                            00-060652

Typeset by Type Study, Scarborough
Printed in Great Britain by St Edmundsbury Press Ltd, Bury St Edmunds, Suffolk

Contents

Biographical notes

● **Project directors**

Professor John MacBeath OBE is Chair of Educational Policy and Leadership and Fellow of Hughes Hall at the University of Cambridge. Prior to this he was Director of the Quality in Education Centre at the University of Strathclyde. He has contributed to policy development in Scotland on school self-evaluation and is a member of the Government Task Force on Standards in England. International consultancies include Organisation in Economic Cooperation and Development (OECD), United Nations Educational, Scientific, and Cultural Organization (UNESCO), the European Commission and the Bertelsmann Foundation. He is currently consultant to the Hong Kong Department of Education on school effectiveness and improvement.

Professor Peter Mortimore OBE was the Director of the Institute of Education from 1994 until 2000 and the Pro-Vice-Chancellor of London University for 1999/2000. He is internationally renowned for his research on school effectiveness. He is currently the president of the British Educational Research Association. Among the books he has co-authored are *Fifteen Thousand Hours*; *School Matters*; *The Road to Improvement* and, most recently, *The Culture of Change*.

● **The team**

Dr Brian Boyd is senior lecturer in education at the University of Strathclyde. He was formerly headteacher of two comprehensive schools in Scotland and was chief adviser for Strathclyde. He has published widely on Scottish education and was section editor and contributor to *Scottish Education* (EUP 1999).

Jim Doherty was headteacher of a Glasgow inner city comprehensive from 1982 to 1989. The school catered additionally for children for whom other schools seemed unable to make adequate provision, especially those who had been excluded. He is now an independent consultant specializing in the role of critical friendship in school improvement. He is currently working on a major school improvement project with 19 schools in Newcastle and Gateshead.

Stewart Jardine was headteacher at Carrick Academy from 1982 to 1990 and subsequently a Chief Inspector with Strathclyde's Quality Assurance Unit for five years. He is currently an independent consultant, working with Her Majesty's Inspectorate (HMI) Audit Unit and various education authorities throughout the UK in the fields of self-evaluation, quality management and school improvement.

Professor Jim McCall is in the Department of Educational Studies at the University of Strathclyde and was Dean of the Faculty of Education until 1997. A former teacher, head of department and college vice-principal, his research interests lie in the general area of learning, teaching and assessment and of their interaction with school effectiveness and school improvement. Most recently he has been involved in the development of resources for use in the New Community Schools initiative in Scotland.

Dr Barbara MacGilchrist is a very experienced practitioner and academic. She is the Dean of Initial Teacher Education at the Institute of Education, University of London. Two recent books, *Planning Matters* and *The Intelligent School*, have been extremely well received by practitioners across the school sector. The main focus of her work is seeking to raise standards through improving the quality of teaching and learning in classrooms.

Dr Jenny Reeves is a Senior Lecturer at the University of Stirling and is currently working as National Development Officer for the Scottish Qualification for Headship. Her particular interests lie in the professional development of school leaders and managers and the use of school-based approaches to continuing professional development (CPD).

Pamela Robertson is an English and psychology graduate and has taught in all education sectors. Now a director of Education & Software Consultants Ltd, working on UK, Scottish, national and local authority development and evaluation projects, she was the ISEP manager and a lead researcher in the Quality in Education Centre, University of Strathclyde from 1993 to 1998. Current projects span early years to lifelong learning and many employ innovative information technology (IT) approaches.

Pam Sammons is a Professor in Education at the London Institute of Education and is Coordinating Director of its International School Effectiveness and Improvement Centre. She has been involved in many major studies of both primary and secondary schools over the last 18 years including *Forging Links: Effective Schools and Effective Departments* (Paul Chapman 1997) and *School*

Matters (Paul Chapman 1994). Her latest book is *School Effectiveness: Coming of Age in the 21st Century* (Swets & Zeitlinger 1999).

Rebecca Smees has a background in psychology and statistics and is currently a research officer at the London Institute of Education. She has been involved in value-added projects at both primary and secondary school level, for local education authorities such as Lancashire, Jersey and Surrey. She is also involved in research into pupils' attitudes in Lancashire and Scotland.

Iain Smith is a senior educational consultant with the Quality in Education Centre. He has worked for 25 years in teacher education, in both Scotland and England. He specializes in management development training and consultancy and has worked extensively overseas for a variety of international organizations.

Louise Stoll is Professor in Education at the University of Bath. Previously she was a primary teacher, researcher on *School Matters*, research director on the Halton Effective Schools Project in Ontario, Canada and, until December 1998, Coordinating Director of the International School Effectiveness and Improvement Centre at the Institute of Education. Current and recent projects include the Improving School Effectiveness Project (ISEP), the Capacity for Change project for the European Commission, and Learning in the Middle Years, funded by GWIST. Publications include *Changing Our Schools* (1996 – with Dean Fink), *No Quick Fixes: Perspectives on Schools in Difficulty* (1998 – edited with Kate Myers), and *It's About Learning* (forthcoming – with Dean Fink and Lorna Earl).

Sally Thomas trained as a psychologist and over the last 17 years has worked at both Oxford University and the London School of Economics. She is currently a senior research lecturer and directs several projects including the Lancashire Value Added project. Her research interests include school evaluation, effectiveness and improvement, assessment, multilevel modelling and international comparisons. She has acted as a consultant to various international projects, funded by the Economic and Social Research Council (ESRC), European Union, Ofsted, the Department for Education and Employment (DfEE) and the Department for Education in Northern Ireland (DENI) among others.

David Toal has a background in social sciences and research methods, and is currently a research assistant and postgraduate research student with the Quality in Education Centre at the University of Strathclyde. Most recently he has been involved in a number of national and regional projects, including the New Community Schools initiative in Scotland and the Evaluation of West Lothian Challenge Fund Projects. He has presented papers of his work at the Scottish Education Research Association (SERA), the British Educational Research Association (BERA) and the International Congress for School Effectiveness and Improvement (ICSEI).

Introduction

School effectiveness is an issue that has occupied researchers and policy makers for three decades. No country facing the demands of the twenty-first century can afford to be indifferent to the questions it raises. All countries of the world are concerned to make their schools more effective, to enhance quality and raise standards of achievement. Yet despite an international library of studies we are still unable to say with confidence how ineffective schools become effective, or indeed to agree on what would constitute an effective school for the third millennium.

In this book we try to address these issues, refracted through the lens of a study in one country between 1995 and 1997. The Improving School Effectiveness project (ISEP) took place in Scotland, but its themes were international. However unique the context and history of one country, the issues it addressed had familiar resonances in countries of the Pacific Rim, the Americas, Africa and Europe. The ISEP team, from the University of Strathclyde and London's Institute of Education, brought to the Scottish study experience of work in all those disparate cultures and were able to test the Scottish experience against other systems, other ways of doing things.

This did not lead us to simple or universal solutions. Rather it sharpened our awareness of culture and history as key factors in understanding schools. There was, however, a common determinant which cut across all cultures – the interrelationship of the three sets of players who make schools work – teachers, pupils and parents. It is with these relationships that the story of school effects began and it is with 'the power of three' as Peter Coleman (1998) describes it, that the story of improvement will continue to be told.

The Improving School Effectiveness project was in many respects a classical effectiveness study, applying statistical techniques to a large sample of schools and studying the 'outliers' – those adding most and least values in terms of pupils' achievements and attitudes. In other respects it was, however, quite unique. The impetus for improvement came from the feedback of data – achievement and attitudinal – to schools to explore, refine and use as a basis for development planning and practical improvement strategies. The in-depth study of 24 of the 80 project schools opened the door to more ethnographic methodologies, revealing the inner life of schools and identifying the brakes and accelerators of improvement.

Chapter 3, which describes the project's aims and structure, is one possible starting point for reading this book. An alternative beginning to the story is Chapter 2, which sets the scene in Scotland, describing the place of ISEP in its political and policy context. It includes first-hand evidence from the Chief Inspector who was responsible for commissioning the study, revealing some of the thinking that made it a project of its time.

Chapter 1 provides the international frame for the book as a whole. It considers what we learned from the school effectiveness/school improvement movement and points to some of the lessons still to be learned.

Chapter 4 is a key chapter, summarizing as succinctly as we were able a very large and significant body of quantitative data. It confirms once again that schools do make a difference, but that their effects are more powerful at different stages in a child's career, with differing effects for boys and girls and for different areas of learning.

Chapter 5 shifts the focus from attainment to attitudes. It examines the views of three sets of stakeholders – pupils, parents and teachers – and what those views reveal about a school's vitality and responsiveness to the expectations held of it. Links between attainment and attitudes reveal important issues for both policy and practice.

Chapter 6 explores some of the qualitative data, focusing in particular on the views of teachers and headteachers, grappling with the three themes at the heart of the project – ethos, school development planning, and learning and teaching. How teachers conceptualize these says much about a school's capacity for meeting change proactively and effectively.

This theme is taken further in Chapter 7, which digs deeper into the process of development planning and the different meanings that term assumes in different schools. It raises the question, Does the sophistication of thinking about 'development' provide an indicator of a school's capacity for handling change?

Chapter 8 describes the role and impact of the critical friends who worked with the 24 case study schools. It examines some of the dilemmas they encountered and teases out the dos and don'ts of critical friendship.

The role of the critical friend is further elaborated in Chapter 9, working with one of the school improvement tools – the change profile. The context is one secondary school in an area of multiple deprivation. How the school used feedback of data is also discussed.

Individual case studies of schools are also the focus of Chapter 10. Two primary schools are compared, both in similar socio-economic contexts but meeting that challenge in wholly different ways. Their respective capacities for longer term improvement are considered factor by factor.

The final chapter returns to some of the themes of Chapter 1, but takes a prospective rather than a retrospective look. What of the future? What do we want from our schools in the new millennium and how can we ensure that we get it?

This journey through the Improving School Effectiveness project will, we hope, give an insight into one study in one country, but more than that – it highlights the issues facing all countries of the world struggling to improve their schools.

As a research team, we have learned a lot from this project and applied its lessons in many other contexts. The questionnaires have been adapted and used in major projects in English authorities and in Northern Ireland. They have been translated into many other languages and used by individual schools as well as by state and provincial administrations. The change profile provided the inspiration for the 'self-evaluation' profile used in 101 schools in 18 European countries (MacBeath *et al.* 2000). Most of all, the ISE project has helped us, and others with whom we have worked in the last few years, to appreciate more deeply how good data can be used by schools themselves to grow and surpass their own expectations.

School effectiveness and improvement: the story so far

John MacBeath and Peter Mortimore

We have entered a new millennium with sophisticated science and spectacular technology but still without the knowledge of how to educate all our children. We have discovered how to engineer the blueprint of living beings but we are still searching for an environment in which children can learn with enjoyment and effect.

School has been entrusted with the educational task and been accepted from generation to generation as fulfilling its remit honestly and ethically. Alternatives to school have been tried and for the most part have enjoyed a brief life. Schooling has become such an integral feature of the social and economic landscape that it is almost impossible to conceive of different approaches to educating children, at least in their pre-adolescent years.

Politicians and policy makers have a specific interest in the here and now and are constrained to work within the boundaries of what their constituents expect of an educational system. So, having promoted education to the forefront of policy they have to make schools work, to make them work more effectively and within a political lifetime. 'Raising standards' has retained its pre-eminent place in the transition from the second to the third millennium, proof of which has to be demonstrated within the parameters of school, school curriculum and school assessment. Seeking evidence to support their policies, governments have had a rich fund of effectiveness research on which to draw, not only in the United Kingdom but on a worldwide basis.

From the researchers' viewpoint, it is a matter of concern that policy makers do not draw deeply enough on the well, nor with the caution and circumspection that the data demand. From the policy point of view this appears as ambivalence and equivocation when what is needed is clear-cut answers to straightforward policy questions. In reality, school effectiveness research has contributed massively to policy formation, but the challenge to governments and educational gatekeepers is to have the courage to listen more intently to what researchers in this field are saying and where the research is leading us. While impolitic for those in seats of government openly to change their mind, it is the first moral imperative for the researcher when presented with evidence, new frames of reference and alternative paradigms.

This counterpoint of policy conviction and research caution has been characteristic of the movement of ideas in school effectiveness nationally and internationally over the last two decades. SE (to use an abbreviation that is often applied) has been charged by its critics with being defensive and precious, a charge to which we must on occasion plead guilty. It has at times set in opposition a school effectiveness 'camp' and a school improvement 'camp', as if these two were not integrally and umbilically related. Researchers have too often talked to one another rather than to teachers or parents and their language has often been impenetrable and self-referring. But the movement has also been open to robust critique and has learned from its critics. It has grown in complexity and sophistication. It has expanded its boundaries, widened its thinking, challenged its own premises. In short, we have learned.

We have learned:

- that school education cannot compensate for society and that in making high demands of teachers and raising our expectations of schools we must have scrupulous respect for the evidence on socio-economic inequality and the changing nature of family and community life;
- that schools can make a difference and that being in an effective as against a less effective school is a crucial determinant of life chances for many individual young people;
- that 'effects' are complex and multilayered and that while schools of themselves can make a difference there are even more significant effects at the level of department and classroom;
- that children experience schools differently; that achievement is not a simple linear progression but subject to ebbs and flows over time and in response to the influence of the peer group and pupils' own expectations on the basis of gender, race and social class;
- that the context of national culture is a powerful determinant of parent, student and teacher motivation and that school improvement requires more than simplistic borrowing of remedies from other countries;
- that we are learning, and still have a lot to learn, about how schools improve and what kind of support and challenge from external sources is most conducive to their effective development;
- that a salient dimension of school improvement is helping schools to be more confident in the use of their own and other data, more self-critical and more skilled in the use of research and evaluation tools;
- that we will only make dramatic advances in educational improvement, in and beyond schooling, when we develop a deeper understanding of how people learn and how we can help them to learn more effectively.

● The unequal society

Our country has been exceptional in that the difference between the 'haves' and 'have nots' seems to have resulted from official policies designed to lift the constraints affecting the rich. These policies have sought to penalise the poor in the interest of freeing them from the so-called 'dependency culture'. Britain stands out internationally, along with New Zealand, in having experienced the largest percentage increase in income inequality between 1967 and 1992.

(Mortimore and Whitty 1997: 2)

In the last two decades many countries, the United Kingdom included, have witnessed a progressive rise in standards of living. However, this statistical mean conceals the fact that the number of people living in poverty has increased threefold since 1979. The distance between rich and poor, privileged and underprivileged has grown progressively during the Thatcher and post-Thatcher years and the proportion of children living in poor households is now 32 per cent, compared to the European Union average of 20 per cent.

Writing in the *Independent on Sunday* (19 September 1999) Professor Piachaud of the London School of Economics concludes: 'My research shows that in five years from the election of New Labour, poverty will have been reduced by nearly two million, child poverty by some 800,000. This is real progress, yet poverty in 2002 will still be twice what it was when Labour left office in 1979.'

That still leaves four million children in households below the poverty level. While poverty is both relative and ill-defined, the four million are in families with below half the average income, that is an annual income of £10,000 for a two-children family. While this does not preclude the possibility of a caring and supportive environment for children, it does significantly weight the odds and affect the balance of priorities in both home life and school life.

The beginnings of a movement

It is with the unequal society that the story of school effectiveness research begins. It was the concern for equality of educational opportunity in the 1960s that prompted the first two major systematic studies of school effects entitled *Equality of Educational Opportunity* (Coleman *et al.* 1966) and *Inequality: A Reassessment of Family and Schooling in America* (Jencks *et al.* 1972).

The American Congress in the 1960s was looking to schools to help redress the deep social and racial divisions and, in commissioning the Coleman study, they hoped to find a solution. The solution hoped for was seen as coming through some form of school restructuring. However, Coleman and Jencks were to draw disappointing conclusions from their studies, the singular message being that if greater equality were to be the goal it would have to be addressed by what happened outside schools rather than within them.

The sixties and seventies were decades when the issue was also at its most live in Britain. A retrospective review of educational literature through the

1960s (Mortimore and Blackstone 1982) reflects the tenor of those two major American studies – the pervasive influence of social class as a key determinant of school achievement. However much the Coleman and Jencks thesis might be recognised as valid, there was nonetheless an optimism in Britain that schools could be better, could be more egalitarian, could reach out to the most disadvantaged communities. That was the message of the Plowden Report of 1967 with its promise of educational priority areas to tackle disadvantage at its roots. With the wisdom of revisionism, the 1970s have been characterized as an era of betrayal by the educational establishment, an establishment which put equality before quality and, self-indulgently, lowered rather than raised expectations of working-class children (Phillips 1996). 'Social engineering' it is said, and was said then (Cox and Dyson 1968), is not the job of schools nor the remit of teachers. Their task is quite simply 'to teach'. This is a view that has not only persisted but grown in strength, reinforced through selective use of research which has underlined the importance of classroom-level or individual teacher effects.

Whatever the failings of schools in the seventies and eighties, such a critique is both simplistic and damaging because it turns a fastidious blind eye to the massive changes in society which have occurred in the last two decades. The scale of social transformation presents schools and teachers with a challenge on a scale never before encountered nor foreseen. To be successful, the class-room teacher has to be a clever engineer of attitudes and beliefs, of both children and their parents, and to counteract other powerful shapers of opinion. Ironically, as knowledge has become more widely accessible and more complex, it has been increasingly simplified by the media, widening the information gap between the knowledge haves and have nots (Aronowitz and De Fazio 1994).

The facile appeal of the following illustrates how 'evidence' may be used as a bedfellow of simple 'common sense':

> I do not accept the argument that a child who has a free school lunch is a child who will necessarily find it difficult to read . . . If they are fortunate enough to have it [a good teacher], then, as test and inspection evidence shows, there is no reason why they cannot do as well as children from more privileged backgrounds.
>
> (Woodhead 1998: 22)

The simple, and deliberate, confusion in the quote is one of correlation and causality. It is one that effectiveness researchers have persistently under-scored in an attempt to educate and not mislead either the general public or policy makers. The recourse of researchers to free meal entitlement (FME) is exemplary. It does no more than serve as a proxy for social background but as such presents an easy target for those who choose to misread its purpose. However imperfect a measure/factor, it serves as a pointer to deep-seated underlying sets of connections between families and school, between social conditions and classroom learning, between valued school knowledge and cultural capital.

There is immense potential for a fruitless debate between those who claim that failure is the product of inadequate families and those who counter that it is down to inadequate schools. Much more helpful is the kind of explanation that posits an interactionist perspective. James Coleman puts it in these terms: 'The resources devoted by the family to the child's education interact with the resources provided by the school – and there is a greater variation in the former resources than in the latter' (Coleman 1995: 369).

Our own school and social experiences offer intuitive confirmation that schools vary in the quality of what they provide but that between the most educationally rich and most educationally impoverished families there lies an even greater world of difference. That disparity, a disparity of cultural and social capital, is not merely a matter of income disparity between richest and poorest, but is related to and affected by what families can 'afford' in the widest sense of that term (Feuerstein *et al.* 1980).

Parental income is significantly correlated with school achievement and a powerful correlate of social malaise, but it offers a less telling story than the one whose account interweaves the cumulative inequities of inadequate housing, dangerous communities, chronic ill health, poor diet, and day-to-day struggle for survival. This is the legacy passed through generations. It is the poverty 'trap', as we are used to calling it, a trap made not simply because people are materially poor but because the quality of opportunity offers no obvious avenues of escape. Even the most brilliant of schools cannot compensate for such a society.

Deprivation of opportunities to mature healthily and confidently in early childhood not only constrains intellectual development but expectations of life itself. Expectations and self-conceptions are culturally conditioned, embedded in the society and passed on from generation to generation. This is illustrated by a comparison of British and American social attitudes (Institute of Fiscal Studies 1998). Asked whether they had a good chance of improving their standards of living, 72 per cent of Americans said they had, compared with 37 per cent of British respondents (Freedland 1998: 128). A further finding of that study, that 80 per cent of children from families of unskilled workers left school at 16, illustrates how the aspirational culture reflects and perpetuates itself (Freedland 1998: 129).

Equality of educational opportunity is what schools continue to strive for, even as the gap between richest and poorest, privileged and underprivileged continues to widen. Equality is a fragile concept. Making schools and curriculum 'available' to all was described by Anthony Crosland as the 'weak' concept of equality (Boyle and Crosland 1971: 51) because it comes with no obligation on the part of the school to make it happen. Providing opportunity to learn for all children, on the other hand, requires an immense exercise in engineering on the part of the individual teacher, the team, the department, the whole school working in concert with agencies beyond the school gate. It is a complex and sophisticated task. It requires the school to find the articulation between family and school need. It means recognizing commonalities and differences in priorities and expectations between school and home.

Schools may require, but cannot provide, the prior childhood experiences that lay the foundations for success. They can seek, but cannot vouchsafe from parents, the promise of continuing support for children's emotional stability and academic achievement. Without that, children can find themselves swept along by a sequential age- and competence-related curriculum and, as well documented by Robert Slavin (1995), a self-generating downward spiral of low self-esteem, low achievement and reduced motivation. The direction of the spiral may be reversed when schools reach out to families and communities in new ways with new insights into learning. The good news, as Slavin and others have shown, is that schools can make a difference.

● Schools can make a difference

From a commonsensical point of view it is obvious that schools make a difference, that from entrance at the age of 5 to exit at the age of 18, an educational transformation has taken place. The simplicity of the headline claim masks a much more fundamental set of questions, however. These are the questions that Coleman and Jencks set out to address and that three decades of research studies have since explored in finer and more discriminating detail.

For Coleman and Jencks the question was primarily about social determinism as against school malleability. Could schools promote achievement for all regardless of social background and ethnic origin? While keeping these issues in their sights, studies that followed came at the issue by comparing schools to determine if some were more effective than others. If this could be shown, it would not only undermine the schools-don't-make-much-of-a-difference hypothesis but, more constructively, point to where the key determinants of 'better' or 'more effective' schools lay.

The unambiguous finding from three decades of studies across the world (Brookover *et al.* 1979; Rutter *et al.* 1979; Mortimore *et al.* 1988; Scheerens 1997) is that schools do indeed make a difference. While social background continues to play a strong influential role, schools are not helpless in promoting educational and social mobility. In other words, there is a 'school effect'. While studies between and within countries come to different conclusions about the magnitude of the school effect, there is a broad consensus that it lies somewhere in the region of 5 to 15 per cent. That is, with all other factors held constant, there is a 5 to 15 per cent variance between more and less effective schools.

This is, on the face of it, perhaps disappointing and not as far away from the Coleman and Jenck's estimates as might have been hoped for. However, the *School Matters* study (Mortimore *et al.* 1988) found that disadvantaged students did make more progress in more effective schools than their counterparts in the least effective schools. When translated into life chances for a pupil, or cohort of pupils, its significance becomes more graphically apparent. For example, in England this could be translated as a difference for the average pupil of seven grade Cs instead of six grade Es at GCSE (Thomas and Mortimore 1994).

In Scotland, studies at Edinburgh's Centre for Educational Sociology (Gray *et al.* 1983; Cuttance 1988; McPherson 1992) translated effectiveness as gaining one or more O Grades (GCSEs) more than expected. In the Netherlands it is described in terms of pupils in a five-ability stream school performing at two streams higher (Brandsma and Dollard 1996). In the Belgian context it is described in the following terms, drawing on Grisay's (1996) study:

> Let's say that at the end of your primary school you have a test in Maths and that you are 500th out of 1000 pupils. Now you have a choice of two secondary schools. Chances are that one will be more effective than the other. If you attend the more effective of the two you might rise to 420th out of 1000 after two years in this school while if you go to the second of the two schools you would be about 580th. However, if you attend the most effective as against the very least effective the difference could be as much as a ranking of 680th rank as compared with 320th.
>
> (MacBeath *et al.* 2000)

Findings such as these reflect the methodology of mainstream school effectiveness research which looks for 'outliers', that is, unusually effective schools, comparing these either with the norm or with schools at the opposite polarity – particularly ineffective schools. It is from these more effective schools that factors of effectiveness are derived. While less attention has been given to the characteristics of ineffective schools, research in this area may, in the long term, prove equally instructive.

Characteristics of effective and ineffective schools

Studies of effectiveness are now so numerous that it would take a voluminous publication to list them all. USA studies alone filled 41 pages in a 1995 review by North West Educational Laboratories (NREL 1989). A 1997 review by Bosker and Scheerens of seminal studies (those meeting specific methodological criteria) listed 719 factors that had been found to be associated with effectiveness. In a meta-analysis (Sammons *et al.* 1996), these were reduced to 11 salient factors:

1 professional leadership;
2 shared vision and goals;
3 a learning environment;
4 concentration on learning and teaching;
5 high expectations;
6 positive reinforcement;
7 monitoring progress;
8 pupil rights and responsibilities;
9 purposeful teaching;
10 a learning organization;
11 home–school partnership.

To what extent can we then characterize ineffective schools as lacking in these 11 features? It is, as Myers argues (1994), not that simple. She describes 'troubled' schools as having 'antithetical' characteristics, their cultures a product of myriad influences at work. 'Troubled' schools in her study (1996) tended to have their own individual clustering of factors, a dynamic mix of student ambivalence, low staff expectations, a pervasive negative ethos, weak or inconsistent leadership.

These find close echoes in other studies. Rosenholtz (1989) compared high-consensus ('moving') and low-consensus ('stuck') schools, finding in the latter a lack of attachment, more concern with their own identity than with a shared community of purpose. Their school environments were 'unfree' and characterized by boredom, punitiveness and self-defensiveness. Gray and Wilcox (1994) conclude: 'We still suspect that there are problems and barriers to change which are specific to "ineffective" schools but which the research has not yet teased out' (p. 16).

Reviewing his own research, Reynolds (1995) suggests that it is easy, and mistaken, to make assumptions about what ineffectiveness is and what the differences are between failure on the one hand and lack of success on the other: '. . . people like me have implicitly back-mapped the characteristics of the effective school on to the ineffective school, thinking that what the ineffective school has is the absence of things that make the effective school effective . . . We have, in short, only viewed failure as not being successful, not as failure' (pp. 66–7).

We have not given sufficient attention to the possibility that ineffective schools are driven by factors still to be explained and with an internal dynamic still to be unravelled. Whether our focus is on effectiveness, ineffectiveness or the transition between them, we have had to move on from correlational studies to enquire more deeply into the how rather than the what, not simply what the characteristics are but how they are acquired or lost. Not simply what do effective and ineffective schools look like but how do they get that way?

● Where do effects lie?

Knowing, and being able to demonstrate, that schools can and do make a difference was an important step away from the determinism of the Coleman and Jencks view. However, the general finding that schools matter is tantalizingly elusive because it leaves a host of unanswered questions. We have needed to know more about where effects lie and we have had to test more rigorously what might be hidden more deeply within the 'school effect'.

Consistently outstanding and unambiguously awful schools are the exception. Schools as we know them tend to be a complex mix of good, less good and, occasionally, very bad teachers. In some countries we would find it difficult to detect any overall school effects at all because they could provide little more than a uneven profile of different classes, held together by a common heating system and connecting corridors. In such schools, we might well find very wide differentials between the performance of one class and another, but little influence over and above that which could be ascribed to the school as such.

Schools in the United Kingdom, whether primary, secondary or special, are rarely an aggregation of effective teachers or effective departments. They are led and managed and have whole-school policies, development plans and staff development sessions. There is synergy, and sometimes entropy, at school level, a whole that may either be greater or lesser than the sum of its parts. In other words the school as an organization may add value to that of its individual members or, on the other hand, may subtract value. It may enhance and multiply the skills of its members, or may stifle and inhibit their mutual growth.

In loosely coupled, or virtually uncoupled, schools with little interclass or interdepartmental collaboration, we might expect to find a very large variation in the performance of pupils; in other words, a high degree of inconsistency within the school as a whole. In a well led and managed school, in contrast, we would hope to see less variation and greater consistency both across the school and over time as children move through it year on year – in other words, a quite clearly distinguishable 'school' effect.

This 'consistency' measure has been the focus of considerable research in recent years and is of most relevance to systems, such as in the United Kingdom, where the cross-fertilization from classroom to classroom, subject to subject, is seen as important in enhancing effectiveness at whole-school level, and feeds back down into improved performance at classroom and individual pupil levels.

Teacher effects

The individual classroom and the individual teacher provide a useful starting point for examining effectiveness. An ideal scenario for the researcher would be in a school where children had the same teacher from 6 until 16, as is the case in many schools in Denmark. We might expect to find over a ten-year period a sharp and increasing divergence between effective teacher A and ineffective teacher B which, assuming two comparable classes, might tell a powerful story. We might, on the other hand, find a growing convergence, suggesting other influences at work – school effects or perhaps departmental effects.

Comparison of two, or more, teachers over a lengthy period would offer a measure of two key factors in the assessment of effectiveness – consistency and stability. The different achievements between teacher A's and teacher B's pupils at a given point in time would measure consistency, while the degree of variance over time would provide us with a measure of stability. In practice, both consistency and stability measures are needed if we are to understand the strength of individual teacher effectiveness.

Dutch researchers (Luyten and Snidjers 1996) were able to study two samples of pupils, one who had the same teacher in grades 7 and 8, the other with two teachers in each grade. They concluded that variation is reduced by 20 per cent if the teacher stayed with the class and that 80 per cent of the variation across grades might be attributable to quality differences among teachers.

What most of the research appears to agree on is that teacher effects are powerful and that they are not limited to the time period which pupils spend with that particular teacher. Research tends to confirm what we would expect from anecdotal experience of our own children or our own personal experience – the impact of an effective primary school teacher lingers on into secondary (Sammons *et al.* 1994).

Departmental and subject effects

In secondary schools teachers are members of subject departments. There is normally a subject leader or head and a collegial team that can provide an important locus for sharing of practice, for monitoring, for quality assurance and for professional development. So, we would expect to find at departmental level some effect greater than that of the individual teachers. One study (Luyten 1994) reported a 40 per cent variance at subject department level, with only 15 per cent of the variance attributable to the whole-school effect. In other words, subjects (or departments) make more of a difference to individual achievement and progress than does the particular school attended.

Caution has to be exercised in making such a judgement, however, because we also know something about the different nature of subjects. Children come virtually brand new to some school subjects while others have a longer gestation in their home education. So, for example, reading shows a weaker school effect than mathematics because reading and pre-reading skills are often accomplished before a child starts school while the same is less true for mathematics. This was a finding of Mortimore and his colleagues (1988) and a clear conclusion of ISEP a decade later.

A number of studies in secondary schools (Smith and Tomlinson 1989; Thomas 1995b) found that there was a generally positive correlation among different subjects and between individual subject departments and whole-school effectiveness. But these correlations were not consistently high, some departments within a school being significantly more effective than others. Similarly, across a whole sample of schools, some subjects tended to correlate more consistently with whole-school effects. English and science, for example, related more closely to the composite GCSE score than other subjects. In Scotland there was a similar finding in a 1987 study (Cuttance) and in 1989 (Willms and Raudenbusch). In Chapter 4, Sally Thomas and her colleagues describe the range of positive intercorrelations between subjects in ISEP, but also show that as many as one in three primary schools, and one in four secondaries, have a positive value-added residual in one subject but a negative residual in the other.

Whole-school effects

As the department can add value to the achievements and effects of individual teachers, so the school may be more than a collection of subject enclaves. It may create a synergy, a whole-school effect, by drawing strengths from each department, cross-fertilizing and amplifying best practice across the school. Alternatively, improvement may come from the top down, from directive leadership, school policies, a vision or plan to which departments and teachers 'sign up'. In either case the school effect is of the further value added by the organization as a whole, through its ethos, culture, policy and planning.

Once classroom and departmental effects have been taken into account, most studies tend to show a relatively small school effect. However, the more we move towards a learning organization, the less easy it will become to separate out specific school effects from departmental and classroom effects. In a highly collaborative school in which people teach together and learn together, the differentiation of specific influences will be more difficult to locate. The further we move away from the model of the individual teacher in her classroom, towards teamwork, shared responsibility and corporate professional development, the less easy it will be to isolate the specific contribution of the individual teacher. The high-achieving teacher may not easily be separated from the context in which the achievement takes place. This is why the rewarding of individual achievement, either through 'Platos' (teaching awards) or through performance-related pay, is problematic and resisted by schools which see themselves as collectives and see their achievements as jointly owned.

● Children experience schools differently

Effective schools tend to be good for all their students while all students tend to perform poorly in ineffective schools. While that was a clear finding from the Junior Schools Study in 1988 (Mortimore *et al.*) and in a follow-up ESRC study (Thomas *et al.* 1995a), this is, like many findings, a generalization which is tested by its exceptions. A more recent study (Sammons *et al.* 1998) did find exceptions to the 'rule'. That general principle, sound and commonsensical as it seems, does not appear to hold true in every context or country and may perhaps be subject to change along with changes in the political and cultural climate. For example, pressure on schools to invest heavily in those students most likely to show transparent returns (borderline A–C GCSE students, for example) might achieve that goal at the expense of others who would thrive in a school stronger on learning support.

Some studies have reported varying effects for different types of students. In Scottish schools, Raudenbush and Willms (1988), for example, found that some schools were effective for students of high ability but not low ability and vice versa. In another study, Willms and Kerr (1997) found that some schools were better for girls and some better for boys or for some social groups as against others.

In a recent study, Pam Sammons and her colleagues (1998) have explored the 'differential effectiveness' of schools, showing that not only do some groups of pupils perform better than others but that they do so at different times in their school cycle. Some pupils show spurts of achievement while others reach a plateau and stay there. Others actually regress. Some pupils do well in some subjects and not others, with individual teachers and not with others. In ISEP, as in other studies, we found that girls tend to outperform boys, in some cases allowing boys a head start but gradually overtaking them. There were complex patterns of achievement which became more discernible as pupils moved up through the system.

The evidence from both ISEP and the Sammons study suggests that the longer pupils stay in school, the more pronounced becomes the influence of social class. Is this a school effect or a background effect? That is, does the social background which pupils bring with them exert itself more strongly over time, or is a school constructed in such a way as to accentuate the difference progressively?

While we are able to separate out social class, ethnicity and gender for the purposes of research, it is also clear that it is the interrelationship of these that is truly significant and how they play themselves out in the day-to-day life of classrooms and schools.

> The experience of a low attaining English middle-class girl with parents of Indian background needs to be probed with a more textured understanding of peer group affiliation, racial and sexual harassment, ascribed roles, sub-cultural tensions and parental and teacher expectations. High achieving, African-Caribbean boys may experience particularly acute difficulties in adjusting to the different expectations of peers, teachers, their families and the group identity which defines them not only as a threat to the authority of teachers but to that of the police and others in positions of power.
>
> (MacBeath 1999: 22)

A review of recent research (Gillborn and Gipps 1998) provides a rich and detailed picture of the intersect between individual experience and school life. Drawing on both school effectiveness research and ethnographic studies, the authors conclude that we have still some way to go in understanding how the internal culture of the school works and how it connects, in multiple, interwoven strands, to the world outside.

Martin Thrupp (1999) has criticized effectiveness research for its blindness to the importance of 'social mix', arguing that the key to our understanding is limited only by our ability to probe with enough sensitivity the complexity of peer social interaction. This thesis receives overwhelming support from Judith Harris (1998) in her controversial book *The Nurture Assumption*. Her contention, supported by a considerable body of research, is that the child's identity as a person, her capacity as a learner and her motivation as a student come from the way in which she defines herself within the immediate peer reference group. Gender, race, ability, class, 'academic' or 'non-academic', anti-school or pro-school may be the salient characteristics of one's identity, but only when school structures and the nature of the school social mix push that feature into social prominence.

In an all-girls school, gender is not a salient feature, just as race is not a salient feature in an all-black school and the undesirable status of 'swot' has less currency in a school where selection is by ability. However, in a large racially and socially heterogeneous comprehensive school what becomes a salient feature of a pupil's self-definition arises from a complex social dynamic, constantly shifting as new friendships form and old ones disappear, as the social mix of the school and peer group changes or stabilises. In Harris's thesis young people's most essential experience of schooling is one of defining and redefining themselves in relation to their peers.

Children experience schools differently because they meet different teachers and engage in different ways with the curriculum, but the alliances they form with others may, in the end, prove to be equally or even more powerful in shaping their expectations of achievement. In fact the compositional, or contextual, effect has been recognized by effectiveness researchers for some time. It was identified in a 1985 study in Scotland by Willms and his CES colleagues at the University of Edinburgh (Willms and Cuttance 1985) and returned to in subsequent studies. In 1997 Willms described how the contextual effect had become highlighted and intensified as a consequence of interschool mobility: 'When a pupil with an advantaged background transfers from a low social class to a high social class school, the contextual effect is strengthened for the chosen school and weakened for the school the child left' (Willms 1997: 3).

'We do not fully understand the contextual effect,' concluded the CES team, warning that there may be spurious effects due to inadequate statistical models, 'but taken together with the evidence from other sources we can conclude that it exists and may even be much more powerful than we had previously thought.'

A recent study in Grampian schools was unequivocal in its conclusions about the contextual effect. The researchers (Croxford and Cowie 1996) reported: '. . . serious inequalities in pupils' examination results. The attainment of an average pupil may be raised or lowered by two or three Standard Grades [GCSE equivalent] by differences in school social context' (p. 5).

They go on to say:

The effects of school social context were not the same for all pupils. A school with a high social context has a greater effect in improving attainment of a pupil whose own family background is relatively disadvantaged than of a pupil whose own family background is advantaged. Conversely, a school with a low social context has a more depressing effect on the attainment of a pupil whose own family background is relatively disadvantaged.

(Croxford and Cowie 1996: 5)

In Chapter 4, Thomas *et al.* provide evidence of the compositional effect at work in our 80 ISEP Scottish schools. As researchers we recognize that this is a factor which we may have underestimated in the past or failed to examine with exploratory tools which were sensitive enough. It is clear that the sub-cultural dynamics identified by Hargreaves (1967) in his *Social Relations in a Secondary School* are still as powerfully at work. It is a challenging area for further in-depth inquiry not just by researchers but more critically by schools themselves as they become more experienced and expert in self-evaluation.

● National cultural context is a powerful determinant

As school effectiveness studies have become more international we have become more aware of those aspects of effective schools that 'travel' across cultures and those that don't. Factors such as home–school partnerships and purposeful teaching, for example, appear to have strong international currency, but deeper probing reveals the extent to which structural features of different national systems play a significant part. Scheerens *et al.*'s (1989) reanalysis of data from the Second International Mathematics and Science study found that in some countries there were relatively small differences between one school and the next while in others there was a much higher level of variance. In systems that were vertically differentiated, that is systems in which pupils entered different tracks or schools at a given age, there were large differences in the mean achievements of pupils across schools. This was true of Belgium and the Netherlands, for example.

In more horizontally integrated, or 'comprehensive', systems where pupils moved up together within the same structure (Scottish, American, Swedish, Finnish and New Zealand schools, for example), there were relatively small differences between schools but relatively large differences between classes within schools. France, Canada and Israel belong to this second group insofar as there is relatively little variance between schools, but they also reveal comparatively little variance among classes within schools.

Some of the characteristics identified by Sammons and her colleagues (1998) appear to travel well. Others do not and other factors not in that list emerge in other countries' studies. For example, a French study by Cousin and Guillemet (1992) compared the English results with those in a French context and found some common factors but an equal number that were country-specific.

Postlethwaite and Ross (1992) compared 27 countries on 51 indicators, drawing two key lessons: one, no matter how rigorous and controlled the study, the findings are necessarily exploratory and tentative; two, there was considerable difficulty in using indicators which meant the same thing in different cultural and linguistic contexts. For example, leadership does not emerge as a significant factor in Switzerland or the Netherlands, in part to do with conceptions of 'leadership', in part explained by structural factors.

Researchers may all too easily equate leadership with the person of the head or senior management team, ignoring shared leadership in flatter, more democratic organizations. In the Postlethwaite and Ross study, for example, 'educational leadership' was evaluated on four variables all to do with the behaviour of the principal in consulting with staff and evaluating teachers' work. On the structural side, decentralization to cantons, Länder or regions, and the wide variety of practices within countries, should alert us to the inherent dangers of generalization.

A four-country study of leadership (MacBeath 1998) revealed how differently the Danes, Australians, English and Scots thought of school leadership. While for Scottish and English schools leadership was uncontroversially represented in the person of the headteacher, the Danes insisted on their leadership team (head and depute) being involved in the project. In Australia students saw themselves as exercising an important leadership role in their schools (Dempster and Logan 1998). If leadership as an effectiveness characteristic is assessed by a focus on the head alone, it will inevitably narrow the compass of the study and possibly miss out on the more complex aspects of how leadership expresses itself in day-to-day school and classroom life.

Studies of other countries' practices also run the risk of confusing causality and correlation. For example, many of the high-achieving nations – Singapore, Taiwan, Hong Kong – have large classes, but few would argue that high achievement is a direct product of that factor. More convincing explanations are to be found elsewhere, in the national, community or home culture. Comparing Taiwan with England, Reynolds and Farrell (1996) note a wide range of achievement on entry to junior school in England: 'The heterogeneity of English society and the variation in parental environments, pre-school experiences and infant school quality are likely to be explanations for this' (p. 57).

Japan, another high-achieving country, also benefits from a national culture of achievement. Describing Japan, with its 35,000 private tutorial schools, Gerald Bracey writes: 'Children in Japan often come home from public schools at 3.30 in the afternoon, eat and go on to private school or tutor. They attend school on Saturdays and many go on Sundays as well' (*The American Prospect*, March–April 1998, 37: 68).

In their conclusion to the Ofsted report *Worlds Apart*, Reynolds and Farrell (1997) describe some of the cultural factors that make a difference from one country to another:

- the high status of teachers and the recruitment of high-achieving students into teaching;
- religious traditions and cultural aspirations that place a high value on learning and education;
- Confucian beliefs on the role of effort, striving and working hard;
- high aspirations of parents for their children;
- high levels of commitment from children keen to do well;
- the prevalent belief that all children can acquire core skills.

They point out:

... there is no need for a 'trailing edge' of low performing pupils. This contrasts with the belief in Western societies of the normal distribution, with an elongated tail and 'built in' failure of fifty per cent of the distribution to acquire more than an average level of skill.

(Reynolds and Farrell 1997)

In a case study of Singapore and London schools, the research team draw four key lessons (Mortimore *et al.* 2000: 142):

- There is no single recipe for turning a school around but there are common elements which include motivating staff, focusing on teaching and learning, enhancing the physical environment and changing the culture of the school.
- Improvements must fit in with the grain of society rather than go against it. Indiscriminate borrowing may not achieve the desired results.
- Resources in themselves do not guarantee improvement but help convince staff, parents and students that society believes in the school and is willing to invest.
- Change has to be carried out by the school itself. Friends are important, but change has to come from within.

Sensitivity to history and context does not preclude learning from other countries. Indeed, in a context of globalization this is becoming an educational imperative. But in any borrowing, whether inter-classroom or inter-school, national or international, the message is 'watch and learn, don't copy'.

● How schools improve

Schools change over time. Headteachers come and go. Good teachers are promoted out of the classroom. Weaker teachers sometimes replace stronger ones. Student cohorts change with housing and demographic shifts. Some schools lose direction while others grow in confidence. Schools are subject to so many external pressures that for some it is a difficult task to maintain stability, let alone demonstrate improvement.

One way in which effectiveness researchers have tried to measure stability and improvement is through fluctuations in examination performance. In a 1995 ESRC study (Sammons *et al.* 1995) it was found that schools' results tended to be relatively stable over time (a correlation of 0.8) but that there was variation within subject departments (correlations between subject and whole school of between 0.38 and 0 .92). Gray and his colleagues (1999a) found a progressive rise over the decade of the 1990s in examination performance, with one in ten schools improving at a rate 'ahead of the pack'. Underlying this analysis the research team make a crucial distinction about improvement, identifying tactics, strategies and capacity as three key distinguishing measures of sustainability. Improvement, as measured by student performance, was in most cases at the tactical level – that is, focusing teachers' energies and efforts on how to improve performance. The strategic schools had longer term goals and had delved deeper into student learning. The capacity-building schools were a small minority. They had gone beyond incremental change to restructuring with an emphasis on collegial self-evaluation.

Drawing on Hopkins's (1994) definition of school improvement as 'a strategy for educational change that enhances student outcomes as well as strengthening the school's capacity for handling change' (p. 3), we may posit a two-dimensional matrix, with the vertical axis representing low to high student outcomes and the horizontal measuring low to high capacity for handling change. The improving school, by definition, is located in the high-outcome/high-capacity quadrant, the 'ineffective/stuck' school in the low-outcome/low-capacity quadrant. As Gray *et al.* (1999b) suggest, schools that have and use outcome data in a positive, active way to enhance the capacity of the school as an organization are those most likely to be truly self-improving in the longer term.

Five years ago, Fullan (1995) described the notions of inclusive self-improving schools as 'a distant dream'. Certainly researchers, critical friends and school development teams have found the job of improvement less easy than the politicians would like. These improvement efforts have, however, furnished us with a fairly extensive lexicon of obstacles to improvement. One project (Reynolds 1991, 1992), which failed to 'turn round' a school in Wales, provides some useful insights into blocks to improvement. These included:

- teachers projecting their own deficiencies on to children or their communities;
- teachers clinging on to past practices;
- defences built up against threatening messages from outside;
- fear of failure;
- seeing change as someone else's job;
- hostile relationships among staff;
- seeking safety in numbers (a ring-fenced mentality).

These features were not hard to identify in some of the ISEP schools in which we worked as critical friends. Drawing on Senge's (1990) notion of 'organisational learning disabilities' we identified eight of these (MacBeath 1998) which were so ingrained in the school culture that they militated against any notion of a quick fix. In Chapter 10 some of these issues are explored in more detail in case studies of two primary schools.

School improvement is a slow process because it is about maturation. David Hargreaves (1999) uses the horticultural metaphor of sowing, germinating, thinning, shaping and pruning, showing and exchanging, to describe the process of improvement. We may add to that the most delicate and subtle aspect of progress: grafting – the process by which an organism allows an external source to take root and flourish, and forever change its organic nature. Where there was clear evidence of growth in our ISEP schools, it was in those schools where good ideas were able to take root and flourish. An example of this process in one secondary school is described in Chapter 9.

We were to discover the truth of Argyris and Schon's (1978) dictum that organizations are often less knowledgeable and skilful than their members, and sometimes 'cannot seem to learn what everybody knows' (p. 71). But organizations can also have a collective wisdom that exceeds that of their individual members. A vital indicator of a school's capacity for improvement is its increased learning ability, because as we move towards the learning organization, the culture of the school becomes the knowledge carrier, spanning generations of staff. Writing about 'the attrition of change', Dean Fink (1999) comments:

> Change has to be built into the processes. Change identified with a person has the roots of its own destruction. There has to be loyalty to broader issues. Life cycles of many 'lighthouse' schools have been shortened because people could not shift loyalties from the individual to broader concepts.
>
> (Fink 1999: 277)

The challenge of continuous improvement is to marry culture and structure. Structures without an underpinning culture of improvement are doomed to be ineffective. Strong cultures without sustaining structures will not survive from one generation to the next.

● Schools becoming confident, self-critical and skilled in evaluation

Policy makers have been keen to rank schools, to pinpoint weaknesses and identify areas for improvement. They have been slower to put the tools in the hands of schools themselves, despite the fact that tools of self-evaluation are potentially powerful. A more cynical view might be that it is precisely because of their power that they are best left in the hands of those with a need to circumscribe and control teachers and teaching.

School self-evaluation is, however, developing an unstoppable momentum and schools are gradually becoming more confident in the use of data, more self-critical, more skilled in the use of research and evaluation tools. It is increasingly commonplace for schools to have attainment data for all of their students, including value-added data at the level of the individual pupil, class, department or whole school. With these data at their disposal teachers have the means to track the progress of their pupils and to make more informed and skilled interventions.

This tells only a part of the story, however, and schools more advanced in self-evaluation complement the quantitative data with deeper qualitative probes. For example, using performance data as a basis for sampling, teachers can systematically examine students' work across subjects, across classes and across teaching staff. This may reveal inconsistencies at individual student level, pointing to differential quality of teachers or departments. For example, a student may perform well in one subject but not in another, or with one teacher but not another. Effectiveness researchers are accustomed to uncovering such differential effects, but when used at school level by teachers for teachers it is salutary and revealing. The sensitivity of such self-evaluation within a school presupposes either a very high level of openness and trust among a staff or requires the support of a critical friend to help in the interpretation of data and may require him or her to mediate the impact of unwelcome news.

Schools are also increasingly likely to have attitudinal data from parents, students or staff. This is typically gathered through questionnaires, sometimes complemented by interviews or focus groups. Schools are becoming increasingly skilled in the customizing of questionnaires or other research tools and often benefit from a resident expert who has taken a course, has statistical expertise or a research background. All of these methodologies, once the sole province of researchers, are now accessible by teachers and management. Again (as described in Chapter 9), the support and guidance of a critical friend can help to avoid some of the pitfalls and hazards of home-made research tools or unscientific modes of data collection.

The most powerful use of data for school self-evaluation is as a tin opener for analysis and discussion within a staff, a management team, a group of students or parents.

It is significant that teacher evaluations of Ofsted, however negative, are consistently positive about the *New Framework for School Inspection* (Gray and Wilcox 1997). This is in large part because it puts into the hands of teachers a tool they can use for themselves, whether in preparation for inspection or their own self-evaluation. In a study for the National Union of Teachers (MacBeath 1999) the Ofsted framework was used in a playful way to explore what these criteria really meant to people and how important they were in the daily life of the school. Working with Ofsted criteria and ranking them in order of importance for a school was engaging for people, not only because it began to give them some sense of ownership, but because it generated dialogue and exposed different viewpoints. People did not immediately agree as to what words meant or how important things were. But they didn't want to arrive at a consensus that concealed their differences. They wanted to find patterns of meaning which lay in the spaces between words. This is one of the strengths of self-evaluation and where it takes root. 'A culture attuned to the multiplicity of particulars or differences, in which it seeks to find patterns, may process information more easily than a culture searching for universal and uniform attributes' (Hampden-Turner and Trompenaars 1993: 114).

External evaluators are sometimes prone to make claims for objectivity, as if their vantage point is a more elevated and panoramic one, more far-seeing in its vision than those inside the school, with all the subjective attachments which that implies. However, Hampden-Turner and Trompenaars warn: 'The problem with "objectivity" is that those who claim to have it believe they need to look no further, need listen to no one else, and never alter their convictions. They have the "data" or the "givens". But those pursuing polyocular knowledge will never be satisfied, never know enough' (1993: 114–15).

Clumsy as it may be, the term 'polyocular' draws our attention to the multifaceted nature of knowledge and the deficiencies inherent in singular ways of seeing. When we open up the school to different ways of seeing we have to acknowledge our neglect of the student insight, the student voice. Jean Rudduck's (1996) approach to school improvement through student participation has seemed at times like a single strand in the school improvement tapestry but helpfully reminds us of the inner struggles and search for meaning which tend to elude more quantitative approaches:

> Our broad understanding of what pupils have told us in interviews is that the conditions of learning that are common across schools do not adequately take account of the social maturity of young people, nor of the tensions and pressures they feel as they struggle to reconcile the demands of their social and personal lives with the development of their identity as learners.
>
> (Rudduck *et al.* 1996: 10)

As we begin to appreciate how students make meaning of their school life we learn how different the school can be for different children. Qualitative researchers such as Dennis Thiessen (1995), Michael Fielding (1999) and Susan Groundwater-Smith (1999) have shown us that there are still deeper layers to be explored. Thiessen (1997) draws distinctions between 'knowing about students' perspectives, 'acting on behalf of students' perspectives, and 'working with students' perspectives. We are increasingly skilled in the first of these – speaking on their behalf. We have to become better at the third of these – helping students to speak for themselves and to work with them in the business of school improvement. Groundwater-Smith has added a fourth level to Thiessen's trilogy – 'acting with students in partnership, to improve and change their lifeworld conditions' (1999: 4).

The ISE project provided us with an opportunity to do more and learn more in this respect and gave us greater confidence to build on this in future work (for example, MacBeath *et al.* 2000).

● Deeper understanding of how people learn

The more we peel back the layers of effective, and less effective, schools, the closer we get to the core of what makes a school work – a commitment to, and joy in, learning. The more we do this with anticipation of surprise, the greater our chance of discovering something new and challenging, perhaps even in the most unlikely of places.

Every year brings new discoveries, sometimes adding scientific endorsement to grandmother's claims (carrots, greens and cod liver oil), often shattering old myths. Year on year we contest prior assumptions about underachievement, learning difficulties or bad behaviour. Year on year new etiologies are found. With each new discovery the convenient labelling of children by ability or potential is exposed and evidence produced to demonstrate its insidiously destructive effects.

We know more today than we did five years ago about the relationship of mind and body, thought and action, emotion and reason, physical and psychological health, what we eat and what we are (see, for example, Ornstein 1993; Le Doux 1997; Martin 1997). Yet we are still on the verge of plumbing their mysteries. We have little knowledge of what school learning people actually draw on in their daily lives. We do not have measures of the resilience or durability of knowledge. We do not as yet have a theory of learning and until we do our theories of teaching will always be tentative and propositional. This may be viewed not as a problem or matter for regret but as an exciting, continuing challenge.

In their document *Teaching for Learning* (SCCC 1997), the Scottish Consultative Council on the Curriculum suggests the following set of questions for teachers to put to themselves on a regular basis:

- How often do I encourage pupils to think for themselves and try out new ideas?
- What techniques do I use to help learners be more aware of how best they learn and why?
- What assumptions do I make about the individual learner when I teach?
- On what are these assumptions based?
- How would I describe the climate I am trying to establish in the classroom?
- What do I say and do to establish this climate?

These questions provide a stimulus for teachers to probe more deeply into their classroom practice, emphasizing the importance of having tools that can assist in that quest for more effective learning. Again borrowing from the researchers' repertoire, observation is being used increasingly frequently, either for performance monitoring by management, for peer assessment or, more occasionally, by students. The SCCC set of questions suggests a form of reflection, or observational framework, which focuses on learning rather than teaching, that is on what the pupils are doing rather than on what the teacher is doing. This is not only less threatening to teachers but, entered into in a spirit of inquiry, may lead to significant discoveries about the how, when and what of learning.

This is the significant challenge for the future and one we return to in the last chapter of this book. Our imperfect research will only improve as we probe more deeply into this area, gaining a better understanding of the when and how of learning. It is critical for school effectiveness and improvement because it will furnish insights, provide new lenses through which to view the school and provide new points of departure.

2

The policy context

John MacBeath and Jim McCall

When the history of the twentieth century comes to be written the last two decades will be seen as a seminal and turbulent period in educational policy making. This has been true not only within the United Kingdom but across the world. Schools worldwide have been swept into the main current of social and economic change. Through the eighties and nineties the character of the educational system experienced a transformation, in Gerald Grace's words, into 'a hierarchical form of executive leadership driven by the vision of the self-managed market-orientated school' (1997: 313).

This is a 'mega-trend', write Caldwell and Spinks (1992), an integral piece in a much larger picture. School reform has been carried on the tide of globalization, a more accurate description of which is 'global capitalism' – a market-driven set of forces which requires of governments that they put financial objectives first, that they intervene less and that they require the public sector to obey the inexorable laws of the market. As Harvard's Rodrik (1997) warns socialist, or would-be socialist, administrations, 'Financial markets stand ready to pounce on any government perceived to be sacrificing financial prudence to social objectives' (p. 47). Or in blunter terms by Haq and Kirdar (1986), 'Poverty can wait, the banks cannot'.

Throughout the eighties, the United Kingdom government was not a bystander or bit player, but a leading actor in this international movement. The reformation of the education system was so far-reaching that it has not been overturned by a Labour government but instead coopted by New Labour into a 'Third Way'. As Michael Barber, Head of the government's Standards and Effectiveness Unit puts it: 'Diversity, co-operation, equity and commitment to tackling disadvantage have been given priority alongside the market values of the previous government' (1999: 1). This attempts simultaneously to ride the economic tiger and to tame it.

The centrepiece of the Thatcherite vision of the future has survived and grown strength and conviction under New Labour. The vision is of a loosely coupled, or entirely uncoupled, system of self-managing schools, founded on three essential premises:

1 that governors and headteachers are better placed to determine priorities than their education authorities;
2 that schools should be the unit of improvement and accountability;
3 that good schools will survive and the best schools will thrive in a market opened to parental choice.

This philosophy is put in its starkest terms by Sexton (1987: 8–9): 'The key principle was that schools obliged to fight for survival would raise standards.' This thinking is explicitly stated in a Departmental document of 1992, three years after the Education Reform Act 1988 (DES 1988): 'To put governing bodies and head teachers under the greater pressure of public accountability for better standards and to increase their freedom to respond to that pressure.'

Freedom to respond to pressure is a provocative concept but nonetheless a fairly accurate description of what has, in fact, occurred in the decade since the introduction of the Baker reforms and local management of schools (LMS). This blueprint for the future, as envisaged by two American commentators on the UK scene (Chubb and Moe 1992), saw schools, operating in a full-blooded open market, with the following salient features:

• legally autonomous;
• free to govern themselves as they see fit;
• selecting their own student bodies;
• appointing their own staff;
• legally empowering parents and students to choose their schools.

(Chubb and Moe 1992: 226)

While such a vision has not been fully realized, there has been, nonetheless, a radical shift in the balance of educational decision making at national, local authority and school level. The power of central government has extended, while that of authorities has diminished. Latitude for decision making at school managerial level has increased, while autonomy and flexibility for individual teachers has commensurately decreased. Schools have been liberated within the wider market while simultaneously constraining teachers within tighter curricular and methodological boundaries. But, as Gerald Grace observes, 'democratic accountability to an external market need not result in greater internal democracy in a school' (1997: 315).

These shifts in the balance of educational decision making have been profound in their influence. They have brought benefits as well as burdens, opportunities as well as privations. The competitive market has brought with it a new set of profits and losses. Many of the freedoms offered by local management have been welcomed, in particular greater budgetary freedom. Market accountability and the scope for creative accounting have proved to be rewarding for entrepreneurial heads with the ability and freedom to exploit new sources of challenge funding. Schools with an entrée to local businesses, national enterprises or charities have profited, while those without the local resource or connections have been left behind. With the benefit of strong and influential parent support schools have prospered, while schools without such support and with no community capital on which to draw have run into deficit, having to invest in their communities without promise of return. It is, of course, in the nature of markets to produce differentiation, and through the nineties the divergence among schools has grown (Willms 1997).

This widening divide was given further momentum by what Phillip Brown described a decade ago as 'the rise of the parentocracy' in which 'a child's education is increasingly dependent on the *wealth* and *wishes* of parents, rather than on the *ability* and *efforts* of pupils' (1997: 65). Michael Adler and his colleagues at the University of Edinburgh showed that, in the early nineties, differences were already being exacerbated (Adler 1993) with confirmation of a continued widening of the social class differentiation by the end of the millennium (Willms 1997).

● The brave new world

This brave new world, in large part the product of the Thatcher–Reagan coalition, succeeded in sweeping away the perceived public policy failures of the sixties and seventies. Educators, cast as the main villains of the piece, were, along with local authorities, to be reined in and schools liberated from their ideological control.

With the benefit of hindsight, few could deny the need for a more rigorous approach to public spending, greater emphasis on institutional accountability, closer and more accurate monitoring of pupil achievement. While there is an all too easy caricaturing of the seventies as an era orchestrated by the Loony Left and permissive professors of education, the failures of that system are, nonetheless, not hard to find. Ever since the early 1960s when the Newsom Committee coined the term 'Half our Future', there has been a mounting body of evidence to show that schools in this country have been failing too many children. The charge that disadvantage was made an excuse for under-achievement by schools is, in many respects, a sustainable one. Without monitoring and evaluation, teaching could be flaccid and self-indulgent. With virtual classroom autonomy, weak teachers could get by without support, challenge or appraisal.

These were the grounds on which much of the reform rhetoric of the 1980s and 1990s was founded. Restructuring of the system was both advocated and defended on educational grounds, sometimes relying on anecdote, hearsay and impressionistic evidence, sometimes drawing on school effectiveness research. The rhetoric, however, barely concealed the political drivers of change, some of which were subjective sentiment, some frankly retributive in motive. Describing the reforms of the 1980s, Nick Davies writes: 'The most sweeping educational reforms this century, it transpires, had just as much to do with guesswork, personal whim and bare knuckle politics' (Davies 1999).

This bold statement is not journalistic spin, but comes directly from the architect of the 1980s reforms, Kenneth Baker, then Secretary of State for Education. His targets were first the teacher unions, removing their negotiating rights, to be followed by emasculation of local authorities. LMS would, in his view, 'fragment the teacher unions by giving them thousands of different employers to deal with and no chance of collective bargaining, would rob the LEAs of their most powerful function by taking their hands out of the till . . . He went on to give parents the right to choose their child's school, thus robbing the LEAs of their second most important function, the allocation of pupils' (Davies 1999: 2).

Its intent, then hidden but now explicitly acknowledged by Sir Kenneth, was to kill off the comprehensive schools and reintroduce selection, to create a radically new open market which would see poorer schools (possibly in both senses of that term) being forced to close:

> . . . in terms of Conservative statecraft, a governing competence over education was facilitated by identifying post-war liberal-democratic reforms as the cause for current troubles, which provided the government with the argument for radical educational change.
>
> (Brown 1997: 401)

The decade of the 1980s laid the groundwork not only for the next decade but for reforms into the next millennium. While it provided the framework for reforms in Scotland too, the leadership class in the Scottish Office was determined, as far as politically viable, to pursue a somewhat different path.

● **The Scottish context – how different?**

In the 1980s in Scotland there was no Kenneth Baker, no 'Baker days', no personal agenda or scores to be settled, no wildly errant local authorities or disintegrating schools to be brought into line. There was no possibility of radical Conservative policies in such a Labour stronghold where the Tories held only a handful of seats at national level and where education authorities were predominantly Labour-controlled (although in a generally more conservative sense than many of their English counterparts). There was one dominant teacher union, the Educational Institute of Scotland, a General Teaching Council, one examination board, one curriculum council, and one single national locus of quality control – Her Majesty's Inspectorate.

Above all there was, in Scotland, one school system. The comprehensive system, in place since the early 1970s, accounts for more than 96 per cent of the Scottish school population. While in England the principle of comprehensive education never succeeded in winning unequivocal support, in Scotland it is now a matter only for historical debate. There are no grammar schools (in the English sense) to return to, and selection by ability is, for older teachers, only a distant and unlamented memory. For this generation of young teachers, selective schooling is not even within the compass of their thinking. The difference between the more homogeneous Scottish system and that of England can be seen in the OECD data which showed a between-school variance in mathematics achievement of 16 per cent in Scotland and 63 per cent in England (OECD 1992).

The success of the comprehensive system is supported by evidence (Benn and Chitty, 1996; Raffe 1999). Attainment and participation rates have increased very significantly since the introduction of comprehensive schools, with a doubling of numbers entering higher education in the last decade. While these trends hold true for the UK as a whole, progress at Standard Grade (GCSE) level in Scotland has been faster than elsewhere (Raffe 1999).

However, class inequalities appear to be very little different from the 1970s. The performance gap between working-class and middle-class students has actually grown larger between Standard Grade (at 15/16) and Higher Grade (at 17/18). While working-class students are now more likely than middle-class students to enter further education, in higher education middle-class students outnumber working-class students by three to one (Bryce and Humes 1999). This link between social disadvantage and school achievement is very little different from England, but social disadvantage is more acute and more historically deeply rooted in Scotland than in most other European countries.

The social landscape

The demographics of Scotland are also a significant factor. The large land mass called the Highlands, whose gateway is Stirling, itself only on the periphery of 'the central belt', accounts for most of the geography of the country but a small percentage of its population. In most of these rural towns and villages, separated by many miles of land or water, school choice does not exist in any realistic sense. In the central belt, where most of the population resides, there are sharply demarcated boundaries – social, psychological and geographic – between advantaged and disadvantaged areas. Areas of deprivation tend to be highly concentrated, a hangover from slum clearance and housing policies of the 1950s onwards which created estates in greenfield sites on peripheries of Glasgow, Edinburgh and Dundee. Successive reports by Strathclyde's Chief Executive Department (1984, 1994) illustrate just how sharply defined are the disparities between one community and the next. A comparison of two Glasgow school catchments, one a council estate, the other an owner-occupied suburb, tells a story of two worlds of health, welfare and education. The more disadvantaged of the two areas has:

- five times more babies under 2.5 kg at birth;
- four times higher rate of prenatal mortality;
- 25 times more mothers under the age of 20;
- 30 times more births to unmarried mothers;
- five times fewer mothers booking in for antenatal care;
- 20 times higher rate of adult illiteracy;

- six times higher rate of unemployment;
- average life expectancy 30 per cent below average, as against 30 per cent above in the other area.

(Strathclyde Regional Council 1984, 1994)

Populations of these outer estates tended, through the seventies and eighties, to be relatively stable and their schools relatively socially homogeneous. It is only in the late eighties and nineties that parental choice began seriously to alter the social profile of comprehensive schools. There was a continuous and progressive growth of parental placing requests during the decade 1985–95, rising from 20,000 to 32,000 at which level it has remained relatively stable (Scottish Executive Education Department 2000).

A recent study (Mackay 1999) provides some revealing data on movement between schools. The ten primary schools studied were in one authority with a very high proportion of owner-occupied housing but which was, at one of its borders, in close juxtaposition with a deprived council scheme. School A in Table 2.1 is in the middle-class area closest to the scheme. Half of its intake is from the scheme, resulting in a relatively high proportion of free meals and clothing grants. Few requests come from within the authority. School B reflects a similar pattern, although less pronounced. School C is a popular school within the middle-class catchment and (or because) it has few requests from beyond the authority. School J is the most popular of all within the authority and receives no children at all from the neighbouring authority.

These data may be viewed, through one lens, as an encouraging indicator of a desire among working-class parents to improve opportunities for their children. It may also reflect, however, a growing polarization within the comprehensive system. A study by Willms and Echols (1992) found that parents who exercised their right to choose schools tended to be more highly educated and of higher socio-economic status than those who did not. In 1996 Willms

Table 2.1 Parents' placing requests in ten schools

	% placing request from other authority	% placing request within authority	% free meal entitlement	% clothing grant
School A	51	6	20.9	38.2
School B	21	2	19.0	34.4
School C	8	30	9.6	14.0
School D	8	13	7.6	10.8
School E	7	9	5.7	15.2
School F	3	9	5.0	12.3
School G	3	7	3.8	9.8
School H	0	37	2.3	10.9
School I	0	4	1.5	5.1
School J	0	41	0	2.0

was to report that parental choice has contributed to an increase in between-school segregation leading to greater inequalities in attainment.

The effect of this was for schools to become even more socially homogeneous, depriving low-achieving schools not only of more aspiring pupils but of parents with expertise and potential influence. In his earlier study Willms (1985) had shown that if you were a pupil of average ability your chances of exam success were better in schools where your peers were of high ability than in schools where they were of low ability. Further confirmation for this was found in the Grampian study of 1996 (Croxford *et al.*) as well as in our own *Improving School Effectiveness* study (1995). This issue, of 'school mix' or the 'compositional effect', is discussed at greater length in Chapters 1 and 4.

With devolution of finance to individual schools at 80 per cent plus, as compared to a more typical 95 per cent in England, Scottish authorities have been better placed to support those schools most vulnerable to market forces. Strathclyde Region's anti-poverty policies in the 1980s and 1990s, for example, led to the creation of after-school homework clubs and study support centres which have under New Labour become a key feature of national government policy. While important and helpful, these initiatives are unlikely of themselves to reverse the tide which threatens to create a new cadre of 'sink' schools.

The creation of 'new community schools' is another attempt to stem the tidal flow from disadvantaged to advantaged schools. Based on the American model of full-service schools, these will offer a one-door entry (physical or metaphorical) to educational, social and psychological services. They promise something that educational systems have so far never succeeded in delivering effectively – a coherent cross-agency, inter-professional approach. However, critics – for example, Lindsay Paterson (writing in *Scotland on Sunday*, November 1999) – predict that by virtue of their location in disadvantaged areas they are liable to reinforce rather than to blur social class demarcations.

● Making a difference

The extent to which schools are able to counter socio-economic effects was the focus of a series of studies at Edinburgh University through the 1980s and 1990s (Gray *et al.* 1983; Willms 1985; Cuttance 1988; Paterson 1992). Drawing on data from the annual survey of Scottish school leavers, their findings not only confirmed the powerful effects of factors lying beyond the control of schools, but also showed that individual schools could make a significant difference.

One of the factors within schools' own control was the ethos which the attitudes and expectations of teachers could do so much to create. Using the authentic voices of young people to tell their own stories, Gow and Macpherson's *Tell Them from Me* (1980) graphically portrayed the power of school ethos to build, or to undermine, the confidence of young people. Their often poignant descriptions of their schools pointed to deep-lying factors which underpinned differential achievement and divided those who failed from those who thrived.

A second factor, at least partially within the control of the school, is the relationship between teachers and parents, home and school. A two-year study (MacBeath *et al.* 1986) explored attitudes to school of young people and their parents through interviews with them in their own homes. It provided graphic insights into the home–school interface, illustrating how difficult it is without such ethnographic knowledge to understand the significance of value-added studies and to meaningfully separate school, as against home, effects. At the same time it included many examples of what could be done to make schools more parent-friendly and more socially inclusive. A large-scale follow-up survey of parent attitudes (MVA/MacBeath, 1989) found that parental choice of secondary school was on the basis of accessibility (47 per cent), reputation (35 per cent), family/friendship links (25 per cent) and academic reputation (11 per cent). When posed the question, 'What makes a good school?' parents prioritized, in order, good teaching, good discipline, pupil–teacher relationships, parent–teacher contacts, good buildings and facilities. The wide dissemination of the findings in five slim, accessible publications was one element of a Scottish Office strategy to disseminate research, to inform a wider public, to enhance parental awareness and to challenge schools to broaden the compass of their thinking.

A place for authorities

School effectiveness research has largely been blind to the role and effect of local authorities (Riley and MacBeath 1999) but they are potentially powerful allies, supporters and mediators of school improvement. In Scotland schools are still more closely tied to their education authorities than in England, and some councils wield as strong an influence as they did a decade ago. Indeed, the move to unitary authorities has, in many instances, brought an even closer relationship of authority and schools.

The historic coalition between the Scottish Office (now Scottish Executive) and the education authorities is also in some respects as collaborative as it has ever been. While never a simple and easygoing relationship, particularly in the Thatcher–Major years when there were Labour-led authorities and a succession of Conservative Ministers, innovation and policy have, nevertheless, been routinely tested and developed in collaboration. While at times it has been in the interest of authorities publicly to portray their relationship to central government as contested, behind the scenes the authorities and Scottish Office have, for the most part, worked closely together.

This consultative instinct may also be seen as an inherent weakness of the Scottish system. From an English perspective it constrained Scotland from keeping step with New Labour reforms. Scotland has no Education Action Zones, beacon schools, literacy and numeracy hours and, from a previous decade, no national testing, so frustrating attempts to build a value-added system and inform target setting at national Scottish level.

Managing Ministers

Scotland had no Baker but it did have its very own Minister, shaped in an even more radical right-wing mould. Michael Forsyth was a committed Thatcherite, but a Scot with a central Scotland constituency and enough political nous to know what was and wasn't likely to float in a turbulent Scottish sea. He recognized the political mileage in establishing some clear blue water between the Scottish Office and Westminster. He was also alive to the policy culture at the Scottish Office. He recognized its interest in, and respect for, research and the stream of studies in which school effectiveness had played a major role. He drew on them in parliamentary briefings and famously used them to challenge low standards and low expectations in Scottish schools.

Forsyth and his successors were kept well briefed on school effectiveness studies. There was respect among them all for a strong Scottish research culture, although they were often prone to selective use of the data. Willms's 1987 study, which showed that choice of schools from similar backgrounds could make a difference of one to two O Grades (GCSEs), was seized on by Forsyth because it not only reinforced the policy thrust but also put the issue into simple and graphic terms which a wider public would understand.

Forsyth's most cherished soundbite, winnowed out for him by his Scottish Office advisers, came in fact from the Opposition benches. It was Paul Boateng who originated what was to become a winning line and eventually a Ministerial mantra: 'Disadvantage is not an alibi for failure.' Michael Forsyth's exuberant embrace of schools-making-a-difference was, however, to earn him an unhappy reputation with the teaching profession when he infamously made a comparison between Glasgow's most deprived and most advantaged schools, implying that it was simply down to teachers to make *all* the difference.

Managing such a mercurial minister was to provide HMI with a challenge which they have not faced subsequently, but it is widely agreed within the Inspectorate that there has not been a Minister since with the same personal drive, grasp of a brief and keen and critical interest in research, combined with a studied deference to the Realpolitik of Scotland's senior Inspectorate. While from one perspective Scotland has not been as radical as England – too collusive, and too thurled to the softly, softly approach – from another perspective Scotland has steered a steady, less erratic course and in so doing avoided the worst excesses of the Baker years.

● **Going international – looking over the parapet**

Scotland, often parochial in its attitudes, is also internationalist in orientation. It has always been more friendly towards Europe than England and has for decades exported its talent to virtually every country of the world. At national level through the eighties and nineties there was a growing willingness to learn from what was happening in other parts of the world. The Scottish Inspectorate believed in international fact-finding, playing host to visitors from other countries, involving itself in international studies and having a presence at international conferences.

In 1988 members of the Inspectorate made a fact-finding visit to the United States, together with colleagues from what was then the Department of Education and Science (DES). It was to prove influential in shaping policy thinking both south and north of the border. A visit to South Carolina exemplified a state which, once a model of complacency, was in the 1980s beginning to take a strong line with failing administrations. Those in positions of power who had turned an opportune blind eye to the massive school drop-out among the black population were now being called to account. This experience helped to seed thinking about how a getting-tough-with-authorities policy might be employed in England and, more cautiously, in Scotland.

Calling schools and authorities to account was to find a different expression in Scotland from the form it was to take in England. The fact that schools had never been cut loose from their authorities, and the strong central steer from the Scottish Office, allowed a softer, gentler, longer term approach. Both Scottish representatives on that USA visit, Harvey Stalker and Archie McGlynn, were to become Chief Inspectors and Heads of the Research and Intelligence Unit at the Scottish Office in years to come; both were to play a role in using research to shape and test policy and forge stronger ties between those who think and those who do.

The American tour was to help to shape thinking about a distinctively Scottish approach to global issues of school effectiveness, decentralization, inspection, evaluation and VFM – value for money.

Key policy advisers in Scotland were not oblivious to or unimpressed by the winds of change that were blowing through national government. They recognized the import of the change in ethos, the challenge to complacency, not only at school and authority level, but in the Department itself.

An interview with Her Majesty's Chief Inspector (HMCI) Archie McGlynn, who had been instrumental in commissioning ISEP, helped not only to illuminate the context for the study but lent deeper insights into the policy debate in which he played such an integral part. He identified the American study visit, together with involvement in OECD indicator development, as two key factors in affecting thinking at policy level. Impressed and invigorated by his American tour, he was one of the first to welcome the winds of change:

> There was a new ethos. We saw then a need for greater accountability, the need for openness at school, authority and national levels, the importance of stewardship of public money, the value of benchmarking and better use of scarce resources. But remember, this was not all new to HMI. We were already producing school effectiveness documents and launching school development planning.

Scotland was by no means immune to a charge of complacency and self-satisfaction. But the attack on complacency was not to come through a frontal assault on failing schools or failing authorities but through lessons learned from the school effectiveness/improvement movement and its applications to development planning and self-evaluation strategies. This was to prove a slower process, seen more as capacity-building than a quick fix. It was believed that organic, systemic growth would give schools the resilience and self-confidence to deal with the inevitability of a freer educational market.

This developmental pragmatism is exemplified in the Scottish response to local management of schools. As is often the case with change, and radical change in particular, LMS was met with strong and vociferous opposition by authorities and schools in Scotland. However, the eventual implementation followed a pattern that was fast becoming typical. Strathclyde Region, a Labour stronghold, and often most outspoken in public opposition to Conservative policies, began trialling something they called 'DMR', or devolved management of resources. Building on the favourable reception it received from schools, other authorities began to roll out their own variations on the theme, with DSM (devolved school management) finally becoming the accepted wisdom.

A study of DSM in one Scottish region, Fife (MacBeath and Dobie 1995), illustrates on the one hand how carefully Scottish authorities tested the waters and on the other hand what came to be seen as the benefits of measured devolution of control. In 1994 Fife Regional Council piloted devolved budgets for the first time with 14 schools (eight primary and six secondary), each school receiving 80 per cent of the total budget. The authority provided support and training for management, with careful delineation of the respective roles of authority managers and school managers, making clear the interdependency of the relationship. Following the pilot year the authority withdrew some of the devolved powers with the specific aim of preventing a creeping inequality among schools.

This serves to highlight the significance of the 15 per cent difference between the English and Scottish models of devolution. Equalization is still seen in Scotland as an important role for the authority and approached through the holding back of certain powers. A Director of a Scottish authority describes its significance in these terms:

> Pupil numbers, although strongly influencing the size of the school's budget, are not regarded as overwhelmingly the main determinant as happened in England and Wales. Thus, it remains possible to allocate additional resources to schools serving deprived areas. Property budgets normally reflect the extent of the premises and the actual costs of rates, thus ironically helping to sustain declining half-empty schools which would otherwise be unviable. The teacher staffing component is usually based upon average salaries rather than actual costs thus avoiding the difficulty faced by many English schools of having to dispense with more experienced staff as they move up the salary scale.
>
> (Bloomer 1999: 165)

● The reform agenda

Up until the late 1980s school improvement and accountability were seen as jobs of the HMI and achieved through external inspection, allied to what tended to be an equally top-down quality assurance process at education authority level. Schools may be characterized at that time as:

- out of touch with current research and development in the fields of evaluation and organizational development;
- seeing inspection by Her Majesty's Inspectorate and/or the local education authority as the primary and singular source for the evaluation and validation of school quality;
- without the benefit of systematic criteria or tools for evaluating the quality of school culture or organizational development.

A number of things marked a change over the next few years:

- a broadening international perspective – fact-finding missions, cultural exchanges, inter-country networking;
- a growing and widening debate on school quality and performance;
- publication of the HM Inspector of Schools school quality and performance criteria, 'opening the secret gardens';
- stronger emphasis on policy-related research and competitive tendering;
- increasing reference by policy makers to school effectiveness research and to school improvement;
- a strengthening of the researcher/policy-maker relationship.

Creating a new and different national ethos and constituency of ideas was, however, seen by HMI as a process of maturation and a matter of sensitive timing. It was not going to be achieved overnight or by central mandate. Research needed to be brought closer to practice. Schools needed to be challenged with external evidence and encouraged to generate their own data. There was a need not only to reach the classroom teacher with what research was saying, but also parents and a wider public.

The publication of *Effective Secondary Schools* in 1988 (Scottish Office Education Department) was a symbolic landmark in the developmental process. It drew on the state of the art in research and was designed to make accessible to teachers issues that had previously been the province of researchers. It was followed a year later by *Effective Primary Schools* (Scottish Office Education Department 1989). Together these booklets provided the basis for school development planning, seen by policy makers as the mechanism through which greater effectiveness would be delivered. In 1991 *The Role of School Development Plans in Managing School Effectiveness* was published (Scottish Office Education Department 1990), and within two years every Scottish school had a development plan. The same year also saw the publication of *School Effectiveness Research: Its Messages for School Improvement*. Edited by Sheila Riddell and Sally Brown (1991), this brought together the latest thinking from the forefront of effectiveness and improvement research.

The early nineties were significant years in laying the groundwork for a more systemic approach to school improvement. 1992 saw the publication by HMI of the school self-evaluation guidelines. This was a significant landmark, moving away from top-down external inspection to a more school-grounded process of self-evaluation. 'The threefold path to enlightenment' was how one journal described the three sets of guidelines (MacBeath 1993). These consisted of:

- a set of qualitative indicators based on criteria used by HMI in inspections of classrooms, departments and aspects of whole-school policy and practice;
- Relative Ratings, which gave secondary schools formulae for calculating the differential effectiveness of subject departments;
- Ethos Indicators, providing schools with techniques for gauging the more subjective and least tangible aspects of school life from the perspectives of pupils, teachers and parents.

Each of these three documents contained an indicator framework, a set of suggested criteria, guidelines on their use and examples of professional development activities for teachers. These were distributed to all schools in Scotland, giving them for the first time the tools to conduct a full audit at every level of their operation or to focus evaluation on specific areas of school life. They exemplified the close working relationship between policy makers, researchers, authorities and schools, trialling and developing the indicator suite from the ground up.

Although home-grown and Scottish in flavour, the self-evaluation guidelines drew on international research and on insights gained by HMI on their fact-finding visits. They fed into, and drew from, close involvement with the OECD and its international indicators in which Scottish policy makers and researchers played a leading formative role (McGlynn and MacBeath 1995; OECD 1995).

Policy making could no longer operate within a purely national context. It had been given a wider perspective and the question was not just 'How good are our schools?' but 'How well are our schools performing in relation to schools in other countries?' This became a pre-eminent concern of policy makers and in 1996, simultaneous with the publication of the full *Third International Mathematics and Science Study* (TIMSS) (IEA 1998), the Scottish Office published its own document giving clear and accessible illustration of the relatively poor performance of Scottish schools in relation to other countries, 22 of which were ahead of Scotland in the international league table on mathematics (SOEID 1996).

The policy story of the nineties is of testing the system against international benchmarks while still pursuing a distinctively Scottish agenda. There was a progressive attempt to achieve the right blend between central guidance and direction on the one hand and school-led evaluation and development on the other. The intention was that the role of external evaluators would ultimately become one which moved away from 'inspection' towards quality assurance mechanisms, taking as its prime focus the rigour and integrity of the school's own self-evaluation procedures at school and classroom level.

While qualitative indicators published by HMI were intended for school use, they also served a normative purpose, being used by HMI to build a national picture of quality and standards. With the aid of new technology data could be presented graphically to a wider public. Information on relative resource provision or comparative effectiveness among different subjects could be made available, pinpointing areas in which schools needed greater support at authority and national level. Availability of data enabled policy advisers to give efficient and speedy answers to Ministers and senior policy makers on questions about quality or on issues of emerging concern.

For HMI indicators served a dual purpose, for individual school improvement and for a collective monitoring of standards and quality. The Scottish Office was becoming increasingly aware of the importance of having a national profile of performance, not just on examination achievement but across a wide range of school factors. In 1996 this indicator set was slimmed down, reducing it to a more manageable set of 33 generic indicators, applicable to primary, secondary and special schools and to all groups within those three sectors. At the same time, a joint initiative between the SOEID and the Investors in People organization harmonized their approaches to quality assurance, emanating in the publication of a set of 23 joint indicators.

Progressing the improvement agenda

At the beginning of the 1990s, and over a period of two years, the Scottish Office began a series of seminars, inviting school effectiveness/improvement researchers to talk to policy makers and advisers. The purpose was to create a more informed climate, friendly to research and in particular to school effectiveness research. It served also to test the waters and prepare the way for a major national research study. Reflecting on these as seminal in research and policy terms, Archie McGlynn, HMCI, says:

> We wanted to take advantage of evidence of what was happening in Britain and beyond and what makes better schools, and how you can bring about improvement. We wanted to link work already going on in Scotland, bringing this together with a growing body of published inspection evidence. We wanted to be challenged and to challenge the conventional wisdom of what makes good education.

So, through the late eighties and early nineties the various components for a large-scale study of effectiveness and improvement were being assembled piece by piece. In 1992 the possibility of an ambitious Scottish study was first discussed at the highest levels within the Scottish Office. However, it was seen as impolitic at that time with an impending election and the possibility of change in political leadership. Confidence within the Kinnock shadow administration was running high and a change of government seemed a not unlikely scenario. Even with the re-election of the Major government, HMI did not rush to commission the study. The climate had to be created for Ministers to see it as important. As Archie McGlynn described it:

There needed to be time to see which way the wind was blowing with new Ministers and to engage in debate on priorities. Our job was to demonstrate that school improvement was the key issue. We couldn't have simply rushed in. Ministers might have said 'Why spend all this money on one piece of research?' We had to provide the evidence, create the climate and link the proposed ISEP study with Ministers' commitment to improving standards in Scottish schools.

There were to be a further two years of preparation, fact finding and consultation before the Improving School Effectiveness Project was finally put out to tender. The tender was, unusually, not restricted to Scotland, as the Scottish Office Education and Industry Department (SOEID) wanted to attract some of the leading exponents in the field on both sides of the border, seeking if possible a new kind of coalition. The tender succeeded in attracting high-quality researchers and imaginative tenders. Commenting on them, Archie McGlynn says:

These were the most high-quality and competitive bids I had seen in my time. All of them were quite outstanding. It was very important to us that we got it right, doing something that we have never done before on this scale, bringing together different organizations working together across the United Kingdom.

The challenge ahead was for the successful tenderers to deliver. What could they say about Scottish schools, their relative effectiveness and their route to improvement? What light could they shed on policy making at national level, its successes and future directions? These are the issues that we deal with in the following chapters.

3

The research design and methods

Pamela Robertson, Pam Sammons, Sally Thomas and
Peter Mortimore

The Improving School Effectiveness project (ISEP) was the first large-scale attempt to integrate, in Scotland, the approaches of school effectiveness research and those of school improvement (MacBeath and Mortimore 1995). This task was important because, throughout the last decade, academics such as Gray *et al.* (1996) and Mortimore (1998) had argued that such a marriage would not only benefit the common understanding of school quality but would also help practitioners to understand better how to promote it.

School improvement has been defined as the process of enhancing the way the school organizes, promotes and supports learning. It is based on more than twenty-five years of research into school effectiveness and its means include changing the aims, expectations, organization, ways of learning, methods of teaching and institutional cultures of schools. In some circumstances it can mean a change of headteacher or some of the staff but, normally, should not involve the large-scale replacement of pupils (Mortimore 2000). As Hopkins has stated: 'School improvement is a strategy for educational change that enhances pupil outcomes as well as strengthening the school's capacity for managing change.' He has also argued that researchers need to obtain a stronger purchase on two fundamental questions: 'How do schools develop?' and 'What are the key elements of a school improvement initiative?' (Hopkins 1994: 3–4).

The sensitive analysis of what actually happens in those schools that are found to promote high levels of progress, when full account has been taken of the nature of their pupil intakes, should provide answers to these questions. By linking reliable measures of school outcomes with rich description and analysis of school characteristics and improvement initiatives, the project team hoped to be able to gauge the impact of the different school initiatives and programmes attempting to raise achievement levels.

The research specification made clear that the research design should include a wide range of schools in relation to background factors and performance in national tests or examinations. A key potential recommendation from the research would be to suggest how schools that appear to be underperforming might change their internal conditions to improve and thus become more effective. Increasingly, school effectiveness measures are being used at school and departmental level as a resource for planning school improvement. They can identify patterns and trends for different groups of pupils, and in different aspects of the curriculum (Sammons *et al.* 1997).

Through the combination of effectiveness and improvement research, we were seeking to uncover patterns of effectiveness, information about the 'inner' world of schools – in terms of both their unintentional and their planned processes – and make a contribution to the vital question of how schools can *learn* to make a difference.

In their conclusions to an important review of different research approaches – school effectiveness; school improvement; and their combination – Gray *et al.* (1996) set a challenging agenda for development. This includes an extension of studies to track patterns of effectiveness over time. Such patterns are likely to include numerous school improvement processes and priorities. Research needs to identify causal, as opposed to merely associative, relationships between what people in schools actually do and how this affects their pupils' progress. Additionally, Gray *et al.* (1996) urge that those undertaking school improvement should endeavour to understand why some schools fail to improve as well as seeking to evaluate the impact of their own activity.

The Scottish education policy context leading up to the commissioning of the project was discussed in Chapter 2. This describes the predominance of three themes: school ethos, the processes of development planning and a particular focus on aspects of learning and teaching. These three themes featured strongly throughout the ISEP project.

The use of data on pupil attainment (whether or not adjusted to take account of intake) to indicate school quality has been increasing in Scotland over the last decade. The 5–14 Programme, with its regime of testing, is now embedded in Scottish primary schools (Harlen *et al.* 1994) and is increasingly being established in the secondary sector as public scrutiny of school performance becomes more common. The research team, however, also believe it is essential to understand more about the relationship of pupil progress to influences both inside and outside schools. As well as learning more about the impact of 'given' factors (such as age, gender and family background) we believe it is important to explore further the effect of school organization, ethos and culture.

We hope that our study will make a significant contribution to a new tradition – one that combines the most sophisticated statistical techniques with more qualitative school improvement techniques.

This chapter describes the overall aims, design and methodology of the study.

● Aims and objectives of the study

The rationale for the study has been described in some detail by Tibbitt *et al.* (1994). In essence, the study had two major aims each subsuming several more detailed objectives.

To create a valid way of judging the performance of schools taking into account their different intakes

This involved:

• the measurement of school effectiveness based on pupil assessments, taking into account the influence of the 'given' factors (noted above) and the effects of these factors on different groups of pupils;
• the creation, testing and use of instruments to measure non-cognitive pupil outcomes (such as self-esteem and the concept of 'self as a learner').

To gain an understanding of the processes that take place in different types of schools

Achieving this aim involved:

• finding out what school-based characteristics are associated with value-added pupil progress;
• investigating what happens in the classrooms and management practices of effective and ineffective schools;
• suggesting how the staff of schools that appear to be underperforming might change their ways of working to become more effective;
• examining the role and effectiveness of school improvement consultants or 'critical friends'.

In order to pursue these aims and objectives, we designed a study which investigated – through the use of detailed case studies and the systematic collection of the views of pupils, teachers and parents – the learning environment of a sample of primary and secondary schools, and then followed the progress of their pupils over two years.

● Research design

The research design took account of Scottish work (Willms 1985, 1997) and wider reviews of the growing body of international school effectiveness work (Sammons *et al.* 1994).

Our study was designed to draw on:

• knowledge of the Scottish educational context at school, local government and national levels;
• current knowledge of techniques in the field of school effectiveness;
• current knowledge of school improvement techniques;

and to acknowledge:

- the limits set by central and local government policies;
- the perceptions and beliefs of teachers and parents;
- the prominence being accorded to pupils' measured attainments;
- the increasing recognition of the importance of pupil attitudes, experiences and attributes as further indicators of school quality;
- the understanding of school processes – both intentional and unintentional.

The design of our study was underpinned by the belief that the impetus for real change can only come from within schools. The research literature shows that change has to be built from practitioners' views and the perceptions of pupils rather than from top-down diktats. The project, therefore, used several measures of pupils' attainment and attitudes – and tapped into the attitudes of their teachers and parents – in order to provide as full a picture as possible of the different schools.

The research specification ensured that, in order to achieve the first aim, the sample should encompass a range of schools reflecting a full spread of background factors including size and performance in national examinations.

Achieving the second aim – understanding the differences between schools in their day-to-day lives – meant investigating the schools' intentions, internal conditions and processes. We also sought to examine changes in teachers', pupils' and parents' views over the course of the project. Furthermore, we endeavoured to document and categorize school processes in relation to the three project themes noted earlier: ethos building, development planning and learning and teaching. Throughout the whole undertaking we strove to keep the issue of quality – and the challenge of improving it – at the heart of the project.

● The sample

The project began in 1994, two years before the 1996 reorganization of local government in Scotland. A random sample of 200 Scottish schools (including some from all but three local authorities) was drawn from a national database. Of those headteachers who accepted the invitation to join the project, 82 were chosen and all but two remained with the project until its completion in 1998. From these 80 participating schools (44 primary and 36 secondary) we drew two age cohorts of pupils (8 to 9-year-olds from Primary 4, and 13 to 14-year-olds from Secondary 2). There were some 7000 pupils in all, plus 2500 teachers and 5400 parents.

The schools differed a great deal according to a range of dimensions including their attainment profile, pupil rolls, denomination, location (rural or urban) and the socio-economic characteristics of their catchment area. They were broadly representative of schools across Scotland.

We invited the school heads to join the project in the knowledge that it was only possible for a small sample to participate in its second phase. In phase one, all schools would be involved in the collection of quantitative data and would receive feedback on their attainment results and questionnaire information. Because of the limited resources of the research team, involvement in the second phase could only be made available to one in three of the schools. We would study these more intensively and would provide some direct support for school development.

This second phase subset of 24 case study schools was selected to mirror, as closely as possible, the characteristics of the larger set of schools in terms of their size, geographical location and socio-economic profile. We made the selection after the first round of data collection, so that it could be informed by these results. Using questionnaire information, combined with analysis of school documentation, we sought to ensure that the subset also represented a variety of approaches to ethos building, development planning and teaching and learning.

● Background information

In order to examine the impact of intake factors on the achievement of pupils, a variety of individual pupil background data was obtained from project schools. Data were collected on 10 'given' factors, including five measures of pupils' earlier school experience, age, gender and socio-economic characteristics. These data are further examined in subsequent chapters. In addition to information about individual pupils, some measures at the overall school level were also used to estimate the effect of school-level characteristics (such as the percentage of pupils eligible for free school meals and pupil attendance) on pupil progress. In the language of researchers, these data enabled the baseline results to be 'contextualized'. This means that important features of both the pupil body, such as socio-economic balance, and of individual pupils have been studied.

● Measures of pupil attainment: piloting and selection

The first pilot study (Thomas *et al.* 1994) took place over a period of six months in 1994. It involved working in seven schools (four primary and three secondary) with cohorts of 530 pupils and 168 staff. The work involved testing both Scottish and standardized commercially produced assessments. Assessment tasks from the 'Scottish Assessment of Achievement Programme' (AAP) were finally selected as these largely met the criteria for statistical reliability necessary for large-scale school effectiveness work. The AAP surveys also provided national norms that enabled the further anchoring of the ISEP data in a Scottish context.

As a result of the pilot study, the discriminatory power of both the primary and secondary mathematics assessments was improved by the addition of more challenging items. The overall assessment tasks were constructed to match the curriculum aims, levels and outcomes of the Scottish 5–14 Development Programme. With the further support of the Scottish Office, a nationally standardized test – the Suffolk Reading Scale developed by NFER-Nelson – was also used to complement the AAP Reading Test.

Some concern had been expressed, by teachers in the pilot schools, about the use of blanket assessments for young people whose range of attainments was likely to be broad. The pilot study enabled us to develop consistent approaches and procedures for working with pupils with special needs and learning difficulties. We wanted as many as possible to take part in the project so, where pupils were being supported by special 'scribes' and/or adult 'readers', we adapted our methods in order to include them. Our procedures for collecting the multilevel background information about pupils, classes and schools were also refined during these pilot trials.

In June 1996 we undertook a second pilot study in order to test and refine the primary school assessments for the project's second phase of data collection. As a result, we again adjusted the measures so as to include several more challenging items.

While it would have been ideal to examine school effectiveness across a broader range of the curriculum, the project was limited by its available resources to two main areas: reading and mathematics. In order to offset this limitation, the AAP reading assessments had been selected to address the cross-curricular skill of 'reading for information'.

Likewise, in choosing items for the mathematics assessment, we paid particular attention to incorporating skills that were applicable across the curriculum. The mathematics assessments covered both basic numerical and mathematical processes and the applications of these to problem-solving contexts. The resource implications associated with both the scale of the project and the variety of information to be collected also precluded the use of practical assessments in either language or mathematics.

● Estimating pupil progress

Pupils' progress was studied over their two years from Primary 4 to Primary 6 (from 8 to 10 years old). This age range was chosen as the pupils were deemed old enough to take standardized, written, curriculum-based assessments in reading and number. In Scotland, Primary 4 also marks the move from the early years department to the middle school. In secondary schools, pupil progress was measured over the two years from Secondary 2 to Secondary 4 (from 14 to 16 years old) which enabled us to use the regular external school examinations as a terminal measure of attainment.

We used the 1995 baseline assessment as a measure of prior attainment, following up the same pupils in 1997. Judgements about the effectiveness of their schools, therefore, were based on the 'relative' progress of all the sample pupils in each school, once the effects of background factors had been taken into account.

In Spring 1997 therefore, the same cohorts of pupils were again involved in testing. The primary cohort, now in P6, completed assessments in mathematics and reading, again based on the Assessment of Achievement Programme. The secondary cohort, now in S4, did not undertake any assessments specifically for the project. In contrast, we drew on pupils' Standard Grade results in mathematics and English as well as on an overall Standard Grade score. Much of the project's data, therefore, consisted of pupils' individual test and examination scores. Similarly, the academic success of schools was judged by the average performance of pupils in Standard Grades (GCSE equivalent) and Highers' (university entrance exams) examination results.

● The pupil questionnaire

The construction of the pupil questionnaires took account of two main considerations: first the central themes of the project, in particular teaching and learning and school ethos; and second, existing research evidence on the relationship between factors in the affective domain and academic progress. For example, we used the concept 'academic motivation' to try to capture achievement motivation, anxiety, self-concept and locus of control (the learner's concept of how much influence s/he has over learning and success). Such a mixture is supported by the work of Bandura (1982) which integrates into a theory of motivation the constructs of self-concept, self-esteem, self-efficacy and competence motivation.

The study of these affective and attitudinal factors also features in other work (Entwistle 1987; Mortimore *et al.* 1988). A study carried out with 11- and 13-year-olds in England for the National Commission on Education by the National Foundation for Educational Research (NFER) (Keys and Fernandes 1993) focused on the concepts of motivation and disaffection from school. Its conclusions suggest that the attitudes of pupils who are disaffected from school can be conceptualized as a three-tier hierarchy of significantly negative perceptions relating to:

- school work itself;
- teachers and the society of the school;
- the wider value of school education.

This view provided us with an approach for the pupil questionnaires given to both primary and secondary pupils. The questionnaire items were grouped into themes such as, for example, 'engagement with school'.

The primary school version has 24 items. Examples include:

I do my best at school
My schoolwork is interesting
I like answering questions in class
My teacher tells me how I can make my work better
I am happy at school.

The questionnaire for older pupils shares the same core of items. It is largely based on classroom experience and on teacher interactions. It was extended to include more age-relevant and sophisticated concepts such as:

My schoolwork is at the right level of difficulty
Teachers encourage me to think for myself
I have confidence in myself
Teachers listen to what I say.

In both questionnaires, we asked pupils to respond on a four-point scale.

● The teacher questionnaire

The roots of the teacher questionnaire lie in an international study on institutional and organizational development. Many of the principles of organizational development can be traced to current models of self-evaluation (SOEID 1998; MacBeath 1999). These emphasize organizational health as opposed to measuring institutional outcomes: the needs of the individual institution rather than those of the external system; continuous cyclical review and self-correction (Dalin and Rust 1983: 22); systematic self-assessment strategies and instruments; and the use of external consultants.

One of the more common techniques for this kind of school improvement practice involves the use of *bipolar* or *multipolar surveys*. A seminal example is the *Guide to Institutional Learning* (GIL), a survey and feedback instrument used in the 1970s in Norwegian schools as part of the Institutional Development Programme (Dalin and Rust 1983). Such an instrument allows contrasts between the points of view of different groups of respondents but can also reveal the difference between what people think is happening in their organization and what they regard as an ideal situation. Some examples of the statements are:

Decision-making processes are fair
Teachers regularly observe each other in class and give each other feedback
Teachers in this school believe that all pupils can be successful.

Dalin and Rust, in summarizing their concerns about the use of this type of survey instrument, discuss issues of reliability. They write of the 'ongoing dilemma' between pursuing statistical reliability and creating a more useful instrument which 'can be modified and tailored to individual schools' (Dalin and Rust 1983: 71).

In using an instrument derived from these approaches, we uncovered a tension in our research design. We needed – for research purposes – an instrument capable of being used reliably across a range of schools but we also wanted to be able to give feedback which would fit the context and needs of each of the schools. Subsequent chapters illustrate how we endeavoured to resolve this dilemma through the use of a questionnaire with a double-scale structure capable of providing insights into 'how the school is now' as well as 'how it should be'.

Feedback of evaluative data is a strategy for change and improvement, and feedback from these questionnaires provided us with a useful tool for examining and implementing change. The teacher questionnaire is potentially a particularly powerful instrument because, in seeking both teachers' current views and their aspirations for the school, it requires respondents to acknowledge their own roles as agents of 'change' or of 'conservatism'.

The case study schools offered us the opportunity to investigate the practical potential of this instrument. We had yet to discover how much attention school managers and their staff would pay to its outcomes or how its use would reflect on the tension between the demands of the external environment and the internal needs of the institution (Smith and Stoll 1998).

In thinking about the issue of cultural change within schools, it is often helpful to regard teacher outcomes (such as changes in attitudes, beliefs, practices and perceptions) as processes or 'intermediate outcomes' rather than as the final indicators of school improvement (Stoll and Fink 1996). Of course the process indicators are valuable in their own right and can provide a useful indication of school change.

● The parent questionnaire

Parents are now recognized as vital stakeholders in schooling (Sammons and Smees 1998). This has come about through the creation of many formal and informal initiatives during the last decade at both local authority and central government level. It was for this reason that we decided to include parent questionnaires in the study. One questionnaire had been developed for a Scottish HMI school inspection survey. Because of its ready availability and its correspondence with central themes from the ISEP specification it was ideal for our study. It has a number of themes in common with the teacher and pupil questionnaires but places more emphasis on the general ethos of the school and the quality of communication between home and school. The questionnaire has 24 items and uses a four-point Likert scale. Parents are asked to give their positive or negative responses to a number of statements about the school, for example:

> *The school has explained to me how I can help my child's learning at home*
> *Children are treated fairly in the school*
> *I find it easy to discuss my child's progress with school staff*
> *My child enjoys being at school.*

● The case studies

The 24 case studies drew on interview and observational techniques in order to try to capture the richness of the different perspectives of the pupils, the teachers and the school management team. Through the careful analysis of this information, we were able to add several more dimensions to our measures of quality.

Each case study, therefore, is a cameo of how particular processes of change aimed (directly or indirectly) at increasing pupil achievement take place in schools. The case studies describe:

- school contexts and their strategies for change;
- schools' use of external support and intervention;
- school-based processes of change in relation to development planning; ethos; teaching and learning; and management and organization;
- approaches to monitoring change;
- perceived impact on intermediate outcomes, such as teachers' and parents' views; and on pupils' views and achievements.

● Methods of analysis

A variety of quantitative and qualitative methodologies were used in the study. As a result, several large data sets were created and, in order to handle these appropriately, a number of different analytic techniques were employed (Robertson *et al.* 1998).

Quantitative data

The quantitative data – pupils' scores on the various tests; and pupils', teachers' and parents' questionnaire responses – were initially analysed to produce overall summaries. These were fed back to schools in 1996 with explanatory documentation. This information could be used to support school planning. Subsequently more sophisticated, multi-level modelling techniques (Goldstein 1995) were used to tease out the relationship between pupils' attainment and background characteristics (Sammons *et al.* 1998) and eventually, after the second round of data collection in 1997/8, to create measures of value-added progress. These value-added measures provided indicators of school effectiveness (Thomas *et al.* 1998b).

A second quantitative strand of the project sought to relate measures of pupil attitudes to value-added measures of school performance. Comparisons were made, for example, between pupil questionnaire scores on self-esteem and performance in mathematics and reading and, in secondary schools, the average score for each pupil based on their best seven Standard Grades. The use of such statistical modelling techniques enabled the allocation of all ISEP schools to a matrix of value-added performance for each of the areas of the curriculum assessed. These matrices are described in detail in a separate methodological paper (Thomas *et al.* 1998b).

The various stages of the analysis provide the basis for much of the rest of the book. Thus, analyses produced, respectively, information about the impact of background factors and value-added data in the various curriculum areas for schools. Analyses of the teacher, pupil and parent questionnaires aided the identification of school factors and the exploration of the relationship between those data and the value-added data.

Qualitative data

We drew on a variety of approaches to analyse the case study data and the information gleaned from the semi-structured interviews with the pupils, teachers and headteachers. These data include simple judgements as well as the identification of particular themes about teacher/pupil relationships or differential expectations of teachers for different groups of pupils. In our analyses we rated this evidence for what it told us about:

• the quality of the school;
• the potential for improvement;
• improvement as perceived by the respondents.

These ratings led to the identification of 35 subthemes which were then related to the three major themes of the project: ethos; development planning; and learning and teaching. We found so much evidence about leadership that we designated it a fourth theme (Robertson 1998).

This database provided us with a volume of evidence about the schools. It also allowed thematic reporting across schools by respondent group. For example, we could look at headteacher views about staff morale across all the case study schools or secondary pupils' views of teacher expectation (Robertson *et al.* 1998).

We could also use the database to look at thematic analysis within single schools. Across the range of schools' ethos, values derived from teacher interviews might spread from very negative to very positive. In a 'low-scoring ethos school' it would be possible to see, for example, how the low score related to:

• pupil beha viour and discipline;
• teacher responses to challenges emerging from the socio-economic circumstances of pupils;
• pupil–pupil relationships;
• pupil self-esteem and self-efficacy; and
• parental liaison and involvement.

Conversely, in a 'high-scoring ethos school' we might see, for example, the major positive components related to:

• perceptions of teacher expectation of pupils;
• teacher morale and engagement with the school;
• teacher responses to challenges in the socio-economic circumstances of pupils;
• the influence of historical events on present activity;
• pupil relationship with teachers.

Other examples of our qualitative analytic techniques are described in later chapters.

The analysis of quantitative and qualitative data within a single analytic framework provided us with the opportunity to study school culture (Hopkins 1994). For example, we could look at the overall value-added performance for any of the 80 schools in relation to their assessment practices in each separate area of the curriculum. We could also contrast 1995 and 1997 pupil, teacher and parent views of school life. The juxtaposition of these different kinds of analyses enabled us to ask important questions about each school's management. For example:

- Do schools show consistency in their impact on pupil progress?
- Is value added across the curriculum?
- Do some schools under-achieve in one curriculum area but add value in another?
- Do positive pupil perceptions of school correspond with value-added performance?
- Are there consistent patterns in pupil views and perceptions in schools that are under-achieving or subtracting value?
- In general, what school processes seem to be positively correlated with value-added pupil attainment?

The different models used in the analyses of qualitative data ranged from the systematic and detailed analysis of case study data to somewhat looser narratives and a combination of approaches as is illustrated in the following chapters.

● Supporting school development: critical friends and data feedback

Our design incorporated the work of what have been termed 'critical friends' supporting change and improvement in schools (Fullan 1991). The research team had always intended to generate a creative dialogue which it believed was essential to school improvement and this became part of the critical friends' work in schools. Starting with the collection of qualitative information and then feeding both qualitative and quantitative information back to schools, these critical friends worked with case study schools supporting change agendas.

As part of this dialogue, case study schools received guidance about the ways in which change could be handled. As might be expected, schools acted upon these guidelines in different ways according to their individual needs and contexts. One result of this was that levels of engagement with the project varied quite substantially. For example, some schools grasped every opportunity to use their critical friends while others seldom used this potential resource. We sought to evaluate the uptake of the varying expertise and specialisms of the critical friend across schools as we illustrate in a later chapter.

Have schools added value in outcomes and quality . . .

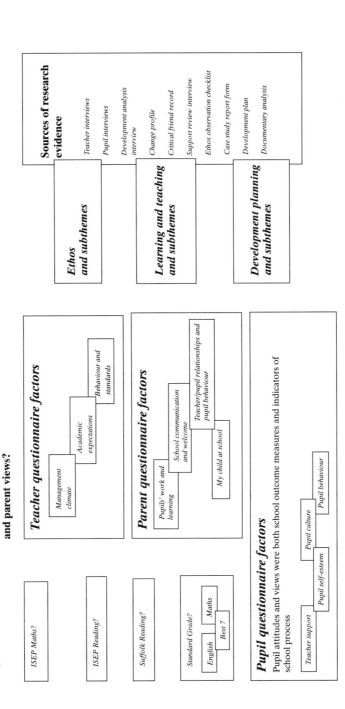

Figure 3.1 Mapping data sets – what do we know about ISEP schools?

● The ISEP postgraduate fellowship

This component of the study was designed to collect supplementary information from staff in the 56 schools which did not participate in the case studies. A special questionnaire was developed for teachers in these schools (Toal 1998). This was used to provide information about teachers' perceptions. This information, in turn, was linked to other data sets. The exercise formed a methodological bridge between the 24 case study schools and the larger set of 80 ISEP schools, enabling the exploration of relationships between school effectiveness outcomes and teacher views to draw on the progress of all 80 ISEP schools.

The questionnaires asked teaching staff and management team members in the 56 schools to respond to 17 items. These reflected aspects of school process and characteristics derived from the analysis of 1995 teacher interview transcripts in the case study schools. In addition to collating overall perceptions within and between schools, this study examined the relationships between teachers' perceptions of specific school characteristics (such as 'parental involvement in the school') or schools' value-added pupil attainment data.

● Summary

This chapter has outlined the project's overall approach and research methodologies. It has described our somewhat eclectic range of strategies for evaluating school quality and has shown how we sought to relate them to each other to provide an overall view of the schools. Figure 3.1 provides an outline of the research design.

The project design brought together the two paradigms of effectiveness and improvement in order to illuminate the relationship between them. We have sought to combine the descriptive, statistical approaches of conventional school effectiveness research with the more fluid and developmental paradigms of school improvement. This 'dovetailing', together with the active involvement of a change agent (Reynolds 1997) has enabled us to explore how some schools are able to promote positive progress and developments for their pupils and to change themselves. Many issues to do with the process of school improvement will be explored in subsequent chapters. We will endeavour to deal with them in clear, non-technical terms. Separate papers – published in educational research journals – deal with technical issues and describe, in much greater detail, our methodological and analytical techniques.

• 4

Attainment, progress and added value

Sally Thomas, Rebecca Smees, Pam Sammons and Peter Mortimore

• Introduction

We all know that children are not randomly allocated to schools. Residential geography, the location of other schools, parental choice, transport and religion can all play a part in influencing catchment areas and, therefore, the characteristics of pupil intakes to schools. Does it matter? All children are unique and bring different 'dowries' or mixes of prior abilities, personal and family characteristics and learning experiences with them. These will influence the reactions of their teachers and schools to them and may affect their subsequent educational outcomes. This chapter seeks to explore some aspects of the importance of such background characteristics.

We begin by summarizing the main findings from our analysis of the general progress of pupils in the sample. Much of the analysis will deal with the impact of various pupil background characteristics on the reading and mathematical skills of the sample of pupils. Our objectives are, first, to investigate the relationships between pupils' background characteristics and their attainment and progress in reading and mathematics and, second, to explore the influence of the schools they attend on their rates of progress.

We will examine our data to ascertain whether any school differences we find are consistent across both reading and mathematics and across both primary and secondary schools or whether they are more effective in one subject rather than another. We will also investigate whether the schools which appear to be the most effective are successful at promoting the progress of groups of pupils uniformly or appear to do better with particular types of pupils. In this way we will address important questions of equity in education. (For further details of these findings the reader may wish to consult the ISEP Policy Papers Numbers 1 and 2 by Sammons *et al.* 1998 and Thomas *et al.* 1998.)

● **The primary sample**

As was noted in the last chapter, 44 primary schools were included in the study. At the start of the project, pupils from Primary 4 year (P4) in 1995 were assessed in reading and mathematics and their progress was tracked through P5 prior to their final assessment in P6. Attendance figures and much background data were also collected for these pupils. Information on the composition of each school's intake of pupils was gathered, providing us with the percentage of pupils in each school for whom English is a second language, those with a Record of Need and those entitled to free school meals. These aggregate percentages are useful indicators of the overall composition of a school's population. They provide an indication of the 'context' of the school for any individual pupil. As previous research in Scotland and elsewhere has shown, the composition of the intake to a school can have an influence on achievement over and above that of any one pupil's own background characteristics (see Willms 1986 and Sammons *et al.* 1996 for a discussion of this issue).

● **The primary pupil data**

Data were originally collected on 1378 pupils of which 47.8 per cent were girls and 52.2 per cent were boys. Most came from Scottish families; less than 2 per cent had ethnic minority backgrounds and less than 1 per cent had English only as a second language. Almost 27 per cent were entitled to free school meals (FSM); 1.7 per cent had a Record of Need; and 15.8 per cent were receiving some form of learning support. Overall, nearly 16 per cent had already changed school (17.5 per cent had been in their current school for less than four terms). Table 4.1 provides a profile of primary pupils in the sample.

By P6, the sample had shrunk to 1096 but the proportion of girls and boys had remained very similar. The proportions from ethnic minority backgrounds – or who had English only as a second language – had also remained close to the original level. The average age was – of course – two years older.

Table 4.1   Characteristics of the primary sample at P4 (1995)

Characteristics	%
Girls	47.8
FSM	26.6
Learning support	15.8
Record of Need	1.7
English as a second language	0.8
Ethnic minority status	1.2
Less than four terms in current school	17.5
More than one school	15.7

● Background factors affecting progress in the primary school

The potency of background influences on the achievement of individual pupils is of considerable importance to those concerned with the administration of schooling and especially to those concerned with the promotion of equity. For example, Brown and Riddell (1992) have discussed the impact of class, race and gender and their implications for policy and practice in Scottish education. These background factors are also relevant to the current government's policy of using benchmarks and target setting as part of its drive to raise standards of literacy and numeracy.

Previous sociological and educational research, conducted over several decades, demonstrates the existence of statistically significant links between pupils' background characteristics and their educational attainment at both primary and secondary levels. Earlier studies emphasized the impact of factors such as low IQ, low family income, low socio-economic status, unemployment, poor housing, low levels of parental education, large family size, single parent status, being in care and other potentially disadvantaging circumstances. It led to the development of such concepts as the 'cycle of disadvantage' which suggested that intergenerational continuities in the probability of educational failure for disadvantaged groups (or, alternatively, success for more advantaged groups) were likely to be powerful. The impact of other factors such as race, fluency in English and having English only as a Second Language (E2L), gender and age (within a year group) received more attention during the 1970s and 1980s (for reviews see Rutter and Madge 1976; Mortimore *et al.* 1988; Brown and Riddell 1992; Sammons *et al.* 1994).

More recent longitudinal research has attempted to explore the influence of such background factors over the long term using more sophisticated statistical techniques. The research has demonstrated the importance of examining the impact of socio-economic disadvantage, gender, race and fluency in English *simultaneously* so that, for example, ethnic differences are not confounded with other differences related to class or income. Such research focuses on pupils' progress over a specific period of time in school and explores differences in the attainment of specific groups of pupils at particular points in time. It has shown that, while the influence of socio-economic factors is fairly stable, the impact of ethnicity is more varied and may change over time (Sammons 1995). Furthermore the impact of background factors has been shown to be more powerful in relation to language-based educational outcomes – such as reading and English – than for more abstract subjects such as mathematics (Brandsma and Knuver 1989; Sammons 1995; Thomas *et al.* 1997a, 1997b).

If meaningful comparisons are to be made between schools on the basis of their pupils' results in any assessment tasks, we believe it is vital to compare 'like with like' in contrast to *raw* league or performance tables. To do this it is necessary to build into the analysis the reality that schools in different areas often receive very different kinds of pupils. By undertaking such analyses, it is possible to explore the relationship between the specific characteristics of schools' intakes and their results, and thus tease out the extent of the school influence.

Detailed research, such as the ISEP study, has an important role to play in explaining patterns of achievement within – and between – schools. Without such research, it is all too easy to assume that poor progress must be the fault of low teacher expectations or, alternatively, to adopt a fatalistic attitude that social disadvantage is so powerful that schools can make little difference. There are important implications for promoting equity in education depending upon the interpretation adopted. The ISEP study provides a rich source of evidence that can help to illuminate such debates about equity. Our findings illustrate both the strength of background influences and also the importance of schools. They suggest we must avoid either of the two extremes of interpretation we have highlighted above.

● Reading skills in the primary years

The Assessment of Achievement Programme (AAP) reading assessment was specially designed for the ISEP research using items related to the Scottish curriculum. The average reading score for the pupils in P4 was 55.2 but this masks a wide range of performance. The variation around the average score (expressed in terms of its standard deviation) was 2.15. The size of this figure indicates the extent of the variation.

Two years later, when the primary sample were in P6, the average reading score was very similar at 54.9 (with a standard deviation of 24.5). Thus the variation had increased slightly as the abler readers had surged ahead while others continued to experience difficulties.

Correlation techniques were used to examine the relationship between the reading performance of the sample at the two separate points in time. In interpreting a correlation, it is important to realize that the closer a correlation is to 0.99, the stronger is the relationship between the two measures. It is not always easy to judge the significance of a particular correlation but a useful guide is that a positive correlation of 0.5 means that up to a quarter of the variation in one measure (say, reading at the later age) can be accounted for by the other measure (reading at the previous age). Our data show that the correlation between the P4 and P6 reading scores was 0.58 indicating a reasonable, but not overwhelming, relationship between the two test results. This demonstrates that, while the early results of a child usually predict later performance, it is still quite likely that the child may do better – or worse – than might be expected from his or her earlier performance. If early results were perfect predictors, the study of the schools' contributions to pupils' progress would be superfluous.

● Mathematical skills in the primary years

The average mathematics score for the sample pupils in P4 was 63.0 with a standard deviation of 20.3. Again, the AAP assessments used were specially designed for the study and relate directly to the Scottish curriculum.

Two years later, when the primary sample were in P6, the average mathematics score was 64.1 (with a standard deviation of 19.7). So, in contrast to reading, there had been no increase in the variance of the scores.

Correlation techniques were again used to examine the relationships between the mathematics performance of the sample at these two time points. As with the reading scores, the closer the figure to 0.99, the stronger the relationship between the two measures. The correlation between the P4 and P6 maths scores was 0.74, indicating a stronger relationship between the two than was found with the reading scores. This suggests that early performance in mathematics is a better estimate of later performance than is the case with reading.

One reason advanced for the different pattern between reading and mathematics is that parents are much more likely to offer help with reading either overtly or covertly – through the provision of newspapers, books and other reading material around the home – than they are with mathematics. Although, in reality, there is likely to be a range of mathematical material, in the form of shopping receipts, bills and bank accounts, parents appear less willing to use this to tutor their children. For some parents this is due to a form of mathematics anxiety while, for others, it is due to an apprehension that they may confuse their children by adopting methods different to those used in the school.

Another factor which might well be playing some part in this difference is the nature of the subject itself. This might make the development of further progress in mathematics more dependent than reading on the mastery of early competencies and understanding. This would tend to lead to a higher correlation between past and subsequent attainment than would be anticipated for reading progress which does not proceed in a linear fashion (see Riley and Reedy 2000).

● **The influence of various factors on pupils' progress through primary schools**

In order to identify and separate the twin influences on their progress of pupils' background characteristics and the individual schools attended, we have found it necessary to use multilevel modelling techniques (Paterson and Goldstein 1991; Goldstein 1995). These techniques provide the most reliable estimates of the influence of any one *single* factor. Thus, for example, the impact of gender can be estimated while controlling – simultaneously – for the influence of other factors such as a pupil's age or socio-economic status.

Such statistical methods allow us to partition the total variation in the scores of pupils between that which is related to differences between individual pupils (which we call the pupil level), and that related to the particular school he or she has attended (the school level). This division of variance is crucially important because, even in a comprehensive system, pupils are seldom distributed randomly between schools. Depending on the areas they serve, their denominational status, and the location of other schools, schools can differ markedly in the kind of intake they attract.

One of the most important ways in which schools differ is in their social balance – the proportion of its pupils which come from socio-economically 'advantaged' or 'disadvantaged' backgrounds. Researchers refer to this social balance as a *contextual* factor. The importance of a reasonable balance of intake has long been recognized by research (Rutter *et al.* 1979) and, since 1997, in government statistical procedures (for example, the use of the percentage of free school meals measure in school benchmarking and target setting in England and Scotland).

We will now report on whether there were statistically significant differences in the attainment of different groups of pupils (for example, girls compared with boys) or in their progress during the two years of the study.

Gender differences in primary schools

There is considerable current interest in the extent of gender differences in pupils' educational achievements across all phases of schooling. In Table 4.2 we show the average mean scores for girls and boys separately. The standard deviations for each group are also shown in brackets. In the analysis of progress, multilevel models were used to take account of the influence of other factors (such as a pupil's age and prior attainment and whether he or she has an official Record of Need – RON – or is receiving learning support). The table illustrates whether the differences in progress – across the two years of the ISEP study – between boys and girls were statistically significant.

Table 4.2 Gender differences in attainment and progress at the primary level

(i) Average reading scores for girls and boys

	Reading P4 1995	Reading P6 1997	Progress 1995–7*
Girls	55.6 (21.2)	57.4 (24.6)	Significantly positive
Boys	54.9 (21.9)	52.6 (24.4)	

Note: * Statistically significant difference in progress 1995–7 controlling for influence of other factors (see Tables 4.15 and 4.16).

(ii) Average maths scores for girls and boys

	Maths P4 1995	Maths P6 1997	Progress 1995–7*
Girls	63.6 (19.9)	64.6 (19.3)	Significantly negative
Boys	62.5 (20.7)	63.5 (20.0)	

Note: * Statistically significant difference in progress 1995–7 controlling for influence of other factors (see Tables 4.15 and 4.16).

We found that there were no statistically significant gender differences in pupil performance at P4 in either literacy or mathematics when we controlled for the impact of other characteristics. This finding contrasts with national assessment results for England (see Thomas 1995; Sammons and Smees 1998; Tymms 1999) where gender differences were found to be significant at the end of Key Stage 1 (pupils age 7 years plus).

Two years later, however, girls – as a group – were noticeably ahead in reading. Our analysis of individual pupils' progress showed that, taking account of other factors, girls made greater reading gains over this period. It should be noted, however, that more boys than girls were identified as requiring learning support or having a Record of Need.

In contrast, when we analysed individual pupils' progress in mathematics (taking account of prior attainment and other factors) we found that the girls in our sample had made significantly less progress than the boys. The more detailed multilevel analysis picked up differences that were not evident if we simply look at the mean scores by themselves. The reasons for these differences in progress during the later years of primary education are probably due to a variety of factors including the different expectations for the performance of girls and boys held by parents, teachers and the pupils themselves. We also found, both in 1995 and 1997, that the reading and mathematics results are more closely related for girls than for boys. In other words, girls who are good readers tend also to do well in maths. Some boys, however, may have a strength in maths without the corresponding reading level.

Age differences in primary schools

It is well known that age differences within a year group affect pupil attainment: those who are 'young' for their 'year' usually perform less well than others at all stages. This has been well documented (see, for example, Mortimore *et al.* 1988; Thomas 1995; Sammons and Smees 1998) and appears to be a function of younger children's immaturity relative to their peers and the likelihood that they have not attended school for as long a time. However, although there were significant differences in attainment, these differences neither increased nor decreased over the two years so that no significant differences in progress were found. This indicates that those young for the school year made as good progress as their slightly older peers. But it also emphasizes the need for all assessments, especially those that affect the school career of pupils, to be age-related.

Socio-economic differences in primary schools

There is evidence from many other studies that socio-economic disadvantage can affect pupils' educational outcomes (Sammons *et al.* 1994, Mortimore and Mortimore 1999). One measure of disadvantage available to schools is whether a pupil is entitled to, or in receipt of, free school meals (FSM). Although crude, this indicator has proved to be relevant in many studies. In

Table 4.3   Socio-economic differences in attainment and progress at the primary level

(i) Average reading scores (standard deviations) for pupils of varying backgrounds

	Reading P4 1995	*Reading P6 1997*	*Progress 1995–7**
Free school meals	44.5 (20.0)	44.2 (24.1)	Non-significant
Other pupils	59.0 (20.8)	58.2 (23.8)	

Note: * Statistically significant difference in progress 1995–7 controlling for influence of other factors (see Tables 4.15 and 4.16).

(ii) Average maths scores (standard deviations) for pupils of varying backgrounds

	Maths P4 1995	*Maths P6 1997*	*Progress 1995–7**
Free school meals	55.8 (20.8)	53.5 (17.3)	Non-significant
Other pupils	65.5 (19.6)	63.4 (17.7)	

Note: * Statistically significant difference in progress 1995–7 controlling for influence of other factors (see Tables 4.15 and 4.16).

Table 4.3 we show the average (mean) raw scores in reading and maths at P4 and P6 for pupils entitled to FSM compared with those of other pupils.

The ISEP data show that pupils eligible for free school meals attained less highly in reading and maths than their peers at both P4 and P6, controlling for the influence of the other factors. There were also some indications that these pupils made less progress in reading across these two years although the results just failed to reach statistical significance.

The overall relationship between poverty and lower-than-average attainment should not be a surprise as most such comparisons – even of international data – have the same outcome (Mortimore and Mortimore 1999). This negative relationship does not imply that pupils coming from disadvantaged backgrounds are less able but rather that they tend to perform less well than others who have experienced greater advantages. It is hardly surprising that those who have enjoyed better diet, housing and healthcare and whose families have been able to buy books and provide outings and holidays generally do better in competitive tests than those for whom family life has always been a struggle against poverty.

The data also demonstrate that the composition of a school's intake, in terms of the percentage of pupils entitled to free school meals, has a negative influence – over and above their own characteristics – on individual pupils' results in reading but not in mathematics. This is why performance levels tend to be depressed in schools where there are high concentrations of disadvantaged pupils in the intake. It is often harder for such schools to raise standards. Interestingly, we did not find this factor to be significant when we analysed progress for our primary sample.

Although evidence of the links between socio-economic disadvantage and pupil attainment has accumulated over the years, the interpretation of these data remains controversial. Our data provide new evidence of the links between low income and low attainment. While this must never be used as an excuse to lower expectations for such pupils, this evidence supports the view that schools which serve such communities require extra help to meet the challenge of raising standards. Targeting such schools (for example, via the creation of Education Action Zones in England, or initiatives such as New Community Schools in Scotland which are intended to provide examples of 'joined up' policy thinking) may help provide resources to enable specially 'needy' schools to provide such extra help.

Learning support in primary years

Information was also collected on whether or not pupils were being given any extra learning support (Table 4.4).

Not surprisingly, those pupils who were identified as being in need of learning support earlier in their primary schooling attained less highly at both P4 and P6. They also made less progress than others in mathematics, though not in reading. This could be interpreted either as indicating that such pupils had been accurately selected or it could show that the process of being identified as having a learning problem actually has a negative impact on the pupils' perception of their own learning skills, as well – of course – as on the teachers' perceptions of them. It may also be that a greater amount of support was provided for reading than for mathematics. Again unsurprisingly, the small group of pupils with a Record of Need performed significantly less well than their peers.

Table 4.4 Differences in attainment and progress of pupils receiving or not needing learning support

(i) Average reading scores for pupils

	Reading P4 1995	*Reading P6 1997*	*Progress 1995–7**
Learning support	32.2 (16.5)	34.7 (21.7)	Non-significant
Other pupils	59.2 (19.7)	57.9 (23.5)	

Note: * Statistically significant difference in progress 1995–7 controlling for influence of other factors (see Tables 4.15 and 4.16).

(ii) Average maths scores for pupils

	Maths P4 1995	*Maths P6 1997*	*Progress 1995–7**
Learning support	39.7 (19.4)	42.3 (19.1)	Significantly negative
Other pupils	67.0 (17.6)	63.9 (16.1)	

Note: * Statistically significant difference in progress 1995–7 controlling for influence of other factors (see Tables 4.15 and 4.16).

● The combined effect of the factors on primary school performance

The combination of all pupil background factors – by themselves – account for less than one-fifth of the variation in their attainment at P6. But when we examined progress by taking account of attainment at P4 as well as all pupil background factors, we were able to explain a substantially greater proportion of the variation (42 per cent of the AAP reading and 57 per cent of the AAP mathematics). Like other studies of school effectiveness, we can now examine the amount of unexplained variance (having accounted for pupils' backgrounds and their prior attainment that can be attributed to the school effect). This ranges from 12 per cent for reading to 33 per cent for mathematics. As we have noted earlier, the *school effect* on pupils' mathematics progress is considerably greater than the effect on reading. As with other studies, this finding is in line with previous research which suggests that school effects are usually stronger for this subject area (Sammons 1993).

The next question gets to the heart of school effectiveness: are there significant differences between individual schools in either their pupils' reading or mathematics progress? We investigate this by calculating a 'predicted score' based on prior attainment and intake for each school. The difference between their actual results and these predicted scores indicates whether or not their pupils had made more – or less – progress than expected given the nature of their intake (what we call residual estimates).

In Table 4.5 we show the difference between the most and the least effective school.

As we can see from the tables, there were sizeable differences in both reading and mathematics progress and these are also reflected in the standard deviation of the school residuals (AAP reading = 5.7; maths = 6.7 raw points).

Table 4.5 Effectiveness of primary schools

(i) in reading progress (AAP reading)

	Difference in relative progress – raw points
Most effective school	+13.5
Least effective school	−11.1

(ii) in mathematics progress

	Difference in relative progress – raw points
Most effective school	+21.3
Least effective school	−14.2

In order to get a feel for the importance of the school effect we can consider the difference that might be experienced by two pupils with the same level of prior attainment who attended the *most* and the *least* effective schools. In the former case (the most effective school) she or he would obtain a score in English which was approximately 14 raw points *higher than expected*. In the latter case (the least effective school) she or he would only gain a score approximately 11 raw points *lower than expected*. This represents a gap of some 25 points between the most and the least effective school. For mathematics the differences are even more striking: 21 points and 14 points respectively. This reveals a gap of 35 points at P6 between the results for pupils with the same starting performance in maths at P4.

Another way of looking at the effectiveness of the sample of schools is by dividing them into four groups depending on the significance of their effects. Table 4.6 illustrates this grouping. The categories 'effective' and 'ineffective' identify 'outlier' schools where pupil progress was statistically significantly better or worse ($p<0.05$) than predicted on the basis of intake.

As can be seen, the two reading tests produce rather different distributions. More schools appear in the effective category when the Suffolk test is used than with the AAP assessment. However, on both tests the proportions of significantly negative scores are relatively low: 7 and 2 per cent respectively. These differences illustrate the difficulties of producing definitive judgements on schools, if only one outcome measure is used.

In the mathematics test, a larger proportion of schools are identified as more effective (23 per cent) but this is matched by 26 per cent of schools which were classified ineffective. As we have argued earlier, the reading/mathematics

Table 4.6 Grouping of primary schools in terms of effectiveness

(i) in AAP reading (Suffolk reading test results in brackets)

Outcomes	*Number of schools*	*%*
Effective (significant positive residual)	5 (8)	11 (18)
Average – positive (non-significant positive residual)	17 (10)	39 (23)
Average – negative (non-significant negative residual)	19 (25)	43 (57)
Ineffective (significant negative residual)	3 (1)	7 (2)

(ii) in mathematics

Outcomes	*Number of schools*	*%*
Effective (significant positive residual)	10	23
Average – positive (non-significant positive residual)	7	16
Average – negative (non-significant negative residual)	15	35
Ineffective (significant negative residual)	11	26

Table 4.7   Positive residuals by primary schools

Number of positive outcomes	Number of schools	%
None	17	39
One	15	34
Two	12	27

differences illustrate that schools that are particularly effective in one area are not necessarily so in another. The correlations between primary school residuals for reading and mathematics ranged from 0.39 to 0.47 thus allowing plenty of scope for doing well in one subject but not the other. If we look (in Table 4.7) at the percentage of schools obtaining positive – but not necessarily statistically significant – residuals in one or two subjects, we find that only 27 per cent are positive (but not necessarily effective) in both reading and mathematics, while a sizeable minority (39 per cent) have a negative effect on both areas. This means that about one-third of the sample show a positive effect in one but not the other subject.

● Differential effects of primary schools

Interestingly, there was little evidence that primary schools had different effects on different groups of pupils. However, there were significant differential effects for those with different levels of prior ability (the correlations between school residuals for low- and high-ability pupils were: reading = 0.72; maths = 0.97). Overall, therefore, we can tentatively conclude that those schools that were more effective tended to be so for *both* boys and girls, and for those from both advantaged and disadvantaged backgrounds (FSM and other pupils). Likewise, the less effective schools were generally less effective for *all* pupils and not just for specific groups. This is in line with findings from earlier studies of primary schools in England (Mortimore *et al.* 1988; Sammons *et al.* 1993, Sammons and Smees 1998).

● The results of the analysis of the secondary schools data

As was noted in the last chapter, 36 secondary schools were included in the study. Pupils aged 13 from the second year in secondary school (S2) were assessed in reading and mathematics and their progress was tracked through S3 and assessed again in S4 using the Standard Grade public examination results. As with the primary sample, attendance figures and background information were also collected for these pupils.

● The secondary pupil data

Data were originally collected on 5123 pupils, of whom 49 per cent were girls and 51 per cent were boys. One per cent came from ethnic minority backgrounds and less than 1 per cent had English only as a second language. Just over 17 per cent were entitled to free school meals; 2.1 per cent had a Record of Need; and 16.9 per cent were receiving learning support. Only 3.2 per cent had already changed secondary school. In all, nearly a third had spent less than four terms in their current secondary school.

By S4 the sample had 4406 but the proportion of girls and boys had remained very similar The proportions from ethnic minority backgrounds – or who had English only as a second language – had also remained close to the original figure. In measuring progress we were able to draw on the data from the Standard Grade examinations in addition to the AAP assessments. It should be noted that in the ISEP study all Standard Grade data have been converted to points scores (thus, for example, Standard Grade 1 the highest grade is awarded a score of 6 points, while pupils who obtained no Standard Grades scored 0). Thus in the following tables a higher Standard Grade result signifies better performance.

● Reading skills in secondary schools

The average reading score for the sample pupils in S2 was 64.3 but this masks a wide range of performance. The variation about the average score (expressed in terms of its standard deviation) was 21.0. Two years later, when the secondary sample were in S4, the equivalent Standard Grade average in English was 4.02 points (with a standard deviation of 1.21). The average total points score (based on the best seven Standard Grade results) was 27.0 points, with a standard deviation of 9.53.

Correlation techniques were used to examine the relationship between the reading performance of the sample at the two separate points in time. The correlation between the S2 and S4 English Standard Grades was 0.62, indicating

Table 4.8 Characteristics of the secondary Sample at S2 (1995)

Characteristics	%
Girls	49.1
FSM	17.4
Learning support	16.9
Record of Need	2.1
English as a second language	0.8
Ethnic minority status	0.9
Less than four terms in current school	31.6
More than one school	3.2

a relatively strong relationship between the two. This demonstrates that the earlier reading performance of a pupil in the secondary school generally predicts the later one. The correlation with the overall performance in the best seven Standard Grades was 0.66. Thus reading performance remains a good predictor of later public examination success, reflecting the importance of this skill for achievement in different curriculum areas.

● Mathematical skills in secondary schools

The average maths score for the sample pupils in S2 was 52.3 with a standard deviation of 22.9, slightly higher than that found for reading for this age group. Two years later, when the secondary sample were in S4, the average maths grade in the Standard Grades was 3.50 points (with a standard deviation of 1.64 points). Again, these data suggest greater variability in pupils' mathematics performance than was found for English at Standard Grade.

Correlation techniques were used to examine the relationships between the mathematics performance of the sample at the two points in time. The correlation between the S2 mathematics scores and later mathematics results at Standard Grade was 0.80, indicating a stronger relationship between the two than was found with the reading scores. As with the findings for the primary sample, this also suggests that past performance in mathematics can provide a better indicator of future performance than does reading. The correlation with the overall performance in the best seven Standard Grades was 0.73, which is stronger than that found for reading. We also found that reading and mathematics results are more closely related for secondary rather than for primary pupils (a correlation of 0.62).

● The influence of prior attainment and family background factors on pupils' secondary progress

As with the primary sample we sought to use multilevel modelling techniques to provide estimates of the net influence of individual background factors (for details see Appendix 1).

Gender differences in secondary schools

Gender differences in performance were examined.

As can be seen from Table 4.9 i), girls had significantly higher reading attainments than boys at S2, taking account of other background characteristics. Their English and overall Standard Grade performance at S4 two years later was also significantly better. When progress was analysed using multilevel models we found that girls as a group made greater gains in both English and overall Standard Grade results, indicating that the gender gap widened during the period S2 to S4.

Table 4.9 Gender differences in attainment and progress at the secondary level

(i) Average reading/English scores for girls and boys

	Reading S2 1995	English S4 1997 Standard Grade	Progress 1995–7*
Girls	67.3 (20.0)	4.28 (1.15)	Significant positive
Boys	61.4 (22.0)	3.77 (1.64)	

Note: * Statistically significant difference in progress 1995–7 controlling for influence of other factors (see Tables 4.15 and 4.16).

(ii) Average maths scores for girls and boys

	Maths S2 1995	Maths S4 1997 Standard Grade	Progress 1995–7*
Girls	52.1 (22.2)	3.55 (1.63)	Not significant
Boys	52.5 (23.6)	3.45 (1.64)	

Note: * Statistically significant difference in progress 1995–7 controlling for influence of other factors (see Tables 4.15 and 4.16).

(iii) Average Overall Standard Grade performance (standard deviation) for girls and boys

	Overall Standard Grade points score S4 1997 (best grades)	Progress 1995–7*
Girls	28.4 (9.35)	Significant positive
Boys	25.7 (9.70)	

Note: * Statistically significant difference in progress 1995–7 controlling for influence of other factors (see Tables 4.15 and 4.16).

For mathematics, in contrast, there were no significant gender differences in attainment at S2. By S4, however, there were indications that girls were beginning to move ahead. Though not quite significant (at the 0.05 level) the analysis of progress in mathematics suggests that girls may be making more progress in this area also.

Age differences in secondary schools

As we noted in the earlier section, age differences – within a year group – were important at the primary level. Perhaps surprisingly, we found that significant age effects were also evident at both S2 and S4 in all the ISEP measures of attainment. This demonstrates that, even in their adolescence, those young for their school year are at a disadvantage. This has implications for the assessment process and the way that pupils are given feedback about their progress, if age-standardized assessments are not used. Although age-related differences in attainment were evident in each assessment there were no age-related differences in progress, in line with the findings for primary pupils. In other words, the age gap did not increase but neither did it close between S2 and S4. Given the 'high stakes' nature of public examination assessments at age 16 and the large numbers of pupils affected, we feel it is a matter of concern that those young for their school year still obtain significantly lower results than older pupils.

Socio-economic differences in secondary years

As with the primary scores, the data show that pupils eligible for free meals had significantly lower attainment at both S2 and S4 in reading and mathematics as well as in terms of Standard Grade results (Table 4.10). The multilevel

Table 4.10   Socio-economic differences in attainment and progress at the secondary level

(i) Average reading/English scores (standard deviations) for pupils

	Reading S2 1995	*English S4 1997 Standard Grade points*	*Progress 1995–7**
Free meals	53.8 (21.9)	3.24 (1.31)	Significant negative
Other pupils	66.3 (20.5)	4.15 (1.17)	

Note: * Statistically significant difference in progress 1995–7 controlling for influence of other factors (see Tables 4.15 and 4.16).

(ii) Average maths scores (standard deviations) for pupils

	Maths S2 1995	*Maths S4 1997 Standard Grade points*	*Progress 1995–7**
Free meals	41.0 (21.9)	2.47 (1.51)	Significant negative
Other pupils	54.4 (22.5)	3.68 (1.59)	

Note: * Statistically significant difference in progress 1995–7 controlling for influence of other factors (see Tables 4.15 and 4.16).

(iii) Average overall standard grade performance for girls and boys

	Overall Standard points score S4 1997 (best 7 grades)	*Progress 1995–97**
Free meals	20.1 (9.7)	Significant negative
Other pupils	28.2 (9.1)	

Note: * Statistically significant difference in progress 1995–7 controlling for influence of other factors (see Tables 4.15 and 4.16).

analysis of progress, likewise, revealed that pupils from socio-economically disadvantaged backgrounds tended to make less progress across the two years of the study. Thus the gap between the disadvantaged group and other pupils increased in the last two years of compulsory schooling.

Learning support in secondary years

The analysis of secondary pupils' attainments revealed, as might be expected, that those identified as receiving learning support had much lower attainments than other pupils at both S2 and S4. These differences were highly significant. The multilevel analysis of progress also revealed evidence that the gap increased during this time, in line with the findings for both gender and socio-economic disadvantage. Table 4.11 summarizes these results.

Table 4.11   Differences in attainment and progress of secondary pupils receiving or not identified as needing learning support

(i) Average reading/English scores (standard deviations) for pupils

	Reading S2 1995	*English S4 1997 Standard Grade points*	*Progress 1995–7**
Learning support	48.3 (22.7)	3.12 (1.31)	Significant negative
Other pupils	68.0 (19.2)	4.18 (1.15)	

Note: * Statistically significant difference in progress 1995–7 controlling for influence of other factors (see Tables 4.15 and 4.16).

(ii) Average maths scores (standard deviations) for pupils

	Maths S2 1995	*Maths S4 1997 Standard Grade points*	*Progress 1995–7**
Learning support	37.0 (23.7)	2.48 (1.63)	Significant negative
Other pupils	55.2 (21.7)	3.69 (1.57)	

Note: * Statistically significant difference in progress 1995–7 controlling for influence of other factors (see Tables 4.15 and 4.16).

(iii) Average overall standard grade performance for girls and boys

	Overall Standard Grade points score S4 1997 (best 7 grades)	*Progress 1995–7**
Learning support	20.0 (10.5)	Significant negative
Other pupils	23.8 (8.9)	

Note: * Statistically significant difference in progress 1995–7 controlling for influence of other factors (see Tables 4.15 and 4.16).

It should be remembered that schools vary in the criteria they use to determine eligibility for learning support. Nevertheless, this factor was clearly related to attainment and progress at secondary school for the ISEP sample. The results demonstrate that those in receipt of LS continue to be at an educational disadvantage in terms of attainment in public examinations. It is quite possible, however, that such pupils may have attained even lower results without this support. Labelling or reduced self-expectations may also have an influence.

Again unsurprisingly, the small group of pupils with a record of need attained significantly less well than their peers in all our assessments. In addition, their progress was significantly lower in mathematics though not, interestingly, in reading.

● The combined effect of the factors on secondary school performance

The background factors taken together account for between 11 and 15 per cent of the total variation in pupils' Standard Grade results. This shows that these factors are relatively less influential for older pupils (in comparison with the primary sample where the equivalent figures were around 20 per cent). Having taken into account the effects of the background and prior attainment we found that we could account for between 54 and 64 per cent of the total variance in Standard Grade outcomes. The percentage of remaining variance attributable to the schools ranges from 6 to 7 per cent for the academic outcomes. In percentage terms, this sounds relatively modest but its impact can be of great significance.

The next question, as with the primary schools' analysis, gets to the heart of school effectiveness: *how much benefit does attending the most effective secondary school bring to an average pupil?*

As can be seen from Table 4.12, the most effective school added just less than half a grade while the least effective deducted the same amount in both English and mathematics. However, in the measure of the best seven grades, the most effective school added nearly three raw grade points and, correspondingly, the least effective deducted the same amount. These findings are also mirrored by the standard deviation of the school residuals (English 0.19; mathematics 0.19; best seven Standard Grades 1.24). We can loosely interpret these figures to mean that a pupil's performance difference in the 'most effective' school would lead to achieving six Standard Grade 2s while, in the least effective school, she or he would be more likely to achieve six Standard Grade 3s.

The difference of a run of 2s or 3s does not represent a large proportion of the variance but, in reality, it represents a highly significant difference in life chances. For English and mathematics outcomes, the equivalent figure is approximately one Standard Grade difference – on average – between the most and least effective secondary departments.

Table 4.12 Effectiveness of secondary schools

(i) in English progress

	Difference in relative progress – raw grades
Most effective school	+0.44
Least effective school	−0.44

(ii) in mathematics progress

	Difference in relative progress – raw grades
Most effective school	+0.42
Least effective school	−0.50

(iii) in best seven Standard Grade progress

	Difference in relative progress – raw grades
Most effective school	+2.8
Least effective school	−3.2

As with the primary sample, we also looked at the effectiveness of the schools by dividing them into four groups depending on the significance of their effectiveness. Table 4.13 illustrates this grouping.

In English, 14 per cent of the schools were classified as effective and 19 per cent were seen as ineffective (as defined by the measure). In mathematics, the proportions at both ends of the spectrum were larger – at 22 per cent. And in the best seven measure, the figures were 17 and 19 per cent. This illustrates that the schools varied considerably in their effectiveness once all the other factors had been taken into account. As with the primary schools, the mathematics results showed the greatest range, thus illustrating that this subject is more open than English to school influence.

Table 4.14 examines whether schools were or were not consistent in their effects.

Of the 36 schools, 30 per cent had positive (but not necessarily statistically significant) effects. Thirty-seven per cent had a positive effect on one of the outcomes. A further 30 per cent had no positive effects at all. The correlations between secondary school residuals for English, mathematics and overall performance in terms of 'best seven' Standard Grades ranged from 0.49 to 0.67. For a significant minority of schools there were significant departmental or subject differences in terms of mathematics and English/reading effectiveness (e.g. 23 per cent of secondary schools obtained both positive and negative residuals across the two curriculum areas). These differences would not be apparent if only an overall measure of cognitive attainment for a school were used.

These findings are in line with previous research (Thomas *et al.* 1997a) and

Table 4.13   Grouping of secondary schools in terms of effectiveness

(i) What proportion of schools were effective in terms of English progress?

Grouping	Number of schools	%
Effective (significant positive residual)	5	14
Average – positive (non-significant positive residual)	14	39
Average – negative (non-significant negative residual)	10	28
Ineffective (significant negative residual)	7	19

(ii) What proportion of schools were effective in terms of mathematical progress?

Grouping	Number of schools	%
Effective (significant positive residual)	8	22
Average – positive (non-significant positive residual)	9	25
Average – negative (non-significant negative residual)	11	31
Ineffective (significant negative residual)	8	22

(iii) What proportion of schools were effective in terms of best seven Standard Grade results?

Grouping	Number of schools	%
Effective (significant positive residual)	7	19
Average – positive (non-significant positive residual)	11	31
Average – negative (non-significant negative residual)	12	33
Ineffective (significant negative residual)	6	17

Table 4.14   Positive residuals of secondary schools

Number of positive outcomes	Number of schools	%
None	12	33
One	13	37
Two	11	30

emphasize the need to look at schools' value-added performance in detail across secondary school departments. The comparison between school residuals for specific academic subjects and an overall academic measure (for secondary pupils) confirms previous findings and shows that some schools can vary considerably in their effectiveness across two curricular areas (English and mathematics).

When account was taken of pupil intake characteristics, the value-added analysis shows that significant school differences in performance remain, though these are much smaller than the raw differences, especially for English assessments. We also find from the multilevel analysis that the school-level variation is particularly affected by the inclusion of background data about pupil intakes. This is an important message for those concerned with developing frameworks to monitor and report on school performance. It also provides pointers to the way schools may find it helpful to explore the attainment and progress of different pupil groups using their own data and setting themselves targets for particular groups of currently underachieving pupils. However it is important for heads and teachers to consider the statistical significance of the progress results, as well as being aware of other limitations in interpreting quantitative data for the purpose of school self-evaluation (Thomas and Smees 2000).

● Differential effects of secondary schools

A further question for all studies of school effectiveness is whether the school effects are uniform across pupil groups or whether some groups gain more than others in some schools. In other words, are some schools better for girls rather than boys or for the advantaged rather than the disadvantaged? Additional multilevel analyses were employed to examine the schools' differential effects for different groups of students categorized by prior attainment, gender and entitlement to free school meals.

The results showed that some schools obtained significant differences in value-added results for different groups of pupils categorized by their ability. (The correlations between the school residuals for high- and low-attaining pupils were 'best seven' = 0.24; English = 0.60; maths = -0.14.) It is interesting that much smaller differences were found for all other groupings. This is in contrast to findings in some other contexts in England (Thomas *et al.* 1997a) which suggests that, in spite of the relatively small sample, schools in Scotland may be more equitable in their effects on pupil groups categorized by gender and FSM but not prior attainment. Those that are more effective tend to be so for both girls *and* for boys and for those from socio-economically disadvantaged *as well as* those from more advantaged backgrounds.

● The overall picture

Our results suggest that school differences in pupils' attainment and progress in the basic skills are more marked at the primary than the secondary level, again pointing to the importance of this phase in pupils' school careers in determining literacy and numeracy performance. They also suggest that pupils' backgrounds are relatively less important in accounting for variations between pupils in their attainments at secondary level (interestingly these findings are in line with those reported in the longitudinal follow-up of the School Matters cohort; see Sammons 1995). This has important implications for policy makers and practitioners, pointing to the need for early intervention to raise pupils' attainment levels in reading and mathematics, given their importance for later progress and attainment.

We found that gender and eligibility for free school meals showed a significant relationship with Standard Grade performance in English and the overall performance measure. Moreover, in contrast to the primary results, the contextualized measure – percentage of pupils eligible for free school meals – was also statistically significant. It may also be that the degree of disadvantage of a school's intake has an impact upon secondary school culture that is not evident at the primary phase. Again, the importance of the balance of intake has implications for policies on selection, schools with concentrations of disadvantaged pupils having a greater risk that all pupils' performance will be depressed.

The greater impact of primary schools on attainment and progress in mathematics than in reading reported here is in line with earlier studies (e.g. Brandsma and Knuver 1989; Sammons *et al.* 1993; Sammons and Smees 1998), but is especially striking with the ISEP primary sample. Again this has implications for the work of the government's Literacy and Numeracy Task Forces.

By using value-added approaches, we have also explored the impact of background on progress. The results show that background has much less impact on progress than it does on attainment. As we have shown, there were significant differences in school effectiveness across the sample. Some schools added greater value to their pupils than did others. These school effects were more powerful for mathematics than for reading. They were also stronger in the primary sector thus pointing to the importance of the earlier years in education for pupils' subsequent educational careers and long-term outcomes.

This chapter has provided a brief account of the detailed analysis of primary and secondary pupils' attainment and progress over the period 1995 to 1997. The evidence is important in the Scottish context, because of the absence of detailed longitudinal studies of these age groups. We have looked, in some detail, at the link between students' background characteristics and their achievements. We have identified important differences in attainment related to pupils' age, gender, low family income and learning needs. The focus on pupils' educational outcomes was a crucial component of the ISEP study. In order to examine the influence of schools we measured pupils' progress over two school years.

In terms of the progress gained, we find that the *school* has a greater influence than pupils' background characteristics such as age, gender or socioeconomic disadvantage. By identifying outliers (schools which were more or less effective in promoting pupils' progress in particular outcomes) we can explore the school processes in different categories of schools. The remainder of the chapters will focus on pupil outcomes within the detailed qualitative case study data.

Table 4.15 Final value-added multilevel model: pupil attainment at P6 (1997, controlling for prior attainment at P4)

Fixed effects	AAP Reading	AAP Mathematics
Age	ns	ns
FSM	ns	ns
Girls	+*	−*
Less than four years in current school	ns	ns
Learning support	ns	−*
Record of Need	ns	ns
% FSM	ns	ns
Suffolk 1995	+*	+*
Reading 1995	+*	+*
Mathematics 1995	+*	+*
% total variance accounted for controlling for prior attainment and background	42.1	56.7
% school level variance accounted for controlling for prior attainment and background	41.0	34.4
Intra-school correlation	0.122	0.326
p < 0.05		

Table 4.16 Final value-added multilevel model: Pupils' Standard Grade attainment at S4 (1997)

Fixed effects n of schools = 36 n of pupils = 4406	English	Mathematics	Overall performance (best seven)
AAP Mathematics 1995	* +	* +	* +
AAP Reading 1995	* +	* +	* +
Gender (girls)	* +	ns	* +
FSM	* −	ns	ns
Age in months	ns	ns	ns
+Too young	ns	ns	ns
+Too old	ns	ns	* +
% FSM	* −	* −	* −
% total variance accounted for controlling for prior attainment and background	54.3	65.9	64.0
% school level variance accounted for controlling for prior attainment and background	77.6	86.5	85.4
Intra-school correlation	0.0708	0.0609	0.0602

Notes:
+ Measures of whether pupils were chronologically too young or too old for their year group (i.e. outside the 12-month range).
* p < 0.05.
   In order to maximize the secondary sample of schools employed to compare school effects, learning support and Record of Need were not included in the analyses used to calculate secondary school residuals. These variables were however found to be significant predictors of secondary pupils' attainment and progress.

● 5

Views of pupils, parents and teachers: vital indicators of effectiveness and for improvement

Jim McCall, Iain Smith, Louise Stoll, Sally Thomas, Pam Sammons, Rebecca Smees, John MacBeath, Brian Boyd and Barbara MacGilchrist

● Introduction

School effectiveness research has been criticized for the narrowness of its outcome measures and its positivist approach (White 1997; Winch 1997; Slee *et al.* 1998). Such critiques tend to ignore the numerous studies in the school effectiveness mainstream which have paid attention to the voices of pupils, parents and teachers and identified their active participation as key elements of effective schools (Mortimore *et al.* 1988; Sammons *et al.* 1995). The inclusion of stakeholder views and their involvement in the interpretation of data was a salient and powerful feature of ISEP. It built on a tradition established in Scotland over the last decade of school self-evaluation and development planning which emphasized stakeholder participation and provided schools with a repertoire of instruments for such collaborative work (see Chapter 2). It also paved the way for the ISEP approach.

The questionnaires used in the ISEP study drew on half a decade of Scottish experience as well as approaches developed in other countries. The questionnaires served two purposes. On the one hand, they furnished a rich body of information on effectiveness and improvement in Scottish schools, providing insights into school cultures as viewed from three quite different vantage points and perspectives. On the other hand, they provided data to schools for schools themselves, to reflect on and to use in planning and improvement. In the 24 case study schools questionnaire data were complemented by qualitative data from individual and group interviews. Chapters 9 and 10 describe how those data were used by schools with the support of a critical friend. In this chapter we consider how far these data help us in:

- our understanding of school effectiveness and improvement;
- how they link to other process and outcome measures;
- how interview data (in particular pupil voice) illuminates the quantitative questionnaire data.

A place for pupil voice

Giving a place to the views of pupils has assumed an increasing priority in many countries over the last decade or so. In Scotland it was given impetus by a seminal and disturbing study, published in 1980 and entitled *Tell Them From Me* (Gow and McPherson 1980), which gave a cumulative picture of 'flung aside forgotten children', to use the words of one young school leaver writing about his experience of school. The report stung the policy community and convinced Her Majesty's Inspectorate (HMI) that not only were young people's views well worth listening to but of critical importance for the health of schools and further education. Subsequent studies found pupils to be both astute and articulate observers of the school environment (MacBeath and Weir 1991; Keys and Fernandes 1993; SooHoo 1993; Rudduck *et al.* 1996). As SooHoo (1993) points out, we are ignoring a rich plethora of information if we fail to bring pupils into the research process:

> Somehow educators have forgotten the important connection between teachers and students. We listen to outside experts to inform us, and, consequently, we overlook the treasure in our very own backyards: our students. Student perceptions are valuable to our practice because they are authentic sources; they personally experience our classrooms first hand . . . As teachers, we need to find ways to continually seek out these silent voices because they can teach us so much about learning and learners.
>
> (SooHoo 1993: 389)

Pickering (1997) argues that the voice and involvement of pupils is essential to school improvement because it is *their* learning that is under discussion. Involving them in responsible debate reflects the level of responsibility many have in their lives outside school, a world that should be recognized and reflected in what happens within the school gates. The message for researchers as well as for school leadership is that we must take scrupulous and systematic account of pupil views in order to broaden the scope of how we evaluate effectiveness and inform school improvement. As previous researchers have noted, only with multiple indicators can we build up a more coherent picture of a school's effectiveness (Ainley 1994).

Building the picture

As we learned from the Gow and Macpherson study, pupil voice is best heard through spontaneous written or interview comment. With the support of a substantive body of quantitative data from the questionnaires we were able to

Table 5.1   Comparison of questionnaire and interview structures

Questionnaire factor analysis	Interview themes
Engagement with school	Engagement with school
Pupil culture	Pupil–pupil relationships
Self-efficacy	Pupil empowerment
Behaviour	Pupil–teacher relationships
Teacher support	Teacher support for learning

satisfy ourselves of the internal consistency of the data and the validity of what young people were telling us about their school experience.

Pupils in the 12 primary and 12 secondary schools were interviewed in small groups in the summer of 1995, with a second round of interviews in 12 of these schools (six primary and six secondary) two years later. Pupils were drawn from P2, P6, S1, S4 and S5/6. On both occasions comments were recorded, analysed and categorized into themes and subthemes. Interview data were analysed independently of the questionnaire data, giving us a set of cross-cutting themes which could then be matched with those emerging from the factor analysis of the questionnaires. The closeness of match is illustrated in Table 5.1.

● **What do pupils say?**

Engagement with school, which emerges from both factor analysis of questionnaires and thematic analysis of interview data, provides an overarching category for exploring pupil views and their significance. While pupils did not speak of 'engagement' as such, they did give clear messages about those aspects of school life that made going to school either congenial or uncongenial. They described aspects of school and classroom life that engaged, or disengaged, their interest. The mediation of school life, learning and values through the individual teacher was, not surprisingly, a key factor.

Teacher support for learning

Good teachers were recognized and appreciated. Pupils could easily identify their qualities and 'added value':

> 'They care. They give up their lunchtimes to do one-to-one tuition. They want you to do well and they help you all they can.'
>
> (S5/6)

Pupils' comments revealed a sensitivity to the kind of support that worked best and what high expectations meant in practice:

> '. . . they encourage you to try even harder. They don't compare you to anyone else.'
>
> (P6)

'If it's not like you to give, say, not neat work, they ask you what's wrong
– "This isn't like you."'

(P6)

Teacher support was often measured in terms of praise and encouragement:

'If you do good work you get a smiley face on your work but if it's really
bad you get a sad star. Some stickers say "brilliant" or "wow".'

(P2)

'We have an assembly and the headteacher mentions pupils' names and
says "thank you".'

(P6)

While welcoming encouragement and praise, pupils, even from early primary
years, showed that they could also be insightful commentators and trenchant
critics of classroom management and methodology:

'We should know more about how we are doing. You'd know what parts
of the subject to go over to improve. You've got to be able to improve –
you need to know what to do.'

(S4)

Relationships with teachers

There is perhaps only the slightest nuance of difference between the theme
teacher support and *teacher–pupil relationships*. The first tended to focus more on
support for learning while the second tended to refer more to discipline and
control. Pupils were usually reluctant to generalize about teachers. They knew
the ones they respected and were able to identify the qualities that went with
that positive evaluation:

'We are treated fairly by most teachers and the classrooms are happy, not
boring. It is the strict teachers who seem to have most problems.'

(S1)

'Some teachers make fun of you but others are nicer. Some dish out
punishments for nothing.'

(S1)

Some of these comments, on strictness for example, might appear to go
against conventional wisdom, but it was only through these qualitative data,
both from teachers and pupils, that we were able to understand what 'strict'
meant in its various contexts and relationships. Some of us were able to
observe (see Chapter 9) how counter-productive strictness could be.

'Shouting' featured a lot in comments from younger children:

'The teacher would shout at you if you're lazy. She shouts at you a very
lot. If you're really, really bad, she shouts really, really loud.'

(P2)

Placing teachers in their classroom context and within the ethos which they established shed further light on this theme:

> 'The atmosphere is relaxed. We know the teacher really well in small classes and can have a joke with them. Class size is important. It's easier to ask questions in a small class.'
>
> (S5/6)

Pupil empowerment

Pupil empowerment was a theme raised spontaneously by pupils in the course of interviews, often in response to open-ended questions such as 'What do you like/not like about the school?' Empowerment in their terms was the degree to which pupils felt that they were listened to, could play a part in the life of the school or participate in its planning and decision making. In this respect there were significant interschool differences:

> 'It's the headteacher who makes up the rules. We don't have a say in making them up.'
>
> (P2)

In another school, however, there was a feeling of some ownership of school rules:

> 'The pupils help decide the rules. The headteacher picks out the best rules and gets them laminated and puts them up round the school.'
>
> (P6)

Empowerment was not simply an age-related difference, as comments from senior pupils in one school illustrate:

> 'There is a pupil council but the headteacher comes to the meetings so you can't really say what you think – well you can, but he always says you're wrong.'
>
> (S5/6)

> 'We do get a say and they do listen, but not necessarily anything is done about it. It's as if they are trying to prove they are listening but they don't pay attention to what we think.'
>
> (S5/6)

In some schools this lack of power was felt at classroom level too:

> '[The teacher says] "Here's your personal topic; you're going to do Australia" – and some of us might not have wanted to do it on Australia.'
>
> (P6)

Pupil–pupil relationships

Much of the comment about pupil–pupil relationships had to do with bullying and the bad behaviour of the minority that was annoying to the majority who stayed out of trouble. Most pupils wanted to get on with their work and expressed frustration at the disruption and energy that went into controlling the dissident few. On the positive side peer mentoring and help from senior pupils were valued, although this was a feature of a minority of schools at the time of the study. Their comments highlight the issue of social mix (Thrupp 1999) and the 'compositional effect' which we describe in Chapters 1 and 4 as playing a vital part in school effectiveness and which can provide the momentum or inhibition of improvement.

This is, in turn, related to the issue of social inclusion, fairness or divisiveness created or reinforced by selective structures and teacher attitudes:

'Some teachers are only interested in the "brainy" ones.'

(S4)

'I think more attention is given to the ones that teachers know will achieve.'

(S5/6)

'Teachers have been complaining that the brainy people will be held back by the not so brainy people.'

(S4)

The frequency of such comments raises a question of how far the ethos of schools has moved since Gow and Macpherson's critique of 'flung aside forgotten children' two decades ago. As both qualitative and quantitative data reveal, however, schools differed markedly in respect of their ethos and capacity for improvement. These issues are explored further in Chapters 6, 7 and 10.

The differential of experience

Analysis of these themes showed some very clear differences from school to school. What were troublesome issues in one school did not figure in another. The physical environment was a salient issue in some schools but not others. Disengagement and disempowerment were felt more acutely in some schools and classrooms than in others. However, as in most effectiveness studies, it was not easy to find consistent differences across schools. Schools were, as we would expect from differential effectiveness data, seldom internally consistent. No school could present itself as a 'high reliability organization' (Reynolds and Stringfield 1996) with consistently satisfied pupils and 100 per cent committed teachers.

Pupils' views about engagement, relationships and inclusion were usually related, positively or negatively, to specific subjects, classrooms or individual teachers. There were stage differences too. We did not hear the same messages from secondary 1 pupils and secondary 4, 5, or 6. They saw their school differently and school was, in a real sense, a different place for them. Their teachers were different people too. A teacher strict with younger children might be more relaxed and informal with older pupils. In other words, strictness was not an inherent quality of the teacher but embedded in specific relationships and contexts. Nor was good or bad behaviour a stable character-istic of pupils. It was equally responsive to age and stage, context and relation-ships, and the statement 'He is not the same boy in my class' may not have been too far from a literal truth.

In other words the inconsistency among pupil views sheds important light on the subjective nature of school experience and the differential impact which schools have on their pupils and on their teachers over time, not only year to year but week to week and day to day.

The questionnaires

The quantitative data from questionnaires also showed considerable varia-tions – between one school and the next, between different age groups and also within age groups. Some questions provided high levels of consensus while others provided a spread of responses; splits in opinion on any given issue proved to be as important as those for which there were high levels of agreement. The questionnaire data allowed us to gain a more systematic, or system-wide, perspective on pupils. How representative were they? How dis-criminating?

For the purposes of ISEP two new pupil questionnaires were created, one for primaries 4 and 6 and the other for secondaries 2 and 4. The questionnaires built on previous research (SOED 1992a, 1992b; Keys and Fernandes 1993; Barber 1994) but with a specific focus on the key ISEP themes of ethos; teach-ing and learning; and development planning. Questions covered four main areas: 'What I think about school', 'Learning in school and at home', 'What I think about myself, my work and my friends' and 'How I behave at school and at home'. The primary questionnaire contained 26 multiple choice questions and two open-ended ones. The secondary questionnaire contained 42 mul-tiple choice questions and two open-ended ones. The 1997 questionnaires also included five additional questions about changes in the school over the previous two years.

Questionnaires were administered for the first time in summer 1995 and to the same group of pupils in summer 1997 (now in P6 and S4). This gave a total of 1144 primary and 3552 secondary pupils in both rounds of data collection. The resulting data were used in a number of ways. First, the spread of pupil responses for each item at two separate time points was calculated and results fed back to schools to inform school improvement processes. Second, by matching the 1995 and 1997 data it was possible to look at the *relative* progress or change in pupils' attitudes over a two-year period – a key aspect of the ISEP value-added framework (see Thomas *et al.* 1998b).

Results were fed back to schools together with data from all schools, allow-ing staff to compare their own results against the average results for all ISEP primary or secondary pupils. Table 5.2 gives an example of pupil responses to one item in the S4 questionnaire – frequency of bullying within a school.

Such data, revealing as they are, take us only some way along the road and need further analysis and interpretation before they can be useful to schools.

Table 5.2   Frequency of reported bullying in S4 (Item 34)

	% all ISEP S4 pupils	*% school 'Z' S4 pupils*
I bully others all the time	0	0
I often bully others	2	1
I hardly ever bully others	19	27
I never bully others	78	72

They can, for example, be further broken down by categories such as, year group, gender or prior attainment, or fed back to pupils to engage them in interpretation and discussion of the issues, helping in the review and reformulation of policy and practice.

Pupil views – the quantitative data

The questionnaire responses add quantitative confirmation to what pupils told us in interviews – that school is generally a positive experience, that relationships are key, that good teachers are appreciated, and that the experience of school depends on a multiplicity of factors and their interrelationship. For all ISEP schools, both primary and secondary, pupils' attitudes were generally more positive than negative. For all 1997 questionnaire items the average category response was above 2 (where 1 = most negative response; 4 = most positive response). Table 5.3 shows the three highest and lowest ranked questionnaire items at the primary and secondary levels in 1997. Broadly, the results suggest that – at the extremes – primary and secondary pupils' responses are most positive about the absence of bullying and least positive in the area of classroom interactions. However, it is important to note that the spread of pupil responses varies across all items with standard deviations ranging from 0.50 to 0.95 (primary) and from 0.36 to 0.94 (secondary). In other words, there is much more consensus on some items than on others. For example, primary pupils' responses vary least for the frequency of bullying item and most for the item relating to answering questions in class. In contrast, secondary pupils' responses vary least on the item relating to appropriateness of work and most on the truancy item. This is confirmation of differential experiences within schools as well as across schools, a finding not only important for the school effectiveness discourse but for policy makers as well.

Used together with the interview data we are able to say considerably more about what responses to these items mean and to probe the variations we find from school to school and classroom to classroom. For example, in both tables the three most negative items provide telling indicators of engagement with school and prove in many ways to be highly discriminating indicators within and among schools. They take us back again to the qualitative data which serve to explain what pupils mean when they express a lack of interest in school work, the significance of lack of recognition and praise from teachers and the importance of getting to do things you are good at.

Table 5.3   Highest and lowest ranked questionnaire items in 1997

		Mean	*(SD)*
Secondary			
Three most positive items	Frequency of bullying others	3.76	(0.49)
	Encouragement at home	3.72	(0.58)
	Frequency of being bullied	3.63	(0.70)
Three most negative items	Interest in school work	2.49	(0.59)
	Teachers praising me	2.41	(0.76)
	The behaviour of other pupils in my classes	2.20	(0.70)
Primary			
Three most positive items	How much I bully others	3.74	(0.50)
	Feeling safe in the playground	3.62	(0.59)
	Appropriate level of work (difficulty)	3.57	(0.59)
Three most negative items	How well I can do things	2.72	(0.58)
	Getting to do things I am good at	2.70	(0.74)
	Answering questions in class	2.67	(0.95)

Notes: Pupils with missing data excluded
Secondary sample n = 3948; primary sample n = 1254
SD = standard deviation.

Creating ISEP attitude scales

As well as examining the responses of the typical pupil (i.e. mean scores) and the spread of responses for each item (i.e. standard deviations), data reduction techniques were also used to combine results from different questionnaire items. By using this approach the variation across ISEP schools in terms of a reduced and more manageable set of pupil attitude measures could be investigated. This gave us the five attitude scales – *engagement with school; pupil culture; self-efficacy; behaviour* and, for the secondary data set only, *teacher support*. These were created using LISREL (Linear Structural Equation Model for Latent Variables), arriving at a similar set of scales as produced by more traditional factor analysis.

Comparing the views of primary and secondary pupils

When making comparisons between primary and secondary pupils it is important to bear in mind that questionnaire items were not identical but broadly equivalent. Data from primary pupils and secondary pupils did show some similar characteristics. In both sectors they were most positive in relation to the factors *pupil culture* and *behaviour* and least positive in relation to *engagement with school*. However, on three of the four scales – *pupil culture, engagement* and *teacher support* – primary pupils were consistently more positive than their secondary counterparts. For the fourth, *behaviour*, mean scores were similar across both sectors.

At primary level there was about twice the variation in pupil scores for the *engagement with school* scale than at secondary level, suggesting that primary pupils are much more likely than their secondary counterparts to differ in their liking for school. In contrast, secondary pupils were more likely to differ than primary pupils in their rating of their own behaviour. Overall, primary pupils' attitudes vary least for *self-efficacy* and most for *engagement with school*. Secondary pupils' attitudes vary least for *engagement with school* and most for *behaviour*. For policy purposes these findings are important because they suggest that particular aspects of educational policy and processes have a more positive and/or consistent impact on the views of primary pupils than second-

Table 5.4 1997 ISEP secondary pupil attitude scales

	Weights	1997 mean (SD)
Factor 1: Engagement with school		2.5 (0.24)
I always like school	[0.10]	
I always get on well with teachers	[0.28]	
Teachers are always fair	[0.31]	
School work is always interesting	[0.11]	
Teachers are nearly always friendly towards pupils	[0.20]	
Factor 2: Pupil culture		3.3 (0.44)
I always get on well with others in my year	[0.28]	
I never feel left out of things	[0.37]	
I never get bullied	[0.14]	
I find it easy to make friends	[0.21]	
Factor 3: Self-efficacy		2.8 (0.38)
My work in class is very good	[0.63]	
I think I'm very clever	[0.15]	
All my teachers think my work in class is good	[0.22]	
Factor 4: Behaviour		3.3 (0.58)
I always get on well with teachers	[0.08]	
How would you describe your behaviour in class? Good	[0.32]	
How do you think teachers would describe your behaviour? Good	[0.60]	
Factor 5: Teacher support		2.6 (0.37)
Teachers always help me to understand my work	[0.21]	
Teachers always tell me I can do well	[0.19]	
Teachers always tell me how I am getting on with work	[0.19]	
Teachers always praise me when I have worked hard	[0.31]	
Teachers are nearly always friendly towards pupils	[0.10]	

Notes:
Weights = LISREL weights applied to each item (i.e. to calculate attitude scales)
1   = most negative response category
4   = most positive response category
SD   = Standard Deviation.

Table 5.5   1997 ISEP primary pupil attitude scales

	Weights	1997 mean (SD)
Factor 1: Engagement with school		3.0 (0.55)
I always like going to school	[0.39]	
My teacher is always fair	[0.19]	
My work is always interesting	[0.22]	
I always feel happy at school	[0.21]	
Factor 2: Pupil culture		3.5 (0.48)
I always feel safe in the playground	[0.24]	
I never feel left out of things	[0.34]	
Nobody ever bullies me	[0.42]	
Factor 3: Self-efficacy		3.1 (0.40)
My work is just about right for me	[0.10]	
I think my work is very good	[0.25]	
I always do my best for school	[0.10]	
I can do everything well	[0.08]	
My teacher thinks my work is very good	[0.33]	
I think I'm very clever	[0.15]	
Factor 4: Behaviour		3.2 (0.46)
I never bully other children	[0.12]	
Grown-ups at home think I always behave well	[0.14]	
I think I always behave well in school	[0.43]	
My teacher thinks I always behave well	[0.32]	

Notes:
Weights = LISREL weights applied to each item (i.e. to calculate attitude scales)
1   = most negative response category
4   = most positive response category
SD   = Standard Deviation.

ary pupils and vice versa.

This also looks like significant confirmation of the findings relative to attainment discussed in Chapter 4. The social background effect is at its most powerful in the primary years.

At both primary and secondary levels there is a significant correlation between pupils' reported attitudes and achievement. The five attitudinal clusters correlate with pupil attainment. For example, in relation to 1997 ISEP primary school reading scores, pupil culture showed a correlation of 0.5, on teacher support for learning 0.43, on behaviour 0.38, and on engagement with school 0.35 (McCall *et al.* 2000).

However, when we tried to establish a correlation between value-added attainment and value-added attitude, this proved to be a more complex task. Comparing value-added scores on the five attitude scales against value-added attainment scores, we found no correlations to which we could attach significance or confidence.

Table 5.6 Attitude change from primary 4 to secondary 4. Percentage of pupils saying agree/strongly agree

	P4	*P6*	*S2*	*S4*
Liking for school	80	76	74	74
Fairness of teachers	87	83	79	82
Interest in school work	80	77	58	52
Liking answering questions in class	78	54	56	51
Encouragement from the teacher to do well	68	63	74	74

Note: n = 1144 (primary); 3552 (secondary).

This does not, however, invalidate findings about the relationship between attitudes and attainment. What it demonstrates is that attitudes and attainment behave in different ways. While attainment is incremental over time (however inconsistently), attitudes do not improve in a linear fashion, indeed move in a contrary direction at key points in a pupil's school career. This is illustrated in Table 5.6.

While there is a general trend from positive to negative it is not always simply linear nor true for all items. Closer examination of patterns of response reveals again the complexity of schools as social and learning places but provides a rich source of data for schools themselves to use for dialogic and improvement purposes.

Summary

Rudduck (1995) asked 'What can pupils tell us about school improvement?' and concluded that we need to 'provide a context in which it seems legitimate for pupil opinion to be taken into account'. The range and diversity of data in our study would seem to confirm her conclusion. We can conclude on the basis of the data that:

- pupils in Scottish schools are capable of mature and insightful discussion about a range of issues affecting them and their schools;
- pupils enjoy the opportunity to express their views and do not, for the most part, get such opportunities in the normal course of events;
- pupils do not feel that they had much input to decision making and, even when they did, feel that 'sometimes our views get lost';
- while pupil comments tended to cluster around the themes of pupil culture/attitudes to learning/pupil experience, there were significant across-school and within-school variations in pupils' reporting of their experience;
- in general pupils like school, although primary pupils are more positive than those in secondary schools;
- in general pupils in Scottish schools believe their teachers, in the main, try their best to help them to succeed.

● What do teachers say?

As well as gathering views of pupils and their parents, information was gathered from teachers by means of a questionnaire and through interviews with teachers in case study schools. Having access to, and working with, teachers' perceptions is an important part of the process of school improvement, providing one potentially rich source of data (Fielding 1997; Victoria Office of Review 1997; MacBeath 1999). Data on teacher perceptions also appear to be useful in helping to identify school capacity for improvement (Stoll and Fink 1996).

Teachers' views emerging from the interviews touch on some of the themes that preoccupied their pupils but come at these from a quite different vantage point. For example, class size mentioned by pupils is also mentioned by teachers, but through a different lens:

'The continuous funding cuts mean class sizes just go on creeping up. Not that four or five more make a huge difference but I do think it sends a message to teachers about how we are valued. And we usually oblige because teachers are like that.'

(Secondary teacher)

As well as sharing common concerns with pupils, teachers also emphasize aspects of school life, relationships and working conditions that are virtually invisible to their pupils but central to teachers' morale and job satisfaction. It reminds us of their position as 'internal clients' of the school, also with needs to be met – social, emotional and learning needs:

'It's a good school to work in because you get support from your colleagues. As a new teacher I don't feel I'm on my own, that I have to hide my problems from other teachers or my head of department. From that point of view it is a good school. And I'm speaking personally here.'

(Secondary teacher in his second year of teaching)

As we have seen, however, teachers' morale and working conditions are not always invisible to their pupils:

'Instead of treating teachers like adults the rector treats them like children. They don't agree with some things but s/he is the headteacher.'

(S5/6)

Data from teacher interviews were an invaluable source on school and classroom life, providing confirmation and counterpoint to the views of their pupils. In Chapters 7 and 8 we explore these data in greater depth, giving us stronger purchase on the quantitative data that we explore here.

The teacher questionnaire

The format of the questionnaire was based on one developed in Canada for use in the Halton Effective Schools Project (Stoll 1992; Stoll and Fink 1996). Customizing this for Scottish schools meant placing emphasis on the three specific focus areas of the project: teaching and learning; school development planning; and developing a 'moving' school ethos (MacBeath and Mortimore 1994).

Each of the 54 questionnaire items required two responses: the first focusing on the extent to which the respondent agreed with the statement as reflecting current practice ('where we are now'); the second indicating how important teachers felt this characteristic was in creating a more effective school ('where we should be'). A five-point scale was used for each.

Interpreting results

In 1995, questionnaires were returned by 638 primary and 1941 secondary teachers (97 and 75 per cent response rates respectively). Two years later, questionnaires were returned by 440 primary and 1406 secondary teachers, representing 63 and 54 per cent response rates respectively.[1] Overall, the percentage of teachers agreeing (that survey statements represented actual practice) increased between 1995 and 1997. There are several possible reasons for this:

- project activities, including use of 1995 data feedback, could have led to a positive change in perceptions;
- a 'project effect' – as a result of the project, teachers hear that certain approaches and strategies lead to improvement, and their responses are subconsciously influenced by this information;
- disaffected teachers were less likely to complete the survey the second time.

While these caveats urge a degree of caution in interpreting the findings in Table 5.7, it is nonetheless interesting to consider which aspects of school

Table 5.7 Changes in your school over the last 2–3 years

		% Worse	% Same	% Better
• The school as a place to be	Secondary	29	27	44
	Primary	11	20	69
• Expectations of pupils by staff	Secondary	13	49	38
	Primary	2	49	49
• Learning and teaching practice	Secondary	5	43	51
	Primary	1	33	66
• The quality of leadership and management	Secondary	18	34	48
	Primary	9	37	54
• The process of school development planning	Secondary	10	40	50
	Primary	5	31	64
• Monitoring school progress towards goals	Secondary	7	43	50
	Primary	4	28	68

processes appear to have altered, especially relative to one another. (Whatever cautions one may have about the significance of *absolute* shifts, the significance of *relative* shifts may be more robust. For example, the 14 per cent increase in the percentage of primary teachers ascribing 'a clear vision' to their senior management team (SMT) is rendered more significant by the fact that the percentage agreement with other items relating to the senior management team remains constant.)

Primary teachers' perceptions of their schools

Generally, perceptions of current practice were more positive for primary teachers than for their secondary colleagues, in both 1995 and 1997. Primary teachers were most positive (75 per cent or more agreement in 1995 and 1997) with regard to the following items: their schools' focus on learning; monitoring of progress and feedback to pupils; the belief that pupils can learn; the communication of work expectations and of behaviour standards; support from colleagues; relationships with the community; and display of pupils' work.

Conversely, issues showing the highest levels of disagreement (15 per cent or more in 1995, 1997 or in both years) included those connected with: collaboration in planning teaching; cover for joint planning; peer classroom observation and feedback; communication between SMT and teachers; staff participation in decision making; recognition of staff successes; input of pupils and non-teaching staff to the development plan; benefits of extra-curricular activities; and significance of the School Board's role. The general picture is one of high satisfaction generally in relation to teaching and learning, i.e. interaction with pupils; but less satisfaction related to teacher interaction with others, for example, with colleagues and with the headteacher.

From 1995 to 1997, agreement among primary teachers increased on 51 of the 54 statements, with no change in the remaining three. Statements for which there was a 10 per cent or more increase are shown in Table 5.8. Three particular issues are noticeable in the changes in primary teachers' perceptions. First, they seem to indicate a perceived increase in communication and collaboration among teachers, particularly in relation to teaching and learning. More agree that teachers share similar beliefs and attitudes about effective teaching and learning, perhaps related to the reported increase in discussion among teachers, or to an increased perception that senior managers were communicating a clear vision of where the school was going. The percentage of primary teachers reporting that 'the primary concern of everyone in the school is pupil learning' rose from 85 to 92 per cent between 1995 and 1997.

Second, there was an increase in the percentages of primary teachers agreeing with statements related to school development planning, specifically in relation to the achievement of goals and targets and practical ways to evaluate these. These items appear likely to have been influenced by the focus, over this period, of the SOEID and of the local authorities in promoting school self-evaluation and development planning. This theme is further developed in Chapters 6 and 7.

Table 5.8 Characteristics showing the highest percentage increase in agreement (10% or more) – primary teachers

Statements	*% agreement 1995 (n = 638)*	*% agreement 1997 (n = 440)*
The SMT communicates a clear vision of where the school is going	63	77
Pupils in this school are enthusiastic about learning	65	80
Teachers have a say in topics selected for the school's staff development programme	64	77
Standards set for pupils are consistently upheld across the school	51	63
The school communicates clearly to parents the standard of work it expects from pupils	70	82
Teachers believe that all pupils can be successful	61	73
There is regular staff discussion about how to achieve school goals/targets	54	67
Extra-curricular activities provide valuable opportunities for all pupils	53	65
The school development plan includes practical ways of evaluating success in achieving goals and targets	51	63
Teachers in this school believe that all pupils can learn	87	98
Teachers regularly discuss ways of improving pupils' learning	74	85
There is effective communication among teachers	73	84
Teachers share similar beliefs and attitudes about effective teaching/learning	54	65
The school provides cover to allow staff joint planning time	46	56

Third, there appears to be a change in perceptions of expectations of pupils and the communication of standards and expectations.

It is also noteworthy that a statement with which 65 per cent of teachers agreed in 1995 – 'Pupils in this school are enthusiastic about learning' – showed an increase in agreement, to 80 per cent, by 1997.

The issues of least importance to primary teachers were pupils and non-teaching staff having input into the school development plan, teachers regularly observing each other in the classroom and giving each other feedback. The percentage of teachers who considered this mutual observation important increased from 19 per cent to 33 per cent, a disappointing statistic perhaps, given the research findings on the value of this form of collaboration (Little 1990).

Secondary teachers' perceptions of their schools

There was considerably greater divergence among secondary teachers than among their primary counterparts. Perceptions of current practice were most positive (75 per cent or more agreement in both 1995 and 1997) with regard to: staff encouraging pupils to try their very best; and teachers' monitoring of pupil progress. The highest levels of *dis*agreement (20 per cent or more in 1995, 1997 or both years) were in relation to: leadership and management;

Table 5.9   Characteristics showing the highest percentage increase in agreement (5% or more) – secondary teachers

Statements	% agreement 1995 (n = 1941)	% agreement 1997 (n = 1406)
Pupils' success is regularly celebrated in this school	65	78
Pupils' work is prominently displayed	59	67
Parents are clear about behaviour standards expected in school	53	61
There is regular staff discussion about how to achieve school goals/targets	35	42
Teachers in this school believe that all pupils can learn	61	67
The school communicates clearly to parents the standard of work it expects from pupils	55	61
The SMT communicates a clear vision of where the school is going	49	55
Staff participate in important decision making	35	41
Teachers regularly discuss ways of improving pupils' learning	58	63
Staff feel encouraged to bring forward new ideas	55	60
The SMT openly recognizes teachers when they do things well	33	38
Teachers share similar beliefs and attitudes about effective teaching/learning	22	27

staff collaboration and discussion about improving pupils' learning; perceptions of pupils' enthusiasm for learning and respect for teachers; teachers' expectations about the success of all pupils; the consistency of standards; and pupil and non-teaching staff involvement in school development planning. In general terms, secondary teachers paint a more pessimistic view of their schools, both in terms of how they view their pupils and how they view their senior colleagues.

From 1995 to 1997, the percentage of secondary teachers agreeing with 38 of the 54 statements increased, while it decreased slightly for 11 of the statements (and more significantly for one, 'The school development plan includes practical ways of evaluating success in achieving goals and targets'), while there was no change in the remaining four statements. In 12 of the statements, the increase in percentage agreement was 5 per cent or greater. Statements showing the highest percentage increase in agreement (5 per cent or more) are shown in Table 5.9.

Changes in secondary teachers' perceptions, while less marked than those of their primary colleagues, also suggest an increase in discussion among teachers, and in expectations. (There is also an increase in the percentage of secondary teachers who believe it is *important* that 'teachers in school believe all pupils can be successful' – from 76 per cent in 1995 to 83 per cent in 1997.) The changes also highlight two other issues. The first is recognition – that is, in the case of pupils, celebration of pupil successes (including display of their work) and, in the case of teachers, acknowledgement of teacher success. The second is an increase in perceived involvement of teachers: through participation in decision making and being encouraged to bring forward new ideas.

Secondary teachers viewed most of the statements as important. In common with their primary colleagues, the issues of least importance were pupils and non-teaching staff having input into the school development plan, and teachers regularly observing each other in the classroom and giving each other feedback (all viewed as important by fewer than 35 per cent of teachers in both years).

Findings across the phases – role differences

There were consistently significant differences between senior managers, middle managers and classroom teachers across both the primary and secondary sectors (although more striking in secondary). As Table 5.10 shows, these gaps were sometimes extremely wide.

While these discrepancies may be easily explained by reference to status and vantage point in the school hierarchy, they nonetheless speak volumes about structural factors in organizational cultures. When these data were fed back to individual schools together with normative data from all ISEP schools, the response was often to treat these as endemic features of secondary schools. But, given that there is a considerable range of difference within these aggregated data, it is an argument that could not be sustained. Some schools could make a difference to their internal cultures.

Table 5.10   Comparison of perceptions of senior management, middle management and teachers – 36 ISEP secondary schools

	% agreement		
	Teachers	Middle Management	Senior Management
Senior staff are available to discuss curriculum and teaching matters	92	73	62
The senior management team openly recognizes teachers when they do things well	71	35	26
There is mutual respect between staff and the senior management team in this school	69	50	54
Staff feel encouraged to bring forward new ideas	79	56	51
Decision-making processes are fair	79	46	41
Staff participate in important decision making	80	38	29
There is effective communication between the senior management team and teachers	87	48	46

Note: n = 1941.

Teachers' perceptions of change – 1995 to 1997

A more direct approach to teachers' perceptions of change in their schools was to ask them to compare their schools now (1997) with two years previously. Table 5.7 provides a positive picture of change, with only a small minority believing that their situation had worsened. Given the popular perception of low – and declining – morale among teachers, this is an interesting, and perhaps surprising, positive finding.

Apart from the broad pattern, there are interesting details: primary and secondary teachers perceived the least improvement being in the expectations of pupils by staff. They differed markedly in their perceptions of change in the school 'as a place to be': while more than two-thirds of primary teachers felt there has been an improvement, less than a half of their secondary colleagues concurred with that view. Indeed, these six items taken together confirm the message from many of the other questionnaire items: primary teachers generally have a more optimistic view of their school than do their secondary school colleagues.

Teacher questionnaires: structure

Factor analysis was used, as with pupil and parent data, to try and identify underlying dimensions to the 54 questionnaire items. Three distinct clusters, or factors, emerged (Smith *et al.* 1998):

1 *Leadership and management* – effective communication, availability of senior staff, staff participation in discussion and decision making, clear leadership

vision, mutual recognition and respect among staff, teacher input into school planning.
2 *Academic emphasis* – high expectations of pupils, monitoring of pupil work and feedback on pupil learning, teacher collegiality in the planning of teaching and learning.
3 *Behavioural standards* – clear behaviour standards communicated to pupils and parents, respect shown by pupils.

This allowed us to compute for each school a composite factor score for each of these three factors: that is, the sum of the teacher scores on the items belonging to a factor, averaged out for the teachers belonging to that particular school.

In 1995, and again in 1997, these composite factor scores discriminate significantly among schools, showing what amount to radical differences between one school and another, both in the primary and in the secondary sectors.

While these provide valuable indicators of school *processes* in their own right, do they have any systematic link to school *outcomes*?

Linking process to outcomes

So far we have shown that, judging schools on measures which teachers themselves believe to contribute to effective schooling, results show widely differing ratings among schools. This does not necessarily mean that these patterns actually differentiate between schools that are comparatively more or less effective (as measured, for example, by value-added attainment outcomes). We explored, therefore, whether these interschool differences in teacher perceptions do indeed in any way systematically link with differences in value-added attainment outcomes.

Secondary and primary schools were classified by value-added attainment outcomes in 1997. With three cognitive outcomes for each school, both in the primary and secondary sectors, we can see which schools show either positive (high) or negative (low) value-added on all three measures and at a level which reaches statistical significance in at least two of these measures; and we can see which schools have less conclusive results (medium). This gives a pattern for the 44 primary schools and 36 secondary schools (Table 5.11):

If:

- factor scores represent a reliable and valid method of distinguishing between schools which vary in their management characteristics, their emphasis on academic learning and their emphasis on behavioural standards;

Table 5.11   Schools classified by value-added cognitive attainment outcomes

	Primary	*Secondary*
High	5	5
Medium	37	26
Low	2	6

and if:

- Table 5.11 scores represent a reliable and valid method of distinguishing between schools which vary in their effectiveness in producing cognitive gains;

then:

- a large body of previous work would lead us to predict that there should be a correlation between the order of schools observed in the questionnaire factor scores and the order of schools observed in Table 5.11.

For example, the first teacher process factor emerging in this study is the rating of management and leadership climate of the school by its teaching staff. There is good reason to believe that this provides a link with school effectiveness in terms of pupil outcomes (Cheng 1994; Silins 1994; Sammons *et al.* 1995), although not all the evidence is unambiguous (Leitner 1994). A meta-analysis of a large number of studies by Scheerens and Bosker (1997) not only points to the importance of school management/leadership as a factor in school effectiveness, but identifies leadership characteristics which appear critical, including:

- support for teachers;
- shared vision and goals;
- participative decision making, collegiality and collaboration;
- a focus on school-based staff development.

We have, therefore, analysed whether our three teacher process factors are linked with the ordering of the schools in terms of value-added attainment outcomes.

Moderately substantial connections have been found for the primary school sample. Positively value-added primary schools appear to have high scores on Factors 1 and 2 of the teacher questionnaires, and the converse holds. No such connections can be found for the secondary school sample. The absence, so far, of obvious school-level results for secondary schools may be a size factor; or it may indicate that process factors operate predominantly at *departmental* rather than *school* level in the secondary school. In interviews with secondary teachers, for example, questioned about management and pedagogical issues, they often asked whether they should refer to the school or to their subject department.

The aggregation of individual questionnaire items into factor scores does, of course, to some extent conceal information being carried in the individual item scores: so we have also explored, for each of the 54 questionnaire items in both 1995 and 1997, whether individual items distinguish between the positive and negative value-added schools. Some items which showed some kind of significance failed to stand up to more robust analysis (e.g. a requirement that the apparent relationship across the three categories of schools – high, medium and low – was linear; and that the apparent relationship was in the predicted direction: i.e. that high scoring in value-added categorization was associated with high scoring on the questionnaire item; medium with medium; and low with low) and we have concluded that some results are unlikely to be other than the spuriously 'significant' results one obtains at random when using large-scale statistical analyses.

However, for the primary schools, the detailed examination of individual items confirmed that there are 11 management-related teacher questionnaire items (a subset of the 17 items in Factor 1) and nine teaching-related teacher questionnaire items (a subset of the eleven items in Factor 2) which distinguish between primary schools which are high, medium or low in value-added attainment outcomes.

In other words, assuming that teacher perceptions have some objective validity, we have evidence that high value-added attainment outcomes in primary schools are associated with two clusters of processes:

1 *Management and leadership*
   This includes effective teacher–teacher and teacher–SMT communication; fair decision making; encouragement of staff ideas; staff participation in decision making (including development planning); collegial and effective use of staff development time; SMT praise for staff.
2 *Emphasis on learning*
   Teacher discussion of pupil learning/teacher collaboration; encouragement of independent learning; monitoring of pupil progress/teacher feedback to pupils; high teacher expectations of pupils.

Teachers' direct perceptions of effective change

As described earlier, the 1997 questionnaire asked teachers directly whether matters had got better or worse in their school over the previous two years. On three of the five items, there were clear (and highly significant) differences between the primary teachers in schools with high value-added attainment outcomes and those in the schools with low value-added scores. Teachers in high value-added schools reported that:

1 their school was a better place to be;
2 learning and teaching practice had got better;
3 the quality of leadership and management in the school had improved.

Teachers in the negative value-added schools on average reported no change on these dimensions. Again we have clear-cut evidence that primary teachers' perceptions of the processes going on within their school tie in directly with measures of cognitive progress by pupils within the school.

In Chapter 6 we explore further the enigmatic relationship between teacher perceptions and value-added attainment in secondary schools.

Summary

The results of the analyses of the teacher questionnaire data show that:

• three different dimensions of school appear as significant differentiating factors: leadership and management; academic emphasis; and behavioural standards;

- generally, the perceptions of Scottish teachers have improved over a period of two years and many perceive positive change in their schools;
- primary teachers have more positive perceptions than their secondary colleagues;
- there are significantly different perceptions of schools held by senior management, middle management and unpromoted teachers, senior managers holding consistently more positive perceptions than their more junior colleagues;
- in primary schools a subset of the items in the *Management and Leadership* scale and the *Emphasis on Learning* scale are associated with value-added outcomes.

● **What do parents say?**

It is widely recognized that parents' views of their child's educational experience supply a further important perspective on a school's educational quality (MacBeath *et al.* 1986; Bastiani 1996; Coleman 1999). To elicit parents' views a questionnaire was devised based on one used by SOEID for school inspection. Parents were asked to rate their child's school using a four-point scale (strongly agree [1] to strongly disagree [4]) in terms of 24 different descriptive statements such as: *My child enjoys being at school,* and *The school has explained to me how I can help my child's learning at home.*

A random sample of all parents of pupils in ISEP schools (44 primary schools and 36 secondary schools) was sent the questionnaire at the start of the project in 1995 and again in 1997. Parents were assured of anonymity and only school identifiers were used. Due to the random nature of the parent sample on the two occasions, it was not possible to make direct comparisons of any individual parent's responses, nor to establish whether changes in views were due to real changes in perceptions over the two years or to the different samples involved in the two surveys. Nonetheless, both surveys provide useful evidence about parents' perceptions and level of satisfaction with specific aspects of their children's schools.

Differences among schools

Exploratory analyses of parents' responses reveal the extent of variation in responses to individual items and between schools. Differences were identified between primary and secondary parents' responses and items which showed greater variation were identified by referring to the means and standard deviations for each. There proved to be less variation in responses among parents of primary school children than for secondary pupils, while primary parents' views were consistently more positive for all items. While the majority of parents in both sectors and in both years, 1995 and 1997, gave favourable responses, the six items which revealed the greatest variation in views for the primary sample were as follows:

The school makes it clear to parents what standard of work it expects from the pupils.
Teachers are good at letting me know about my child's strengths and weaknesses.
The school has explained to me how I can help my child's learning at home.
I have a clear idea of the school's development plan.
Teachers deal effectively with bad behaviour.
There are opportunities for all pupils to take part in extra-curricular activities.

For secondary schools, 14 items were identified as showing more variation:

My child finds schoolwork stimulating and challenging.
The school makes it clear to parents what standard of work it expects from the pupils.
Teachers are good at letting me know about my child's strengths and weaknesses.
Teachers in this school believe all children can learn.
The school has explained to me how I can help my child's learning at home.
I have a clear idea of the school's development plan.
Pupils' work is displayed in the school.
Children are treated fairly in the school.
Teachers deal effectively with bad behaviour.
Pupils respect teachers.
School buildings are kept clean and in good order.
The school has a good reputation in the community.
Teachers respect pupils.
The school is good at keeping parents in touch with what is going on.

Underlying dimensions

Factor analysis was used to identify underlying dimensions that could explain the consistently positive results in some schools, the consistently negative in others and the mixed responses in the rest. This yielded four factors accounting for over half the variation in the two data sets. The factor solutions proved interpretable and broadly similar for both primary and secondary schools.

Primary parent questionnaires

The 1995 primary analysis was based on 2855 questionnaires from 44 schools (after excluding items with missing data).[2]

- **Factor 1 – School communication and welcome to parents** includes items such as *As a parent I feel welcome in the school* and *I find it easy to discuss my child's progress with school staff.*
- **Factor 2 – Pupils' work and learning** covers items such as *The school makes it clear to parents what standards of work it expects from pupils* and *The school has explained to me how I can help my child's learning at home.*
- **Factor 3 – Teacher/pupil relationships and behaviour:** the item showing

the strongest weight was *Pupils respect teachers*. Other items that loaded fairly strongly were *The school has a good reputation in the community* and *Teachers respect pupils*.

- **Factor 4 – My Child and his/her experiences of school:** the items that load most highly are *My child is encouraged to work to the best of his/her ability* and *My child enjoys being at school*.

Factor analysis of 1997 primary parent questionnaire data (based on 2608 cases) shows very similar results to those found in 1995, giving us confidence in the nature of the underlying dimensions identified.

Secondary parent questionnaires

An equivalent factor analysis of the 1995 secondary parent questionnaires was conducted on 1729 cases from 36 schools for which full data were available. This provided some correspondence with the primary data, although in this case two items were found to contribute little to the solution. *Staff, parents and pupils all play a part in making the school better* loaded on two factors (1 and 3) but in neither case strongly, and *there are opportunities for all pupils to take part in extra-curricular activities* loaded only weakly on Factor 1. These items were therefore excluded in calculating factor scores for parents and mean factor scores for schools.

- **Factor 1 – School communication and welcome:** items that loaded most strongly were *As a parent I feel welcome in the school, Parents' evenings are help-ful and informative* and *I find it easy to discuss my child's progress with school staff*. As in the primary analysis, this factor seems to cover the features of welcome and communication, although the items contributing to Factor 1 are not identical (*Pupils' work is displayed in the school* loading on Factor 2 in the secondary analysis, for example).
- **Factor 2 – Pupils' work and learning:** *The school has explained to me how I can help my child's learning at home* loads most highly, followed by *I have a clear idea of the school's development plan* and *The school makes it clear to parents what standards of work it expects from the pupils*.
- **Factor 3 – Teacher/pupil relationships and behaviour** covered identical items to those in the primary analysis. The item with the highest loading was *Teachers respect pupils*, followed by *Pupils respect teachers*.
- **Factor 4**, as in the primary solution, covers the three **My child** items.

Analysis of 1997 secondary parent returns (a sample of 1527 forms from 33 schools) provided four factors similar to those found in 1995. However, the items that formed Factor 1 in 1995 formed Factor 2 in 1997, suggesting that items concerning **Pupils' work and learning** were somewhat more influential for the 1997 sample than those related to the factor **School communication and welcome**.

Change in parent views

Schools were ranked for each of the four factors in terms of parents' mean scores separately in 1995 and 1997, thus making it possible to look across all primary and secondary schools at differences in rank positions and derive an indicator of stability or change in parents' views over this period. As the data in Table 5.12 show, in the primary sector there was relatively little change for just under half of schools in parents' views, with the other half showing changes, most specifically in relation to Factor 4 questions – **My child.** In secondary schools there was much less stability in parents' views and, as with the primary sample, the greatest amount of change was in relation to Factor 4, with least change related to Factor 3 – **Teacher/pupil relationships and behaviour.**

The significance of these data is open to a wide variety of interpretations – the more complex nature of the secondary school; the changing teacher–parent relationships with the school over time; the changing relationship of

Table 5.12 Change in parents' views of schools 1995–7

(i) Primary schools

	little change		*greater change*	
	n (< 5 places)	*%*	*n (> 14 places)*	*%*
Factor 1 Communication and welcome	16	36.4	7	15.9
Factor 2 Pupils' work and learning	21	47.7	8	18.2
Factor 3 Teacher/pupil relationship and behaviour	18	40.9	4	9.1
Factor 4 My child's experience of school	12	27.3	10	22.7

Note: n of schools = 44.

(ii) Secondary schools

	little change		*greater change*	
	n (< 4 places)	*%*	*n (> 10 places)*	*%*
Factor 1 Communication and welcome	10	30.3	9	27.3
Factor 2 Pupils' work and learning	11	33.3	8	24.2
Factor 3 Teacher/pupil relationship and behaviour	13	39.4	5	15.2
Factor 4 My child's experience of school	8	24.2	14	46.7

Note: n of schools = 33.

parents to their children as they progress through secondary (MacBeath *et al.* 1986). 'My child' may gradually cease to become less of a relevant construct for parents as their children become young adults and become clients of the school in their own right. Again, the greatest value of the data was when fed back to schools to interpret in their own context and to share with their parent body in order to foster dialogue and deepen understanding of the relationship between home and school.

Summary

The questionnaire surveys of parental views in 1995 and 1997 indicate that:

- parents' views were generally very positive;
- overall responses by parents were more favourable for primary than for secondary schools;
- there was more variation in views for some items on the parent question-naire than others. Six questions were identified which showed greater vari-ation for the primary sample and 14 for the secondary;
- school-level variation in parents' views was also evident. For example, among the 24 case study schools, particularly positive responses were identi-fied for four secondary and two primary schools, whereas in three second-ary and two primary schools views were less favourable than the average. In some of the case study schools (two secondary and four primary) parents' views were notably mixed – more positive in some areas but less positive in others;
- factor analysis was used to explore any underlying dimensions in parents' views. Four factors were identified for both the primary and secondary samples. These were **School communication and welcome; Pupils' work and learning; Teacher/pupil relationships and behaviour; My child's experience of school.** These dimensions were found to be broadly stable over time for both samples;
- factor scores were broadly stable in around half the sample schools. In a small minority there was evidence of substantial change over these two years.

● Conclusions

The results reported in this chapter have demonstrated that by using appro-priate instruments it is possible to collect reliable, valid and important atti-tudinal data through the use of questionnaires administered to pupils, parents and teachers. Each of those questionnaires yielded data of interest in its own context, but collectively they provided a rich and complex view of the schools and what happens within them from these very different perspectives. In addition, the data, as explained in Chapter 8, proved to be a critically import-ant resource in promoting discussion and change within the schools and in emphasizing the essential linkages between school self-evaluation and school improvement.

● Notes

1 Clearly the differential response rates between 1995 and 1997 must demand some caution in interpreting apparent changes between 1995 and 1997.
2 A rotated varimax factor analysis produced four factors with eigenvalues greater than 1.

Extending the quality framework: lessons from case study schools

Pamela Robertson and David Toal

One of the major purposes of ISEP was to achieve a set of indicators of school quality which went beyond measures of pupil attainment and value-added. In Chapter 5 we looked at the attitudes of pupils, teachers and parents in order to probe beneath the surface of school life, trying to explore what it felt like to be a pupil at one school rather than the other, attempting to view the school from a number of different perspectives. In this chapter we first examine qualitative data from teacher interviews. Then we move on to set the teacher questionnaire analyses alongside the qualitative analyses in order to understand better the processes of school effectiveness and school improvement.

The messages from the various data sources were never simple and unambiguous. This reflected in part the nature of the measuring tools used and the reliability and validity of different approaches. But the strongest message was that schools are not easily objectified or easy to pin down in time, but are restless dynamic and contradictory places. It reminded us that we have continually to question the nature of the evidence if we are to draw out useful messages for schools, policy makers or researchers.

The qualitative data sets provided us with additional frameworks for describing and analysing school quality. These are enlightening and valid for their own sakes, revealing patterns around the project themes of development planning, ethos, teaching and learning. They highlight differences among schools and signal implications for improving both pupil and organizational learning.

This chapter describes two major strategies for analysing the qualitative data – within and across schools. The focus is on the three areas at the heart of the SOEID's project brief – development planning; learning and teaching; and ethos. What would we learn about these three themes from teacher and head-teacher interviews? How did they think about these issues and their inter-relationship?

Interviews: the analytical framework

Interviews were carried out in all 24 case study schools in 1995. Four members of staff in each school were involved – the headteacher, a member of staff with responsibility for staff development, a teacher with long experience in the school and a teacher relatively new to the school. This selection was made to get the best possible coverage of the three main themes but allowing interviewees to range widely across areas of school life of relevance and concern for them. We allowed the voices of teachers to speak for themselves, not forcing the responses into the three major themes but using these as a backdrop to the interviews. Subsequent analysis of the interview transcripts provided us with 35 subthemes. The data also spoke so strongly about the importance of leadership and management that this was added as a fourth major theme.

From the interview evidence a summary statement for the meaning of each subtheme was developed, along with a scaled set of descriptors ranging from very positive to very negative. This five-point scale with a neutral midpoint was used to reclassify and evaluate each fragment of evidence, assigning them to a particular subtheme and rating them on the two scales below:

- the quality scale;
- the potential for improvement scale.

Ratings on these scales were summed to give current quality scores for each theme and also a total current quality score.

Using one subtheme as an example, a summary statement and associated positive and negative descriptors are given in Figure 6.1.

Response to socio-economic circumstances in the community: summary statement

This relates to the way in which a school responds to the needs of pupils from diverse socio-economic backgrounds.

Positive

There is an awareness of the potential influence of socio-economic factors on achievement but this is seen as a challenge. There is a strong staff commitment to raising standards, increasing pupil self-esteem and motivation, and to raising parental and pupil expectations.

Negative

There is a fatalistic attitude that socio-economic circumstances have such a powerful effect on learning and achievement that the school will not succeed in raising achievement no matter how hard staff try.

Figure 6.1 A quality statement: positive and negative descriptors

A database was built to help us classify, collate, analyse and report on this numerical and textual information (Robertson *et al.* 1998). It provided evaluative reports within and across schools based on the major themes and subthemes of the project. Additionally, the associated text-based fragments linked to these judgements were available for scrutiny, providing a check on the validity of the classification as well as being useful for detailed reporting. Thus the 1995 interview evidence provided an evaluative record of school quality and potential for improvement based on the views of teachers. The creation of this database, customized to match the aims, design and initial findings of ISEP, offers an innovative approach to the analyses of data in large-scale qualitative research (Robertson and Sammons 1997).

In 1997, near the end of the project, samples of teachers and pupils were again asked to provide information around these three central themes. Teachers and pupils were selected largely according to the same criteria as in 1995, although teachers were not always the same people due to staff changes.

Interviews were carried out in 12 of the 'in-depth' case study schools, while in the other 12 schools teachers supplied written replies. This change in methodology came about to accommodate an intensive refocusing of the research and case study design on a subset of 12 schools. The 1997 interview schedules were refined a little to focus more closely on the subthemes arising from the 1995 analysis.

As the classification, scoring and entry into a database of hundreds of fragments of interview evidence in 1995 had been unduly onerous, a new database was created for 1997 with the 35 subthemes used as an organizing structure (Robertson *et al.* 1998). After the evidence had been classified, coded and weighted, a single entry per subtheme was made to the database. Thus any individual transcript might have up to 35 records associated with it.

In 1997, a new scale for rating evidence (Scale C: perceived improvement) was added, providing evidence on perceived improvement in key areas of school life over two years. So, in addition to evidence of trends from qualitative and quantitative data, we had the direct assessment of teachers on aspects of school improvement.

● **Case studies: emerging themes**

Outer ethos and inner culture

What did the data reveal about ethos as seen by teachers? What conclusions could we derive for policy makers for whom it had been such a high policy priority?

It is clear from the interview data that the concept of ethos had been internalized by teachers and had become part of their everyday vocabulary. However, there were conceptual differences and some confusion in the use of terminology and, when put together with other ISEP data, revealed differences between espoused theory and theory-in-use. Many analysts draw a distinction between the concepts of 'culture' and 'ethos' (Torrington and Weightman

1998; Hargreaves 1993) and we found the work of Dalin and his colleagues (1993) especially helpful in disentangling the various strands.

If we accept the notion of 'ethos' as the outward and public expression of a school's norms and values, we may also find matching or contradictory cultures and sub-cultures. Organizational culture, suggest Dalin *et al.* (1993), operates on three levels corresponding broadly to the Freudian concepts of super-ego, ego and id. Applying these to the school, he describes them as:

- *'Transrational'* – values are conceived as 'metaphysical', based on moral and ethical values and codes. Theses are rarely found explicitly in state schools and are more characteristic of Waldorf, Montessori, Steiner or Summerhill-type schools.
- *'Rational'* – values are grounded within a social and perhaps political context on norms and customs, conventional expectations and standards and dependent on 'collective justification'. At this level most values are expressed through daily routines, norms, rules, 'customs and ceremonies' of the school.
- *'Subrational'* – values are based on personal preferences, experiences and biases, grounded in emotion rather than rational thought, direct and personal, 'asocial and amoral'. From his analysis, Dalin finds that culture at this level has a powerful role in the school at any point in time and in its future.

These different levels of school culture, with their varying power, are built up through the history and development of the school. They arise through the history that each individual or group brings to the school. Even a brand new school has a powerful past, composed from the prior experiences that each individual brings. This means that several cultures or subcultures may exist within a school – among different groups of young people, among different sets of staff and among parents. The values and norms of these separate subcultures may be coherent or incongruent; with quite different implications for the school and its improvement. These will operate at many different levels, from the individual level through to the interface of school and community. This public interface is described by Hodgkinson (1983) as the *ethos* level.

Our understanding of these conceptual issues has implications for school improvement. It grows out of our analyses of pupil and teacher interviews, where we often find contradictions amongst teachers themselves and between the ways in which teachers and pupils view things. There are further differences between vision as expressed in school documentation and in the discourse of staff.

A predominant theme of teacher interviews was the importance of a positive school ethos with an associated emphasis on praise for achievement and recognition of effort, reflecting the high profile given to ethos in Scottish educational policy over the last 15 years. Yet headteachers frequently expressed concern about the level of challenge to pupils' learning and the level of teachers' expectations:

'This is beginning to sound negative but there is a definite lack in some areas of rigour and challenge and real engagement with learning. We still suffer from the old school approach to teaching which was if you could control your classes everything was fine. Keep the door closed and you wouldn't get any problems . . . They are on task but the task level is too low. They're not being pushed . . . That is probably my biggest concern. . . the attitude "It's only [School T] kids, you can't expect them to do any better". That was a fairly common statement for some staff to make around the building and I am afraid I got annoyed and said I didn't want to hear anyone talking like that about our young people. Everyone in here needs to be valued and they have something to offer, we've got to find the key to unlock it.'

(Headteacher, Secondary School T)

Another head, speaking about ethos, painted a more optimistic picture, describing ethos as 'an outstanding strength. The development of an enhanced culture of rewarding achievement and a focus on records of achievement in S5/6 is discernible. It is a great delight to see staff's commitment to their extended professionalism . . .' (Headteacher, Secondary School V).

In all case study schools, interviewees spoke about the importance of high expectations and positive teacher attitude, advocating a set of values and beliefs well established in Scottish central and local government policy over the last two decades. This may be described as the 'rational' level of the school culture (Dalin *et al.* 1993). At the same time, in a number of schools in disadvantaged areas, some interviewees spoke about the futility of their professional task, and others (such as the head of school T, described above) provided indirect information about the predominant cultures or subcultures in the school. In other words, there was an implicit acknowledgement of the existence and power of the subrational in determining the nature of school culture. The following three examples of teachers' views of the potential of their pupils, all from schools where low attainment and poverty were persistent concerns, illustrate these tensions and contrasts:

'The children have got worse . . . A big minus is caused by the area . . . the strength of the community influence negates anything we try to do.'

(Teacher, Primary School H)

'There has been no major change in my aims and vision for the school over the last two years. I am still aiming for the children to achieve all that they can – to be all they can be. This means appropriate curriculum, appropriately differentiated and learning support if necessary. It also means making a conscious effort to expand horizons and to nurture talents.'

(Headteacher, Primary School K)

'Given the difficulties these children have in their lives there are small triumphs every day . . . Firstly we have to try and boost their self-esteem . . . We want the best but we have to give the children tasks they can achieve, an appropriate curriculum. One of our problems with Quality Assurance [local authority] was that they came into the school and saw well-mannered children speaking politely and they thought we weren't pushing them enough. They didn't realize that our children can't take a lot of pressure, they are vulnerable and they have to be able to cope with what they are doing so that you can praise them. It doesn't mean that you don't push them further next time.'

(Teacher, Primary School J)

These three schools are all within an area no more than 30 miles in diameter, experiencing similar levels of support at local authority and national level, and are all confronted with the same profound difficulties in the communities they serve. Yet while some schools seem to be marked by a pervasive sense of resignation, in others there is an optimism that schools can make a difference.

Teaching and learning

One of the purposes of the teacher interviews was to explore how, in their opinion, recent initiatives in curriculum approaches to teaching and learning had influenced classroom and whole-school practices. How had these changes impinged on individual teachers' attitudes and perceptions?

Curriculum change has been a major feature of Scottish school education throughout the last two decades. Some commentators have seen this emphasis as damaging the pursuit of educational improvement, as detracting from a focus on essential, generic issues related to learning and teaching (Scottish Consultative Council on the Curriculum 1996). Some critics (for example, Brown *et al.* 1995) have called for school effectiveness research to focus more closely on classroom processes, accompanying our understanding of differential achievement with a systematic analysis of learning and teaching. While fine-grained, observational analysis was beyond the scope of ISEP, questionnaire and interview data helped us to understand how teachers saw the relationship between teaching and learning and ever-changing curriculum. Analysis of transcripts from primary school interviews in 1997 showed that the most frequently mentioned aspects of learning and teaching focused on teaching methodologies.

In interviews with headteachers, the 5–14 programme was a recurring theme. It had become an increasingly accepted part of school life, yet heads reported few fundamental changes in learning and teaching over the two-year period of the study. The significant changes they identified were mostly concerned with development planning, school priorities and, in some cases, the effect of these on classroom activity. They stressed, in particular, the increasingly high profile of assessment and monitoring of pupil progress and the pressure to improve school ethos, especially in respect of management styles and communication issues. Several headteachers also identified changes in personnel as significant, positive in respect of younger staff with fresher ideas but negative in respect of too much staff change – seen as destabilizing for parents, pupils and colleagues.

Despite these reservations, many primary schools seemed confident about their aims and vision. Teachers recognized the obstacles to progress which children were facing in their lives outside school, and believed that they took account of these influences in their teaching and pastoral care. Despite concerns about overload from curriculum reform, resourcing difficulties and lack of challenge for more able children, the overall impression they gave was of children progressing well in relatively successful and improving schools.

Secondary school interviews evidenced a greater quest for new routes to improvement. The fragmented structure and lack of coherence of the curriculum from secondary Years 1 to 6 was a persistent concern. Many secondary staff believed that, for several groups of pupils, schools were not getting it right; that there was a lack of challenge and consistency in the early years of secondary schooling and that many pupils were demotivated, especially in Years 3 and 4. A number of schools, however, had put specific initiatives into practice to deal with these issues, for example 'the enhancement of a more positive approach to recognition of achievement and the S4 boys project' (Secondary School V).

The preoccupation with curriculum change and relative lack of focus on pupil learning was explained by one headteacher in these terms:

> '. . . I don't think we've come to terms with the nature of learning. We've not yet managed to overcome the subject barrier nonsense that goes on around the place with more and more departments wanting a chunk of time in S1. We're still very much a subject-centred curriculum. We haven't crossed over to being anything like a child-centred curriculum. Maybe that is a national problem but certainly it is an issue. In terms of the good practice that goes on in our associated primary schools, I don't think we do ourselves any favours by ignoring that practice. . . I don't think we have got it right in terms of curriculum organization and that is one of the major blows to young people who've been making progress from P1 to P7 to come here. There are so many opportunities to opt out of the learning process and a lack of consistency across the school is a major issue in that. A lack of understanding of how young people learn . . .'
>
> (Headteacher, Secondary School T)

Others spoke of fragmentation and inconsistency, difficulties in reconciling the three main programmes of curriculum and assessment in secondary schools – the 5–14 Programme; Standard Grade (14–16); and the Higher Still Programme (16+). Together, these were designed to provide a continuous progression from age 5 to 18, but many teachers spoke of the difficulty for teachers, pupils and parents to make coherent sense of the varying aims and assessment regimes of these programmes. Many teachers who were not members of senior or middle management teams felt they had a limited knowledge of what was going on in the other departments of their schools. This was also true, in some cases, of whole-school initiatives. The ability to deal with a multiplicity of initiatives was a discriminating factor among schools. Some were overwhelmed but others appeared to have the capacity and flexibility to accommodate change. There were, in sum, significant differences among and within schools.

Assessment as a tool for school improvement

Those few headteachers who identified significant change taking place in learning and teaching, as opposed to curriculum change, also mentioned an increased emphasis on appropriate use of assessment. This was accompanied by a greater awareness of the need for more effective differentiation in teaching approaches and in resourcing. The comment below is fairly typical of headteachers who identified significant change over the last two years in respect of learning and teaching:

'Learning and teaching has developed and differentiation is more evident in planning and practice. Assessment has been carefully looked at and an effective learning and teaching policy has been implemented. An increase in cooperative teaching and our new reading scheme has meant a greater knowledge of teaching reading has been gained through in-service to parents as well as staff.'

(Headteacher, Primary School A)

Several teachers had found the assessment associated with the research project problematic and emphasized this strongly in their responses. This is perhaps because Scottish primary teachers have been accustomed to an assessment regime within the 5–14 Programme in which children are tested only when teachers anticipate substantial success. Consequently the use of blanket testing for all pupils caused teachers some anxiety:

'National testing horrified people at first but now they see it as a real tool. The strands, levels and targets etc. were not a major change here. It is a good thing it is firmly embedded in maths, reading and some writing and teachers are beginning to see that they are reaching these targets . . . It has given a pat on the back to teachers. They [pupils] are tested at their level . . . These tests with ISEP will be very sad, these children will sit these tests, most will fail them, our children will panic when they see them – take them out of what they know and their confidence goes. We have worked hard to build it up and suddenly their faces tell it all and we are not there to help.'

And later in the interview:

'When the staff were hit with the raw results of the testing on children, in particular the infant staff who had taught them for three years, it took the stuffing from them, they were . . . questioning if they had really failed these children.'

(Headteacher, Primary School J)

These comments raised questions about normative testing strategies. Teachers expressed concern because they felt that ISEP's undifferentiated testing put undue pressure on many of their pupils and cast doubt on the school's effectiveness. This was especially the case in disadvantaged areas. In retrospect, however, several heads came to view testing as useful in addressing broader issues of pupil achievement with their staff. In both low-attaining and high-attaining schools it allowed them to look at differences in relative achievement across the curriculum and to set more realistic and challenging targets. The two contrasting commentaries below show how testing can be used by a school to challenge existing notions about levels of attainment and the possibility of raising these:

> 'I knew that the kids were underachieving, I knew they were really poor but a lot of teachers didn't because they had been used to it over the years, they thought that it was normal – it is in some ways for here – but for some teachers it was a shock, – "we knew they were poor but not that poor . . ."'
>
> 'The project has made us look more at testing, look more at research, it has made us question what we do and why we do it.'
>
> (Headteacher, Primary School I)

And in another school with higher levels of attainment the headteacher said:

> The evidence of the range of pupils in our classes from 70 to 130+ on standardized tests came as a shock to some staff. The average level of attainment as a school disappointed many . . . a halo effect from our best pupils who are normally well behaved too. These factors led us to reappraise expectations and the appropriateness of tasks for some pupils.'
>
> (Headteacher, Primary School D)

In most primary schools there was marked consistency between the views of the headteachers and those of the other two members of staff interviewed. Again assessment, reporting and the pursuit of increasingly differentiated resources were predominant in teachers' comments. The need to extend the curriculum to challenge more able children as well as to support the learning of less able children was a recurrent theme. As might be expected, class teachers spoke proportionately more about teaching and learning than did headteachers.

In secondary schools Higher Still was frequently mentioned and several interviewees had attended associated staff development. Some teachers looked forward to this development because it would increase pupils' opportunities in Years 5 and 6 whereas at least an equal number spoke with apprehension about the programme 'looming like a weight': 'I am still left with the feeling that even although effective learning and teaching is a priority in the school, change and improvement is very slow' (Headteacher, Secondary School U).

*Pressure for change: decision making, staff morale and
professional development*

There was a lot of teacher discussion about involvement in decision making
and about teacher morale. As threads of ethos they were among the most
frequently mentioned among staff. Teachers were relatively positive about
involvement in decision making in both primary and secondary schools, and
just under half of the comment in both sectors suggested that there had been
some improvement over the last two years. Many headteachers, particularly in
primary schools, spoke about the helpfulness of the development planning
process in bringing about a greater feeling of involvement in decision making
among staff. This was endorsed by many teachers who shared headteachers'
positive views about involvement in general. This shed light on, and helped
to confirm, quantitative data discussed in Chapter 5. The following comment
is fairly typical:

> 'We have regular maths meetings . . . we have spelling meetings and
> French meetings. It is an important aspect of our style of management
> that we have regular meetings. A few weeks ago we gathered together
> teachers from different areas of the school and used some of our develop-
> ment time to cover classes . . . it gave the chance for teachers from the
> infant end to talk to teachers from the senior end . . . if we could spend
> more time doing that it would be valuable.'
>
> (Teacher, Primary School I)

In secondary schools there was more varied response to questions about
involvement in decision making, ranging from fairly diffident to extremely
positive. In respect of staff relations, there was perhaps an even greater range
of opinion than in primary schools, and of all subthemes in this cluster,
teacher morale and engagement with school is least positive. The situation in
primary schools is quite different, with the majority of comment being highly
positive.

For secondary schools resourcing issues also attracted least positive comment with negative implications for school quality. For example:

> 'The level of resourcing is going down every year in terms of the overall
> allocation to the school. Per capita has been at a standstill for the fourth
> year in a row . . . it's a significant drop . . . a number of things were cut in
> the last round of budgets – property maintenance budget was cut by 50
> per cent which restricts the kinds of projects you can take on board . . . the
> worst one for us is the reduction in staffing . . . the net result is that for the
> new S1 intake we've had to, with an immense regret, abandon class sizes
> of 20 so that we now have 25 or 26 – that's a significant shift because we've
> been enjoying classes of 20 for several years now.'
>
> (Headteacher, Secondary School T)

In secondary schools personnel change was seen as having great potential benefit to schools, bringing in new ideas and enthusiasm. There was recognition too that this might take some time to develop. In both primary and secondary sectors there was an acknowledgement that too much change in too short a time could be damaging for both staff and pupils.

Throughout most interviews there was a strong emphasis on a more tightly defined structure for the curriculum over recent years. There was also a perception that in very recent years stress and anxiety associated with major educational change had diminished a little, although there was still worry in primary schools about environmental studies. Of special concern was time for teachers to learn and, in some schools, acquisition of appropriate resources was also seen as problematic. For many teachers assessment and reporting to parents had become part of a productive but demanding routine.

Development planning, leadership and school improvement

Proportionately, there was much emphasis on development planning by headteachers in both primary and secondary schools. It had become an aspect of their professional lives with a high profile and was generally seen as useful for monitoring and sustaining school quality. Overall in primary schools there was most talk about the effectiveness of development planning in terms of its impact on the quality of the schools. Almost every teacher interviewed in the 12 case study primary schools, whether established headteacher or teacher new to the school, had something substantial to say about this: 'It clarifies your thinking . . . it is good to see how much we had actually achieved. It has given us confidence. Setting priorities is helpful. All the staff are involved in this' (Headteacher, Primary School J).

Schools were at very different stages in development planning. Because of local authority differences in relation to timing its introduction, some schools were relatively near the beginning of the process whereas other schools had the process underway for more than five years. Mobility of headteachers also gave an added impetus in some schools, with individual heads carrying expertise and commitment from one post to another:

'I think development planning is at the core of what we do. I was very much involved in the original [local authority] development plan format, which was drawn up after the Scottish Office guidelines came out . . . it has been going on for about five years but I think that there are very important debates that need to be engaged in . . . it can very easily be quite a sterile process or activity where the headteacher . . . draws up a plan and sends it round everybody, saying "Is this OK?" and then everybody says "Aye" and it basically gathers dust . . . What we are trying to do is . . . school aims and goals clearly linked under headings such as ethos and teaching and learning, if you like . . . It gives us the ability to link the planning closely into the aims . . . And the authority's priorities . . . performance indicators will be used to focus the discussion at the development team meeting . . . the development plan would be a running agenda item. . . reviewed continually.'

(Headteacher, Primary School G)

And in the same school, a teacher new to the school, a member of the development team, said:

'. . . everything happens. Everything has a time . . . It's a very structured school and they know where they're going and they know where they've been, they know what they have to improve.'

(Teacher, Primary School G)

These quotes, which speak for many of the schools, show a clearly articulated relationship between the effectiveness of development planning as a process, the perceived clarity of school aims and goals and the pursuit of improvement.

Many headteachers and teachers saw development planning as useful in redefining objectives or methodologies rather than in articulating and refining broader and more fundamental aims or goals:

'I don't think there's anything changed in terms of strategic aims, [rather] changes in the terms of *how* we've tried to achieve them . . . looking closely at our own practice in terms of effective teaching and learning . . . and management systems.'

(Headteacher, Primary School G)

Indeed, aims and goals were largely seen as fixed, described in terms of two central features:

1 maximizing the academic attainment potential of all young people within their schools;
2 supporting personal development, self-confidence and self-esteem.

Maximizing attainment was seen as guaranteeing young people greater economic, personal and social opportunities throughout life. As a consequence school aims tended to be articulated in a way that was largely outcome-dominated. While there was a great deal of talk about the importance of effective teaching and learning, very few teachers mentioned the nurturing of effective learners as part of their school goals or vision. Although much talk was process-dominated, aims were articulated differently, dominated by a perceived need to implement various wide-ranging curriculum initiatives. One primary school teacher, for example, cited seven recent curricular priorities, including French, health and early literacy work.

Throughout the primary sector there was an increasing emphasis on curriculum and a notable tendency over the duration of ISEP for primary teachers to move closer to secondary staff in the way they talked about planning for learning. For some teachers this was an area of deep concern.

Together with this emphasis on attainment outcomes, teachers and heads spoke about the development of the person and the importance of building young people's self-esteem and self-confidence. This was evident in schools in all areas, although in many schools in disadvantaged areas there was a predictably greater emphasis on the importance of a pastoral role:

'. . . there has been no shift at all. What we thought we had then we still have. That could have been changed with a changed staff but it has not . . . The ethos of this school has overflown into them . . . a very safe caring environment. We work very hard at providing that for both the parents and the children. A lot of parents. . . do not always have pleasant experiences [of school] . . . It should also be a caring place for the staff – that is part of my role. I would highlight it – relationships, dealing with and working with people.'

(Headteacher, Primary School G)

In secondary schools it was more common for staff to stress academic outcomes rather than the process of learning itself. There was markedly less emphasis on developing learners except when it came to discussion of personal and social development. In that context process was emphasized often, with a keen focus on teachers as role models, exemplifying characteristics such as fairness, respect, diffusion of aggression, listening, reinforcing desired behaviour.

Conspicuously absent from interviews were references by teachers to themselves as learners. On the few occasions when teachers did reflect on their own learning it was seen as part of the adult culture of the school. The sharing of learning did not seem to extend to young people. In planning too there was often a commitment to sharing ideas with colleagues and parents, to consultation and ownership of planning and development processes. Only rarely was such consideration extended to pupils. In a few secondary schools there had been initiatives to take pupils' views into greater consideration.

One of the most noticeable aspects of teacher talk about development planning was their emphasis on recent improvement in monitoring and evaluating the plan itself. In general there was an increasing awareness of the need to prioritize according to the school's circumstances although a small number of schools wanted to tackle everything in the national and local government agenda. In schools like this there was an explicit commitment to development, together with an underlying concern for consolidation:

'. . . do we need to revisit the aims of the schools? Do we need a clearer sense of direction? Do we need to make it more meaningful to staff and pupils? We need to be re-evaluating and reinforming . . . More emphasis on assemblies . . . articulate aims . . .'

(Headteacher, School S)

And later: '. . . perhaps we need to prioritize more, perhaps we have tackled too much. But it's difficult to decide what you put out' (Headteacher, School S).

The ambivalence with which headteachers, in particular, spoke about reduced formal provision and the quality of occasional support provided by advisory or directorate staff was notable. However in schools where there were especially serious concerns about pupils with behavioural or learning difficulties, the anxieties of headteachers were quite explicit. In terms of its contribution to school quality, the subtheme of support from local authorities is the least positive in the area of development planning. Support from local authorities was conceived as a mixture of documentation, training and personal advice and support for headteachers and their staff, with the emphases leaning towards the staff development and personal support agendas. Discussing support from the Scottish Office, there was a recognition that the quality of written support for schools had increased markedly in recent years. Publications that helped with school audit, review and planning were particularly welcomed: 'I think that *How Good Is Our School?* is essential to what we are about' (Headteacher, Secondary School P).

While advocating the value of such publications, many headteachers recognized that support for school development from the SOEID was not a familiar concept among unpromoted staff. They also recognized that it was the responsibility of headteachers and management to disseminate both information and strategies. This is borne out by teachers themselves feeling it was something about which they had scarce experience and little to say. Headteachers wanted more advice and support on the practicalities of using such documentation and several commented that they often hesitated to take forward ideas from national education policy, awaiting local authority guidance. Sometimes local and national strategies conflicted, to their regret.

● Case study indicators of school quality

In all ISEP schools we were able to analyse teachers' perceptions and experiences through the teacher questionnaire. Additionally, in case study schools, we could cross-tabulate these analyses with judgements based on the richer, but less extensive, case study evidence. Interviews go deep while questionnaires spread wide. We found that comparing and cross-tabulating these contrasting qualitative and quantitative analyses, illuminated the meanings, validity and reliability of both. Furthermore, we explored the relationship between teachers' perceptions of school quality and school performance based on pupil attainment.

In Chapter 5 we described three main factors (statistically coherent clusters of items) emerging from the analysis of teacher questionnaires. These were also fairly coherent, semantically and educationally, and have been labelled accordingly:

- **Factor 1 – Leadership and management climate:** this includes 17 items related to decision making, teacher morale, communication and consultation with staff.
- **Factor 2 – Academic expectations/learning emphasis:** the 11 items here

relate to teacher attitudes, expectations and relationships with pupils; and dialogue about learning and teaching.

- **Factor 3 – Clarity in standards: behaviour and work:** five items concerned with pupil behaviour and consistency in standards.

We found these factors consistently across primary and secondary sectors in both 1995 and 1997.

As part of the research design (Chapter 3) we included teacher views as particularly important intermediate indicators of school quality. We saw them as potential measures of organizational health and of the worth of the educational process. While schools are judged by their overall effectiveness, it is teachers who are the executors of the teaching task. The quality of their professional lives, their job satisfaction, the depth of their understanding of learning and teaching, are all central to the quality of education which schools provide.

Comparing measures of process with school outcomes: case study and teacher questionnaire evidence

The total current quality score derived from the interview analyses and also the teacher questionnaire factor scores were plotted against mean pupil attainment scores (1997) for each of the 12 primary and 12 secondary case study schools. The correlation coefficients obtained by relating the ISEP current quality scores to raw pupil attainment are relatively high (0.56 in secondary schools and 0.60 in primary). These suggest a link between teachers' perceptions of school quality and measured pupil attainment.

The reproducibility of the current quality correlation scores with raw attainment measures in mathematics and English/reading across both primary and

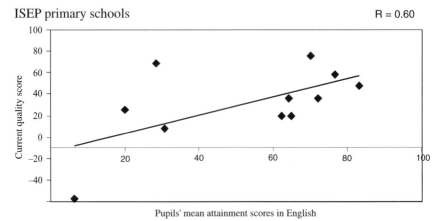

Figure 6.2   Current quality score v. primary school mean score for English (1997)

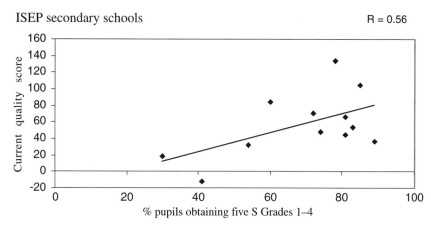

Figure 6.3   Current quality score v. % pupils gaining five Standard Grades at 1–4 (1997)

secondary sectors is clear (see Figures 6.2 and 6.3). However, this does not hold good for correlations between the current quality scores and value-added attainment. In other words, a school struggling against a background of social and economic disadvantage, even when performing significantly beyond expectation, may still be seen by teachers as not succeeding. Teacher views do not implicitly contain a value-added perspective.

Socio-economic disadvantage and teachers' perceptions of school

The hypothesis that teachers do not infer or internalize value-added judgements is given further credence when we look at the correlation of both current quality and teacher questionnaire factor scores with free school meal entitlement (FSME). Figures 6.4 and 6.5 illustrate the relationship between the quality score for the case study schools and free meal entitlement.

This gives a fairly strong correlation coefficient in primary schools (0.58), suggesting a significant association between teachers' perceptions of their schools and the socio-economic profile of the school population. The regression line is in a negative direction, indicating that the greater the socio-economic disadvantage (using the proxy measure of FSME), the more negative teachers' views of school are likely to be.

Turning to the relationship between the teacher questionnaire factors and school performance, we found similar associations. These are particularly marked in secondary schools regarding Factors 2 and 3. Teachers' views of learning and teaching and behavioural standards, in particular, are therefore less directly related to the value the school may be adding to pupil progress, than to the socio-economic composition of the pupil population. This might be partly expected when we remind ourselves of the composition of Factor 3,

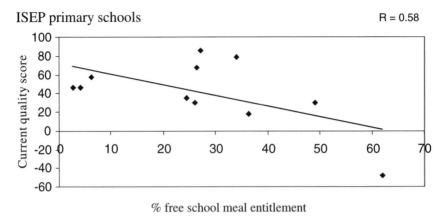

Figure 6.4   Current quality score v. free school meal entitlement

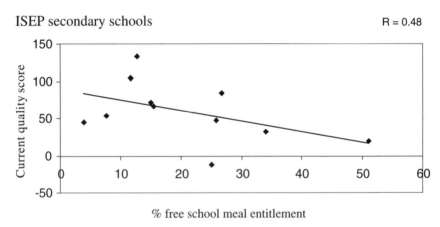

Figure 6.5   Current quality score v. free school meak entitlement

consisting of issues related to behaviour, discipline and pupil respect for teachers. However Factor 2 is more directly connected to teachers' own activity than to pupil performance.

These associations, if robust and borne out by further research, have significant implications for school managers and policy makers. They suggest that, where pupils' educational opportunities and progress are already disadvantaged by extraneous socio-economic background influences and relatively low levels of attainment, then generally the school climate and learning/teaching are viewed less positively. Teacher expectations too are lower.

Validating measures of process: teacher questionnaire and case study interview data

As part of the research process we were interested to find out how well the teacher questionnaire factor scores and the current quality score correlated. A significant correlation would tend to validate the instruments themselves and the analysis techniques used by the research team.

With the exception of Factor 1 (leadership and management), the current quality scores correlate well with the questionnaire factor scores in both primary and secondary schools. The lower correlation for the sum of factors in the secondary school sample may be explained by the fact that only three teachers in each school were interviewed. In secondary schools this represents a small proportion of the total staff whereas in primary schools it is proportionately greater. This may also help to explain why the correlation between the current quality score and Teacher Factor 1 is stronger in the primary school sample. Views of management and leadership in secondary schools may be expected to be less homogeneous than those in primary schools, due to their differences in size, structure and management strategies.

We wanted to seek further evidence of the validity and reliability of both the ISEP teacher questionnaire and the case study analysis. To achieve this,

Table 6.1 Primary and secondary schools: correlation coefficients

Current quality sub-scores v. teacher questionnaire factors

	Teacher Q Factor 1	*Teacher Q Factor 2+ Factor 3*
Primary schools: current quality *Ethos + learning and teaching*	ns	0.90
Primary schools: current quality *Development planning + leadership and management*	0.6	ns
Secondary schools: current quality *Ethos + learning and teaching*	ns	0.63 0.79*
Secondary schools: current quality *Development planning + leadership and management*	0.30 0.48*	ns
Secondary schools: current quality *Leadership & management* only	0.38 0.56*	ns

Note: * $p < 0.05$.

we tested sub-components of the current quality score against the teacher questionnaire factors. These sub-components or subthemes for comparison were selected because they seemed to represent similar and coherent areas of schools. For example, combining Factors 2 and 3 from the teacher question-naire, with their emphasis on learning and teaching practice, teacher expec-tations and behaviourial standards, corresponds with the case study themes of ethos and learning and teaching. Factor 1, with its components of leadership, school development culture and staff relations seemed to correspond roughly with the case study theme of leadership and management.

The high correlation (0.90) in primary schools between Factors 2 and 3 summed and the current quality score is striking. It suggests a remarkable degree of consistency in judgements about school quality derived from two independent and very different evaluation and analytic approaches.

● Summary

The case study research, in conjunction with information from the teacher questionnaire, suggests that teachers' attitudes and perceptions of major school processes are associated with the attainment level and socio-economic balance of the school; that teachers' views of the quality of their schools are significantly associated with factors other than value-added status. This might at first sound self-evident and commonsensical; schools in affluent areas are generally regarded as effective and efficient; schools in less privileged places are generally seen as less effective in terms of pupil achievement.

When we begin to look more closely at the components of the ISEP case study analysis, the implications become clearer. The case study and teacher questionnaire analyses do not represent global statements about school quality that might be dismissed as impressionistic, superficial or rhetorical judge-ments. The three teacher questionnaire factors consist of 33 items and the case study analysis clusters around 35 subthemes. The subsequent analysis and meta-analysis of both data sets has been carefully structured to reflect on the themes at the heart of the project, while not obscuring other important messages that the evidence might throw up. At both macro and micro levels, the case study evidence suggests that teachers think that teaching and learn-ing practice, teacher expectation and consistency of standards are of poorer quality in lower achieving schools, regardless of value-added status. In other words, value-added is not a concept that has significantly permeated the perceptions of teachers. Stronger influences are those well established in the history and ethos of schools and in the nature of their pupil population. There are important implications for education and school managers. In schools faced with the challenges of low prior attainment and socio-economic dis-advantage, low teacher expectation and low morale may be additional obstacles to improvement.

There is much evidence that schools can contribute differentially to pupil progress in the formal curriculum, that some schools are more successful than others in countering extraneous influences on pupil achievement. If schools are to make increasing improvements in pupil achievement, it may be that these issues of staff attitude and expectation require greater attention, particularly in disadvantaged and low-attaining schools.

Chapters 9 and 10 explore these issues in greater depth and explore some exceptions to test the general rule.

7

Change leadership: planning, conceptualization and perception

Jenny Reeves, Jim McCall and Barbara MacGilchrist

In order to explore the connection between development planning and school effectiveness we used the development analysis interview (DAI), an instrument that enabled the project team to gather accounts of the development process from two respondents in each case study school. We asked for the headteacher to be present together with another person who had been closely involved in the initiative which the school chose to describe. Schools were not given any guidance as to what they should select as a topic – the choice was left entirely up to them. In most schools it was the headteacher and the depute (ten primaries and six secondaries) who were the respondents. In three schools it was the headteacher on her/his own and in the other four[1] a mixture of promoted staff. We shall refer to this group of people as the change leaders in the discussion that follows.

● Background

Because we were attempting to predict which of our sample of 24 schools would prove to be effective, the initial analysis of the DAI data focused on developing a quantitative measure which could be used to rank the schools on the basis of the quality of their planning. From the detailed account of each development, a strategy impact score was derived for the school. It was calculated on the basis of the likely change impact of the various stratagems that the school staff described to us. As such, despite the use of the word 'strategy', the measure largely concentrated on the operational level of planning (Reeves 1999).

The kinds of impacts we were looking for were whether the activities used to bring about the initiative the school chose to describe to us would be likely to influence staff by changing:

- their attitudes;
- their knowledge and understanding;
- their teaching skills;
- the resources they had to work with;
- their management skills;
- their monitoring and evaluation skills.

The development of the measure was based on three assumptions:

- a school's approach to development would be likely to be consistent and to be applied to a variety of initiatives;
- schools with a high strategy impact score would be more likely to increase the capabilities of the staff and the capacity of the school to accommodate new developments;
- schools which invested more in capability and capacity were likely to be more effective than those which did not.

(Hopkins and Harris 1997)

On the basis of these three assumptions, the prediction was that schools in the sample with relatively high strategy impact (SI) scores would prove to be more effective than those with relatively low strategy impact scores.

The strategy impact measure gave a range of scores across the sample. For instance, in the primary sector, some schools saw the changes entailed by the implementation of the 5–14[2] curriculum as a relatively superficial matter of swapping from one set of materials to another or purchasing a new scheme to fill a curricular 'gap':

'What we did was we felt that the 5–14 document was too difficult for us to handle like that so we tried to write down what we did at each stage because we felt we weren't all that far away from it. So it was to make 5–14 a practical document and we actually made big sheets out on reading, listening and talking and that was over two in-service days. We looked to see if we were covering 5–14. When we looked at what we did and then looked at 5–14 we found one of the things [we didn't cover] was listening so that's when we bought all the tapes and the books.'

(Headteacher, School C, DAI, 1995)

Others used and interpreted the guidelines in order to pursue more fundamental goals. In the following discussion about the introduction of problem-solving in mathematics, the head and the deputy of School B clearly have a broader target in mind:

'The teacher was very much autonomous in her own classroom – there was a sort of trichotomy: there was the nursery which was a separate entity, there was the infant department as a separate entity and the rest of the school. We really had to establish a basic approach – that problem solving and enquiry had to be a major feature in teaching and learning and that we couldn't work solely to workbooks. There had to be a whole rethink of what we were doing in maths and that actually tied in with a whole rethink of what we were doing in teaching and learning.'

(Headteacher, School B, DAI, 1995)

In School B the change in maths became part of other innovations in terms of content, i.e. forward planning, personal review and monitoring and evaluation, whereas in School C the initiative remained very tidy and self-contained. In the former there was the clear possibility of a systemic impact, whereas in the latter the effect was likely to be 'atomistic' and confined within its own bounds.

While this contrast was fairly typical of the two ends of the range in the primary sample, the picture in the 12 secondary schools was rather different, with less of a focus on curriculum development. Generally respondents who talked of a whole-school initiative reported using a greater number of stratagems with a wider range of impacts than those who talked of sectional reforms.

The account from one of the schools at the higher end of the range showed that the procedure for the initiative was carefully planned and that orthodoxies about the management of change, at least in the initial stages, were clearly understood and adhered to. Another feature of this school's approach was careful attention to structures for involving the staff in the change process.

The impression in this case of cautious development and a concern with procedures was typical of the secondary schools at the higher end of the SI range. In part it demonstrated the somewhat bureaucratic nature of the headteachers with an emphasis on the values of efficiency, clarity and consistency (Handy and Aitken 1986).

Comparing this type of approach with that of a potentially less effective school, there was much less opportunity for participation in the anti-bullying initiative which was described. Although the staff were made aware of what was going on, they were not actually involved in the process of development, nor did the anti-bullying group seek or act on their responses to the initiative. This was a characteristic of several of the low-impact accounts where there seemed to be a 'ginger' group which was clearly committed to and interested in the innovation but which worked in relative isolation from the rest of the staff. This phenomenon fits with Dalin, Rolff and Kleekamp's description of 'project schools' in the typology they used in *Changing the School Culture* (1993).

When the value-added attainment results for the case study schools became available in 1997, there was a correlation with the strategy impact scores (Reeves 2000) in both sectors. Schools with high strategy impact scores were more likely to show positive value-added attainment than those with low strategy impact scores.

● Associated factors

To further explore possible explanations for the variations between schools, a second content analysis of the DAI data identified 23 items which were linked with the accounts of change across the sample schools.

Table 7.1 Significant factors associated with change

Primary	*Secondary*
Relevant course attended by change leader/s	Talked of a whole-school initiative
Placed change in a context for improvement	Took a managerial stance
Mentioned the importance of being new/new people	Placed change in a context for improvement
Change leaders had particular interest in content	Mentioned the importance of being new/new people
Talked of the wider effects of the change	Change leaders had particular interest in content
Gave evidence of a high level of resistance	Relevant course attended by change leader/s
Involved pupils	Miscalculated level of complexity
Involved parents	Used alliance with Learning Support
Talked of simple technical solutions to change	Had problems with sustaining resources Gave evidence of a high level of resistance

Note: Shaded portions indicate negative factors associated with low strategy impact scores.

In order to discriminate between those features associated with either high or low strategy impact scores, the list was refined by eliminating those items which were not linked to either end of the SI scale to produce the results shown in Table 7.1.

The factors which are of most interest are those which relate to the motivation and thinking of the respondents because they would be likely to have a bearing on the change leaders' approaches to planning. The bulk of this chapter will be concerned with discussing the significance of these conceptual elements.

In addition to this data we also had some instances where heads gave relatively coherent and holistic accounts of what they saw as significant elements in the school's functioning, either during the DAI or the headteacher interview. Although this evidence was inconclusive in terms of any linkage to effectiveness, nevertheless it gave an interesting insight into what might inform the planning of some heads at a more strategic level.

Lastly we explored the possible dynamics in the school which might have contributed to positive or negative effects of planning practices using the results of the teacher questionnaire and the transcripts of the teacher interviews, both of which posed questions about development planning.

On the basis of the scores on the teacher questionnaire (Chapter 5) and the tenor of the interviews, schools were placed in three categories:

Positive   – staff gave a positive response to questions on the nature of development planning in the school;

Mixed/neutral – staff gave responses that were neither particularly positive nor negative;

Negative – staff responded unfavourably to questions about the quality of development planning.

● Conceptual and perceptual influences on planning for development

There were two conceptual/perceptual factors that were derived from the second content analysis of the DAI data. One was about the level of interest, commitment and expertise a respondent had in the content of a change and the second was the level of interest and expertise s/he had in the process of bringing about change. Both bear an obvious relationship to leadership. The usual textbook definition of leadership as the ability to motivate people within an organization to achieve organizational goals implies that its key characteristics are:

- the ability to set the agenda for the organization;
- the ability to win commitment to that agenda;
- the ability to motivate and enable others to carry out the required changes to achieve the agenda.

(Du Brin 1995: 2–4)

Within this definition, the content factor in change leadership relates most clearly to setting the organizational agenda and the process factor to the ability to engender action.

It is worth looking in greater detail at the evidence to see what was included within each of these change leadership categories, both positive and negative, in terms of links to school effectiveness.

Content leadership

There were three items indicating expertise and interest in the content of a change on the part of change leaders that were associated with schools which had positive effects on pupil attainment:

- *A relevant course had been attended by the change leader/s.* Respondents in six primaries and five secondaries mentioned attending a course relevant to the development they chose to describe and said that it had influenced them. Most of these courses were fairly substantial, either involving postgraduate study and/or work in school.
- *The change leader/s expressed a personal interest in the content of the change.* Several respondents said that the content of the change had interested them for some time and they also related the change to their own beliefs about teaching and learning or schools. They regarded the development they chose to discuss as desirable as well as necessary.

- *The change leader/s talked with a degree of expertise and a reasonably holistic understanding of the content area.* The respondents had a relatively sophisticated view of how the content of the development related to a wider framework. For example, where they talked of writing or spelling, it was in the context of a holistic approach to language development rather than as an isolated feature of the curriculum; or if they discussed a change in discipline policy, they saw this as part of a wider effort to improve relationships and ethos.

Combining these features seems to justify the identification of content leadership as a factor in effective planning for development. Much of the literature on school development emphasizes the importance of the process of planning, which is often discussed as though divorced from content. This study indicated that the content of a change and how change leaders (and others) feel about it is a crucial parameter in the planning process.

Looking at the negative side of this factor, schools with low strategy impact scores were associated with change leaders who expressed no particular interest or expertise in relation to the content of the development they chose to discuss. Often their concerns were pragmatic rather than educational and focused on compliance with external demands.

Process leadership

There were two items under this heading which were associated with positive value-added results:

- *Change leaders took a managerial view of the development.* Respondents talked about the processes for change and tied these to general principles for change management. For instance, they would talk about the need to consult staff and respond to feedback if they were to secure ownership and commitment. They gave importance to the identification of staff development needs at a variety of levels.
- *Change leaders placed change in a general context for improvement.* Here the respondents saw the particular change or/and the approach to its implementation as part of a broader strategy for school improvement. For example, a particular curricular development was seen as part of a wider strategy for changing the approach to learning and teaching within the school. In the primary accounts in particular, ways had been found for welding together external and internal priorities so that the respondents felt committed to the development because they saw it as meeting their own school's needs in addition to fulfilling external demands. A number of those expressing a managerial stance also linked this to undertaking professional development in aspects of management. The evidence for this factor, as well as that for content leadership, supported the notion of the importance of change leaders demonstrating extended professionalism (Hoyle 1974).

Associated with positive value-added attainment in the secondary sector:

- *Change leaders talked of a whole-school initiative.* School representatives who chose to talk about whole-school developments gave accounts of actions with higher strategy impact scores than those who talked of initiatives based in particular departments or cross-curricular units.

Two further items associated with negative value-added results in the secondary sector were where:

- *Change leaders described problems in sustaining resources;* and
- *They appeared to have difficulties predicting and allowing for the complexity of a change.*

These were additional to the lack of a direct expression of interest in change processes and a sectional rather than a whole-school focus.

In introducing and implementing new practices and procedures, good management skills and an understanding of the process of facilitating change have a strong face validity. As with content leadership, having the skills and understanding to undertake the various tasks and an interest and expertise in the processes required to do so would be likely to add to a person's chances of success compared to those with neither an interest in, nor any articulated understanding of, such matters.

Change leader roles were differently assigned in the two sectors. In primary schools heads often exercised both kinds of leadership although the major emphasis here was on content leadership. In secondary schools the roles were more likely to be split between the headteacher and another member of the senior management team, and usually the head expressed the process leader interests while the other respondent placed a focus on the content leadership role. This reflected one of Mintzberg's findings that the leaders of small organizations were more centrally involved in operational issues and had a more entrepreneurial role than the more bureaucratic and managerial focus of the leaders of larger organizations (1979).

Discussion

What this evidence seemed to show was that there were two identifiable change leader roles. One related to the content of an innovation and expertise and belief in the worth of that content. This in turn reflected the person's commitment to their own professional development and interest in the particular field. The other role was process-orientated and reflected an interest and a degree of expertise in the management and the facilitation of change. Positive aspects of both these types of change leadership were expressed in schools with high strategy impact scores. Where only one aspect of change leadership was positively expressed, this was not necessarily linked to high strategy impact. The exceptions to this were three secondary schools where the emphasis was on process leadership, probably because the topic they chose to discuss was the introduction of development planning.

The strategy impact scores also seemed to indicate there was a connection between the strength of commitment and understanding of the change leaders, and the level of investment in the development. Content and process expertise and interest may have given change leaders possessing these qualities:

• the courage and drive to undertake more fundamental approaches to improvement than those change leaders who lacked these qualities. Change leaders who were neither confident nor committed to a particular development may have elected to take the line of least resistance and not risked tackling any fundamental change;
• the know-how to use a more powerful and effective process of implementation as well as the ability to confront and deal with problems and difficulties.

There is an interesting link here between the personal and the organizational level. Moorman and Miner (1998), talking of organizations that showed the ability to improvise and respond successfully to their environment, identified two forms of organizational knowledge which seemed to be significant. One of these was procedural knowledge, or 'know how' about how to set about things, which links to the process aspect of change leadership. One of the major changes which development planning had brought about in schools, where it had been fully implemented, was the greater involvement of teachers in managerial processes: planning, decision making, organizing, etc. – in this sense it could be seen as increasing their 'know-how'. The other type of knowledge was labelled declarative knowledge – 'know-what' – that Moorman and Miner describe as a theoretical knowledge of the core business and which in our case relates to the notion of content leadership. Organizations with a good memory of 'know-how' and 'know-what' were more successful at improvising and responding proactively to the environment because they had a basis for both creativity and action.

One of the features of sound content and process leadership was that it engendered a more strategic approach to development because goals tended to be more long-term and holistic in relation to the functioning of the school. Thus, in schools where the positive aspects of both roles were expressed, developments were more complex and took longer to accomplish than those in schools where the performance of these two roles was not in evidence.

Those who demonstrated a lack of positive change leadership attributes tended to be reactionary rather than proactive in their response to change and to focus on achieving short-term goals. Because they took a fairly simplistic and superficial approach they often described a development as being successfully implemented in a short time with relatively few problems. The low strategy impact scores in these schools may indicate that development was easy because little of any significance was actually happening.

Strategic orientation

A possible link from the operational to the strategic has already been established in the schools in which positive change leadership expressed a longer term and more cohesive approach to change than was evident in schools where the change leaders showed neither content nor process expertise.

Although we had asked people to explain the reasons for adopting particular stratagems, we had not asked them to give us an overview of the school or to explain their general approach to development. Nevertheless, some head-teachers volunteered such an overview. Five of these heads were new in post and one had just returned to his school after a secondment.

In these six cases there appeared to be a strong relationship between the head's diagnosis of the school situation and the subsequent action which they described. How they framed and interpreted the circumstances of the school seemed to be key to some of the biases that showed in their choice of actions and therefore it gave an indication of the strategic orientation of the individuals concerned. These heads' diagnoses also provided an insight into how planning at the strategic and the operational level might relate to each other.

The statements also came nearest to giving evidence of 'vision', which is described in many texts as the key to effective leadership, and it is worth pursuing what the ISEP results seemed to indicate in this regard.

There are broadly three meanings given to the word 'vision' in the literature:

1 a common goal which can be embodied in a simple statement that serves to unite everyone by providing the common and shared purpose for their work (McNay 1995; Morrison 1998);
2 the ability of leaders to take a holistic view of the organization. To quote Senge (1996: 292): 'An accurate picture of current reality is just as important as a compelling picture of a desired future';
3 the ability of the organization, through its leaders, to 'see where it is going'. Senge (1996) ties this version of vision to the notion of the leader as a designer, building a sense of direction into the aims and policies of the organization.

Several of the school development plans did contain mission statements but these were not mentioned in the interviews, so there was no evidence that they were an integral part of people's approach to planning. Equally, links between school aims and priorities were seldom articulated either in development plans or in the oral accounts.

The teacher interview data was similarly bare of evidence. A search through the responses to the question 'What is the most important thing this school is trying to achieve?' in the 1995 teacher interviews (TIs) revealed very little.

Turning to the small sample of headteachers' descriptions of their school's situation was more illuminating:

'My analysis of the situation was that we needed to get people involved instead of waiting for things to be dictated to them. After all we have an all-graduate workforce and we should be using their skills, not treating them like imbeciles. Valuing and empowering staff was something I brought with me – all groups were chaired by the SMT and nobody else got a look-in, which made my hackles rise. The starting point was really confronting what was happening. A number of staff had been in the job for years and a number were really comfortable. They blamed the outside environment for all the problems. Real negative stuff, so there really had to be a cards on the table session. I used the critical friend to do that, giving the information from ISEP, and then told them what I'd discovered. I had staff who'd told me they were so apathetic about the school they couldn't be bothered getting out of bed in the morning. I pointed to the attainment level and the responses of youngsters 'cos I'd talked a lot with them as well saying, "This is a minging school." We don't want to keep on this downward spiral. We've got to move things forward from this.

(Headteacher 2, School X, DAI, 1997)

This analysis centred on issues that relate to culture of the school and to relationships. The headteacher chose to tackle the issue of attitudes as a first step and to link this closely to action to improve pupil outcomes. This school showed evidence of improvement over the ISEP period.

This link between perceptions of school's position, diagnosis of the problems and action can also be seen in another school. Headteacher 1 at School T emphasized structural features in his analysis of the school's problems and this way of 'seeing' the school was reflected in his solutions:

'What attracted me to T as a school was the fact that it had an appalling reputation but it had 1000 pupils and most schools that are perceived to be in a failing situation have very small rolls and thus have great difficulty in manoeuvring themselves out of their problem area because they simply do not have the flexibility that comes from having sufficient per capita allowances – both the flexibility in terms of curriculum and funding – so this is a very unusual situation to have in a school which is widely regarded as an awful place and yet has the structural capacity for changes to be made. When I came most people were referring decisions to me – I think that is a suggestion of a rather hierarchical structure and the timetable itself was an absolute classic of add-on where it was really a mess – a real classic example of something that was addressing yesterday's problems, rather than tomorrow's.'

(Headteacher 1, School T, TI, 1995)

The head then recounted how he went on to change the structure of the timetable and the curriculum. In this case the head did not carry the staff with him and the teacher questionnaire results showed a school in crisis.

In these first two examples, the change leaders have a strategic focus on the future improvement of the school but this is not always the case. A headteacher may adopt a very straightforward diagnosis, picking on a pragmatic approach to a particular feature of the school's functioning that later develops into a more strategic focus:

'The place was a tip, expectations were very low, children weren't given ownership of anything, the behaviour was atrocious, something had to be done with kids literally swinging from the lights. We had to get discipline right. I set about educating myself – I asked the behaviour support teacher's advice and visited schools. We came back with a lot of enthusiasm – that was when we started the caring and sharing assemblies and we had a ladder of success going up the wall. Once we had decided where we were going we met a lot to discuss how we would do it.'

(Headteacher, School I, DAI, 1995)

This marked the prelude to integrating the special unit in the school, getting more classroom auxiliaries and providing in-class support throughout the school as well as introducing a positive discipline policy. Again there is a very clear link between perception and action.

The final example is different again:

'The background in the mid-eighties was of an extremely divided and unhappy staff. It was a very, very stable staff which had seen off a number of heads. My coming back to the school has had a very big impact, with three people reverting back to substantive posts. [Setting up a single decision-making forum] came about through a desire to set up a system that everyone felt included in but, by doing that, the very opposite would happen for people who had traditionally considered themselves the senior management team. I spent up till Easter picking up the vibes – I did the groundwork and I took it to the EIS[3] rep. to see what she thought and to an influential member of staff. I was lobbying before the meeting but that's what effective leadership is about. You duck and you dive.'

(Headteacher, School G, DAI, 1997)

Here the head circumvented the senior staff who had been acting up in his absence and agreed with the rest of the staff a decision-making forum that allowed him to regain a dominant position within the school: a political solution to what was seen as a struggle to reassert power. In this case, unlike the other three examples, the head's diagnosis did not really focus on how the school could improve.

The third sense of vision was where a view of the future direction for the school was formulated and, as the previous section shows, this was likely to be expressed in defining current reality. However, the final example also indicates that it is possible to have a diagnostic statement about current reality which does not relate to school improvement – it may be confined to achieving personal rather than organizational goals.

We have called this amalgam of the definition of current reality and a possible future the strategic orientation of the change leader. Partly this is because the term does not carry the same evangelical overtones as 'vision' but, more importantly, because it also hints at the complexities of the process by which such a view is formed and it acts as a bias on the change leader's responses to events and circumstances, i.e. it has a direct and intimate link to the way in which developments are operationalized (Lindell *et al.* 1998).

To sum up, the evidence showed that there was a connection between the quality of the planning in the school and whether the change leaders had some longer term view of what was required. The articulation of a clear direction for the school and an understanding of how various initiatives fitted with 'moving the school forward' was positively linked to school effectiveness where, additionally, the understanding and command of process issues was sufficient to secure the cooperation of staff.

In those schools where the staff were not persuaded of the direction the headteacher wanted to adopt, the 'vision' could lead to conflict. Under these circumstances, vision was decidedly not linked to effectiveness. In two of these schools (W and T), the change leaders had a clear view of what needed to be done but, due to a breakdown in the process of managing change, failed to take the staff with them.

● The dynamics of change leadership

Linking perception to action

The identification of these conceptual/perceptual characteristics of effective change leaders is all very well, but the essence of organizational development lies in action and it is the link between these factors and organizational activity which remains elusive. In this there are two elements:

- the effects of these factors on the behaviour of the change leader; and
- the effects of the behaviours of the change leaders on colleagues and pupils.

Research, largely in the field of social and cognitive psychology, shows that there is a strong link between people's perceptions and judgements and the actions that they take (Wright and Taylor 1994):

Perception is an active process which provides structure, stability and meaning to our interaction with the environment. This reduces uncertainty and assists prediction. Finally as the directive for action, it is intimately and integrally related to our successful adaptation to the environment we live in.

(1994: 66)

It could therefore be argued that the cognitive change factors – interest and expertise in relation to the content of a change, and interest and expertise in relation to the process of change – would be likely to have a direct impact on the perception and judgement of change leaders and therefore on the action they would be liable to take.

This gives a possible explanation for a connection between the two cognitive change factors and strategy impact scores.

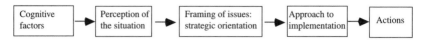

Figure 7.1   Cognitive factors affecting approaches to planning

The link between the cognitive factors and action is critically determined by the nature of the change leaders' strategic thinking, which in turn links to their capacity for formulating a workable direction for development, and this would underpin the two strategic stages in Figure 7.1:

1 *perception of the situation* – links to the way in which change leaders attend to particular elements in their school and the wider environment as a basis for envisioning the current situation; and
2 *framing the issues* – links to the way in which they identify a direction for the school by linking their view of the current state of affairs and their view of a desirable future.

So there is a basis here for examining the individual change leaders' biases for action but this still does not give us the mechanisms by which they may have influenced the behaviour of others.

The postulation has been that strategy impact provides the link because by analysing the actions change leaders say they have taken we can make a connection between:

• the possible impact of those actions on other people's capabilities and capacities; and
• the perception of the staff of being fruitfully involved in the change process.[4]

In relation to the first point we have to rely on the literature to provide possible explanations since we did not ask teachers directly about their responses to the changes discussed in the DAIs.

One difficulty we have is that although a focus on teaching and learning is cited as a key to success (MacGilchrist *et al.* 1997) in most instances in our sample, even where the development process had a high impact it was difficult to identify stratagems which would have a very direct effect on classroom practice. A possible key here to improved effectiveness may lie in the area of cultural change. Our findings are congruent with some of the general arguments in the management literature for the power of culture as a control mechanism: 'Culture, with its related norms, serves as a control mechanism to channel employees' behaviours towards the desired and away from undesired behaviours' (Hellreigel *et al.* 1989: 312); and 'When they participate in decision making about tasks, goals, plans and procedures subordinates learn more about the tasks and have a better chance of successfully achieving them' (1989: 285).

It is argued that the same kind of connection could also exist between the effects of strategy impact on capability and teacher/pupil behaviour.

Where a new development was implemented through a programme that had high impact on a range of the capability/capacity factors, this may have had a variety of beneficial effects. The activities may have helped to win commitment, lower fear of failure through training and feedback, improve communication and lower ambiguity and uncertainty. These in turn are all effects which should be helpful in decreasing resistance to change and facilitating improvement (Hatch 1997).

In addition, the adoption of a strong content leadership role makes a number of key contributions to facilitating the change process (DuBrin1995; Jirasinghe and Lyons 1996):

- the leaders are committed to the area of interest and feel ownership of it and therefore pursue the improvement with greater energy and persistence;
- by displaying enthusiasm and expertise they have a greater likelihood of convincing their colleagues of the desirability of the change;
- by displaying confidence and conviction they may be able to engender a greater feeling of security among their colleagues about their capacity to cope with the new practice.

Obviously this linkage does not always follow – some individuals frighten others with their enthusiasms. However, generally, people are more likely to follow the lead of someone with recognized expertise and enthusiasm than they are to be convinced by someone who displays limited knowledge, understanding and conviction. In the leadership literature these factors which underpin the way in which the change leader or leaders give purpose and meaning to the implementation of new practices are linked to high performance in organizations (Vaill 1996).

In relation to staff's perceptions of their involvement in planning and implementation processes, both the teacher interviews and the teacher questionnaire contained items which explored opinions about development planning and levels of staff participation in each of the schools.

We found seven schools where there seemed to be a generally positive response towards the development planning process and its management, and 17 where this was not so clearly the case. Of this 17, four could be distinguished as quite clearly negative while the others varied from schools where there was a difference of opinion about the process to those where there was a neutral attitude toward it.

Generally there was a reasonable match at the positive and the negative ends of the scale between the teachers' responses to planning issues, the value-added results and the strategy impact scores. Most of the teachers who responded favourably to the development planning process saw the major benefit of involvement as being that it gave them 'a sense of direction', a better understanding of what was going on and/or what was required of them. Where, in one school, a teacher linked these outcomes of participation in planning to a general tightening up of procedures and raising expectations of performance, there is some clue to the mechanism for improvement, even though she is not talking of direct leverage on classroom practice or pupil conduct. Improvements in practice can occur simply through a sharpening of focus and through a sense of increased accountability brought about by a change in cultural norms and what counts as acceptable professional behaviour.

There was an interesting group of schools where the strategy impact score and value-added results were at the high end but where attitudes to planning were in the 'mixed' category. In all of them there was a more negative attitude towards the senior management team in the teacher questionnaires than was characteristic for the sector. There were also intimations from the interviews that the management style in these schools was perceived as fairly directive and/or remote although there was not the level of hostility which was evident in the schools with openly negative attitudes. This association between high strategy impact and a view of senior management as overly dominant would lend credence to the controlling effects of development planning. Although participation in planning and high strategy impact processes may lead to enhanced performance, this does not necessarily ensure that staff feel personal ownership and a sense of empowerment (Ball 1996).

The argument

It is our contention that how effectively planning is undertaken depends to a significant extent on how well the change leaders in the school understand the content and process of change. This understanding is often the outcome of their own motivations, and the resulting combination of developed expertise and commitment gives effective change leaders the impetus to use more powerful and persistent approaches to change and to maintain a strategic focus. Simple operationalization of initiatives which are neither fully understood by change leaders nor personally engaging to them results in superficial change which has little real impact on the school.

A tendency to overemphasize the importance of management processes has perhaps obscured the significance of change content as the basis for securing commitment and motivation both in the leaders themselves and in those who follow them. In the recent argument for the separation of leadership and management, our results seem to show that both are needed for successful planning. Having a sense of direction without the wherewithal to implement it is ineffective. Managing prescribed change without having a sense of educational purpose is liable to be equally fruitless.

The study points to the need to think more clearly about what effective planning entails and how school leadership in relation to this function can be supported and developed. It also indicates that maybe there is a need to move away from a technicist 'dumbing down' approach to educational management to something more personally and cognitively challenging. The evidence from ISEP backs commercial sector research which shows that leaders who attend to their own development, who engage and invest intellectually as well as emotionally in the purpose and nature of their business, make a difference.

● Notes

1 DAI interview data were only available from 23 schools.
2 5–14 is a reference to the centrally prescribed curriculum structure in Scotland for primary schools and the early years of secondary education.
3 The Educational Institute of Scotland – the main teachers' union.
4 It is also at this stage that the importance of a whole-school focus becomes particularly salient. Logically, influencing matters at the organizational level is likely to be facilitated by actions which impact on a wide range of staff.

8

Do schools need critical friends?

Jim Doherty, John MacBeath, Stewart Jardine,
Iain Smith and Jim McCall

● Introduction

The ISEP project described in earlier chapters employed three distinctive
techniques:

- examination of school effectiveness outcomes;
- in-depth qualitative examination of the processes of improvement in 24
  case study schools;
- intervention and support in these 24 schools.

This chapter examines the role, experiences and value of those who were
involved in the third activity – intervention and support in 24 schools – as *'critical
friends'*. They worked alongside *researchers* as a team of two, attached to each
school. The distinctions between the roles and functions of the two are described
in this chapter along with a more extended analysis of the critical friend's role
and impact. This draws on data gathered from critical friends themselves, from
researchers, from schools and from an independent evaluator appointed purely
to assess the work of critical friends in the participating case study schools.

● Definitions

Costa and Kallick (1993) characterize a *critical friend* as:

> a trusted person who asks provocative questions, provides data to be
> examined through another lens, and offers critique of a person's work as
> a friend. A critical friend takes the time to fully understand the context of
> the work presented and the outcomes that the person or group is working
> toward. The friend is an advocate for the success of that work.

With this definition in mind we defined their purpose and role within ISEP as one which would offer support and challenge to the school in a way that would make it more able to:

- understand itself;
- understand the process of change;
- become more open to critique;
- engage in genuine dialogue;
- become more effective at managing change;
- be more effective at self-evaluation and self-monitoring;
- be more thoughtful in defining and prioritizing targets;
- develop greater self-confidence at self-management and self-improvement;
- learn how to use outside critical friends, networking and other sources of support;
- learn how to sustain 'habits of effectiveness'.

Two ISEP team members were attached to each school – one as a researcher and one as critical friend. Each, however, had a distinctive role. The role of the critical friend was primarily to support the process of change. The researcher's purpose was to document and interpret what was happening in the development process, including appraisal of the activities of the critical friend. In a sense both researcher and critical friend may be seen as 'catalysts of change' insofar as their presence, and their willingness to listen and probe, raised issues to the surface and increased levels of awareness.

● Ground rules, guidelines and assumptions

In the early stages of the project certain ground rules were agreed which may be summarized as a list of 'dos and don'ts'.
Critical friends *will*:

- facilitate and support;
- have positive regard for the school and its community;
- negotiate shared understandings with the teaching community;
- influence process (as opposed to content);
- encourage collegiality, including the sharing of ideas among teachers;
- support the senior management team and heads of department in any moves to encourage and enhance participative decision making;
- be prepared to help with change strategies;
- advise (but only advise) on which school initiatives might enhance cognitive or attitudinal outcomes.

Critical friends *will not*:

- assume a directive or 'expert' role;
- be evaluative (while encouraging evaluation);
- teach pupils;

- attempt to teach teachers in any directive, expert, content-led way;
- provide instant 'solutions' or 'quick fixes' to school problems;
- influence content (as opposed to process);
- break individual confidentiality or anonymity.

The focus of activity for critical friends was categorized broadly within the three themes – ethos; learning and teaching; development planning. The selection of theme(s) to be pursued by each school was agreed at the outset. Schools knew the terms of reference of both researcher and critical friend, although there were some differences of understanding and expectation of what their roles should be.

● Initial contact

The normal pattern was for researchers and/or critical friends to visit the school to establish initial contacts, negotiating ground rules for future relationships, arranging for data collection, agreeing the broad parameters within which the school and project staff would work. In these early stages it was important for the critical friend to be aware of the power of first impressions, his/her 'passport' into the school, his/her perceived allegiances and alliances. We felt it important that he or she came first as a friend, in a listening mode and open to approaches from virtually all quarters; not as an expert but not denying expertise. In these early stages it was important to be available in as many situations and contexts as possible, not to be seen as always in the head's room or construed as an ally of senior management. Being in the staff room or having lunch with support staff or pupils were more than symbolic acts. They established the critical friend from the start as a resource for the school as a whole and all its constituencies.

This required a delicate balancing act because headteachers and senior staff often saw the critical friend as their ally and proponents of their agenda. In other cases, staff saw the critical friend as an instrument which they could use to attack the head. Yet again, some tried to involve the critical friend in their own internal factional disputes. By their words and actions, critical friends had to establish the independence of their role.

This was helped where critical friends were known to staff through national or local reputation and a number of schools mentioned this as an important factor. While there was some initial resistance to 'people from ivory towers coming to sort out our problems', in general, critical friends were made welcome in schools. The remark from one school – 'You're wasting your time coming here' – was an exception. That is not to say that critical friends met with universal or unqualified support. Resistance and obstacles had to be surmounted and critical friends had, in some instances, to work hard to win the trust of staff and allay fears of hidden agendas.

● The first hurdle

The first tricky hurdle was the feedback from the data collection exercise. The most contentious aspect of this was the attitude questionnaires from parents, pupils and teachers. It was not only important for the critical friend to be totally familiar with the data and feel comfortable with handling them, but to create a climate in which staff, or parents or pupils, could also deal with them positively and constructively and come up with their own alternative interpretations. This was not always achieved. In some cases staff were unwilling to accept the validity of the data or the credibility of their sources (see Chapter 10). One headteacher informed the critical friend that the data from staff were, in fact, totally spurious since he had personally checked with every member of staff individually and they had, to a man and woman, denied having given a negative response! Defensive and self-justifying responses were not difficult to understand where the headteacher had been the brunt of serious criticism from staff (rarely from parents or pupils), but helping the head to accept and deal with it called on a high level of diplomatic and interpersonal skills. As a critical friend comments:

'The staff questionnaires, while generally pretty positive, included a considerable level of criticism of the school in general and the Senior Management Team in particular, especially regarding communication and liaison between the senior staff and the more junior staff. The reaction of the SMT to this was striking and I vividly recollect the difficulty I had in trying to talk to them in a fairly neutral way, suggesting that they should not necessarily confuse the message with the messenger.'

The experience of this member of the ISEP team is typical of the challenge of helping staff to accept data when they were the brunt of criticism. He goes on to say:

'It was clear that the headteacher, while surprised and dismayed by some of the apparent feedback from the questionnaires, was prepared to deal with it in a fairly open and positive manner. Some of the reactions from her senior colleagues, however, were of a rather different order, suggesting that some of the results were what you would expect to find in any secondary school. (Despite the fact that the data fed back to the school gave them not only the responses within their own school, but also comparative data on all 36 secondary schools taking part in the project.)'

Defensive reactions could sometimes be defused by accentuating the positives and discussing how these could be built upon, but in the worst case scenarios a head or staff had to come to terms with the bad feeling or low morale that existed and seek to find constructive ways of addressing the issues. Directing schools to others within the project was sometimes useful in addressing problem areas so that schools could see that their issues were not unique and that there could be escape routes. Because of their joint involvement in ISEP and sharing of a mutual critical friend, two schools were put in touch with each other in such a way that one, which had progressed from the same starting point at which the other now found itself, was able to offer not only support and hope but also share some approaches to tackling the problems. This kind of networking was an important element of the project.

Seeing how data could most profitably be presented, without compromising the integrity of the project, was one of the foremost challenges to the skills of the critical friend because it began to move people out of their 'comfort zone', and began a transition in role from friend to critic. Illustrative examples of this were in schools where, having examined the data, the school was reluctant to engage further with the process, in some cases because of a perceived 'destabilizing' effect of making the data more widely known among hard-pressed staff. 'Don't call us, we'll call you' was the message to the critical friend.

This posed a dilemma which was discussed at meetings where the critical friend team came together to exchange views and review progress. How 'interventionist' or persistent ought they to be in such cases? Should they be proactive or reactive? Accepting or assertive? Even devious? Some argued that in such circumstances the critical friend ought simply to withdraw and respect the school's wishes. Others argued that the schools concerned had contracted to take part in the project and critical friends, therefore, had a responsibility both to the school and to the project to ensure that persistent efforts were made to engage, or re-engage, the school in the work of the project. Failure to do so, it was argued, might be seen as a betrayal of those staff who wished these issues to be confronted and not simply ruled out of order by the head on their behalf. Where the reluctance to continue apparently emanated from the headteacher, it was suggested and attempted (with varying degrees of success) to enter the school by 'another door' (not literally) and to look for ways of engaging other members of staff. This did prove to be successful in some cases.

In one case a school did not so much resist further involvement by the critical friend, as 'absorb' her into the comfortable ethos of the school. Despite very poor results in the attainment tests, the school had a very strong pastoral tradition which was welcoming and reassuring. Poor attainment was accepted – 'I know. Isn't it terrible?' – yet the school seemed very satisfied with the job which it was doing. No amount of presentational skills on the part of the critical friend seemed to have an impact on deeply entrenched complacency. Persistence over a two-year period appeared in the final analysis (as reported by the school) to have had some impact on people's thinking but perhaps not commensurate with time and energy costs.

● What next?

The subsequent challenge for critical friends was to move the agenda forward, not to close the book on the exercise but to see it as merely the first chapter. In trying to negotiate with staff what the 'change agenda' was to be, another dilemma presented itself – the conflict between content and process. There was an inclination on the part of schools, particularly primary schools, to look to quick and effective ways of addressing the issues raised, to create new procedures, put in new structures when clearly, to the critical friend at least, the problems lay at a cultural rather than a structural level. Where there were low levels of attainment, heads often looked to the critical friend for a solution, manifesting itself in attempts to find a new course – a kind of 'magic wand' solution. While critical friends understood and felt some sympathy for this reaction, they saw their task as helping staff to dig deeper and more critically into the *why and how* as much as the *what* of their teaching. In some cases, this dilemma was more easily resolved where the critical friend had no particular subject specialism in the area of operation, as in the case of the secondary English specialist who worked with primary teachers on mathematics.

Indeed, this presented a real *paradox* which is central to projects designed to assist schools to improve their effectiveness. It is this: if the measure of effectiveness is pupil attainment, why not simply help schools to put in place courses and methods which might improve performances in such measures of attainment? In short, since ISEP attainment measurements had been in English and mathematics, why not simply concentrate on English and mathematics so that attainment levels could be improved? (Gray *et al.*'s 'tactical' improvement – see Chapter 1).

Improvement which is more strategic and capacity-building is concerned with helping teachers themselves to focus on processes involved in effecting real improvement. It aims to help them understand how such skills can then be transferred to any aspect of children's learning. When negotiating their role in the school improvement process, critical friends had to be aware of the importance of the 'internal context' of each school (Stoll and Fink 1996) – its nature and history, its community, its pupil population and current programme; teachers' professional, personal, political and learning experiences and the school's current culture. One aspect of this internal context was school policy documents which had sometimes been arrived at consensually but just as often had been written and imposed. Another not insignificant aspect of the internal context was the nature of the leadership of the school. This was often a matter of style and personality, vision and conviction. Some heads were directive or authoritarian. Some were consensus builders. Others were more laissez-faire. This often had a significant effect on the reaction of individual teachers, their level of defensiveness or openness, their wariness or willingness to embark on reflection or critique. In some circumstances questioning might be construed as criticism or complaint. Therefore, absolute respect for individual confidentiality was crucial in developing relationships, although critical friends had to exercise discretion in feeding back information to headteachers, resisting pressure to reveal more and giving information in general terms where appropriate.

There was also the 'external context', represented by the SOEID, local authorities, other initiatives and expectations. These included policy priorities such as *How good is our school?* (frequently referred to in both primary and secondary schools), the 5–14 Development Programme, Higher Still developments, school development planning, devolved management of resources (DMR) and so on. The 5–14 initiative loomed large, particularly in the primary schools, where new curriculum initiatives were pressing concerns, while development planning initiatives were a common concern in secondary schools.

Whatever the agreed 'improvement agenda', critical friends knew that they had to be seen to be a part of the school's efforts to change. They were not simply observers nor were they inspectors. They were participants in the improvement process, alongside their colleagues in the schools, working with them, hopefully with a common aim, a belief that had to be proved through deeds rather than words.

Critical friends worked with schools in a wide variety of contexts and in an equally wide variety of ways. They worked with whole staff groups (more often in primary schools where this was easier to achieve) and with departments in secondary schools and with groups of teachers for the different stages in the primary schools. They sat as members of short-life working groups, cross-curricular in composition (for example, on promoting positive behaviour) and took part in the work of specialist teams such as guidance staff and those responsible for careers education. In primary schools, where a common pattern was for teachers to work in pairs, critical friends often worked alongside them. They sometimes found themselves engaged with individuals who sought them out, sometimes looking for guidance, sometimes seeking clarification, sometimes simply in order to have a gripe in a receptive ear. On a number of occasions, they met formally with parents to discuss the project, to explore the data and what the school was trying to do. In one school, formal consultation with pupils was established (again, as part of the promoting positive behaviour initiative) and the results of the consultations were fed back to a working group which then incorporated them into aspects of a new policy initiative.

In all of this, critical friends were asked to keep a log of their activities from which it is possible to discern certain patterns of support and intervention and varying styles of approach. In none of the logs is there evidence of critical friends assuming a directive role. They were not evaluating, but helping others to do so. When asked, they would typically respond with examples of good practice from elsewhere, but usually offering more than one example so that teachers would have to reflect on the relative merits of each and their relevance to their own situations. Similarly, they would offer examples of schools where different practices operated, inviting teachers to ascertain for themselves what these might be in detail and what benefit could be learned from them.

Critical friends would, on occasion, invite teachers to consider options available to them, to assess the strengths and weaknesses of each and the opportunities and threats inherent in them. They would, on occasion, sum up a discussion, but only as a means of allowing participants to agree around certain points. They would help participants to chart out their next series of actions and try to assist them to set realistic targets and timescales. On the odd occasion, they 'refereed' heated discussions, but did not take sides (no matter what their private views). At times, they acquiesced in decisions legitimately arrived at with which they themselves might have disagreed.

A particularly perplexing situation arose where a school seemed to have assumptions and practices that had become institutionalized and remained unchallenged and, for some staff at least, were unchallengeable. In one instance the problem lay in the deeply institutionalized belief that some children could not achieve success. The critical friend had to find a way of unlocking this particular door and the answer lay, in part, in the data for that school. The teacher questionnaire had sought views on what an effective school might look like and staff had expressed the overwhelming view (150 responses) that it was crucial (78 per cent) or important (22 per cent) to believe that all children could be successful, yet only a small minority thought that this was true of their school. This large and significant gap between the ideal and the real provided the space for the critical friend to intervene and suggest the possibility that closing the gap might lie in their own hands.

In some cases the critical friend found herself or himself in the role of therapeutic counsellor, a role which it was easy to become locked into as in the case of a school whose existence in its present form was under threat, and in another case where the headteacher had serious personal difficulties with a senior colleague. In one case, the critical friend was described as a 'saviour' by the headteacher and in the other as the headteacher's 'only true friend' in the situation.

At times such difficulties could overwhelm all other concerns and critical friends had to work hard to try to keep focused on the main task. It is difficult to work seriously at improving the effectiveness of an already struggling school when its very existence is threatened (and this in a school where staff numbers had been slashed from 19 to 9 in one session) – or when key players in the change process refuse to communicate with one another!

Critical friends also found themselves in the role of confidant with some headteachers who would share personal problems with them, seeking their reassurance or advice. This sometimes took place directly in the school, by telephone or in the evening over a meal. The decision about how to respond in these situations was a personal one for which there was no rulebook or clear-cut set of principles. There were other occasions too when critical friends had reaffirmed headteachers in their pursuit of a strategy despite adverse data results and hostile criticism from some staff. A case of this was one recently appointed headteacher who was so in awe of his predecessor that he was unnecessarily tentative in his approach.

Another persistent problem both for critical friends and for schools was time and the management of time. Critical friends would typically spend the equivalent of six days on the 'nitty-gritty' of the work in schools but given sickness and other eventualities this meant that, in some schools, this time was reduced and that time lost could not easily be retrieved. Geographical problems further complicated the picture as trips to outlying areas, the Highlands and Islands for example, often meant overnight stays with the consequential loss of time. Even where none of the preceding difficulties obtained, there was real difficulty in matching the busy diaries of critical friends (who continued with their normal workload) with school needs. Schools themselves had the very pressing demands of school timetables and other commitments to be taken into account. It was, therefore, remarkable that critical friends and schools were able to achieve so much in terms of time management and sustained levels of commitment, and schools commented on the commendable efforts critical friends made to overcome difficulties.

There are, however, lessons to be learned from this aspect of the project. The reality was that the practical developmental work of critical friends in their schools did not really begin until the project was well in progress. This left a very short timescale in what was only a two-year project to achieve the results the schools hoped for and the project wished to achieve. For sustained improvement work to be effective, critical friend involvement needs to be sustained over a period of time long enough to embed processes within the structure and culture of the school.

● Embedding and disengaging

From the very early stages of the project, critical friends were aware that part of their task was to try to leave behind them schools more self-sufficient and self-confident in sustaining improvement. Throughout, they had tried to help staff to understand and define issues, plan priorities and set targets, reflect on their actions, evaluate them, change direction as necessary, review procedures and monitor accurately.

At the end of the project's direct involvement (and some critical friends have continued their connections with the school in an unofficial capacity – at least as far as this project is concerned), critical friends were anxious to identify achievement where it had taken place and give credit for it. Schools were encouraged to evaluate their work with the project and to see what lessons had been learned. Interviews were conducted with schools by an independent consultant in order to document changes over the previous two years and to comment critically on the activities of the critical friend.

This review revealed an almost universally favourable response, but in too short a timescale to say a great deal about the long-term outcome or effect of the critical friend's support. It would almost certainly be necessary to revisit the schools, and all of these issues particularly, to obtain an accurate view of how the critical friend had helped schools to 'continue' (in terms of Fullan's model; Fullan with Stiegebauer 1991) the improvement processes.

● Views on change in the schools with critical friends

Final collection and analysis of data from schools indicates objectively (certainly in comparison with baseline data) what change or otherwise there has been in terms of attainment and attitudes. Schools (in the person of the headteacher or other person in close contact with the critical friend) were asked to comment on change and other developments over the last two years. Of course, such changes could not exclusively (or predominantly) be attributed to the school's association with ISEP, nor necessarily be due to the presence of the critical friend. However, it is interesting to note how often schools make reference to the ISEP themes and in the broad context of the original ISEP briefings. Where specific questions were asked about ISEP's involvement, schools talked about the value of being involved with the project in terms of knowing where they stood, of providing them with a focus, of keeping them focused and of providing meaningful support in a wide variety of contexts.

It is impossible here to attempt to cover all of the 24 schools in detail. However, it is possible to isolate trends which give some indication of how schools viewed change in their own contexts. This last point is important. It is very clear that schools were not really interested in studying and mastering theories of change in the abstract. While they may have wished to understand the background, they also wanted to move on as quickly as possible to finding and applying solutions within their own environment. It was a real challenge for critical friends in this situation to try to help and support schools in such a way that they would begin to move in the direction of embedding the processes of change rather than simply looking for the 'quick fix'.

In some ways, the comments on change reflect the model of the school's readiness for change referred to earlier. It is clear that some remained at the superficial level (even at the level of resistance). Others had clearly moved along the line a little and had begun to look more closely at why change was necessary. Yet others had begun to put into practice some more reflective techniques with colleagues and were attempting to analyse and to share good practice. Some had become much more aware of monitoring and evaluation and the need to be prepared to take new directions in the course of the change process. There were schools, too, which were very concerned that changes should remain viable once introduced. Many schools seemed to have looked more closely at the development planning process and the need to involve staff more widely in it. Genuine dialogue does seem to have opened up in a number of cases (although there is no way of judging whether or not it would be maintained). There is also evidence of continuing resistance to change.

However, in the majority of cases, schools were willing to engage in the process of change in a constructive way. There was also evidence, in some schools, that the challenge of change caused a degree of staff unease and uncertainty. In some cases, staff saw this as an affront to their professionalism and a dent in their morale. Schools and critical friends had to work at re-establishing confidence. There is evidence of a 'pulling together' by staff to overcome their difficulties and a significant number of schools seem to have given priority to 'team building' as a result – a kind of 'siege mentality' in reverse.

A critical friend, writing about his involvement with a secondary school, described significant improvements in pupil attitudes and in teacher and parent questionnaire responses, which in 1995 had been more critical than the generality of Scottish secondary schools. Although there was no value-added evidence in terms of attainment, questionnaire responses were now uniformly up to at least the average Scottish secondary school and in many aspects beyond it. In 1998, the school, now having exited from the ISEP project, at least in a formal sense, had a full-school inspection, culminating in an extremely positive inspectorate report. Invited as a principal guest to the school prize-giving, the critical friend recounts the speech given by the head and then by the depute to assembled parents and pupils.

'After describing [to the inspectors] what was happening in the school, I was faced with the killer question, 'How do you know?' It took no-one by surprise as this is an area to which HMI pay close attention. Fortunately I was able to prove *how* I knew by referring to the evidence of the Improving School Effectiveness Project in which the school was involved over a two-year period. As a project school we acquired a critical friend to work with us. His involvement with the school was stimulating, productive and enjoyable as he worked closely with us in tackling a development plan priority – in this case, promoting positive behaviour to change attitudes and create a positive climate, enhance self-esteem and hopefully improve attainment.'

The critical friend also recounts the vote of thanks given by the depute head at the end of the evening:

'The most remarkable part of that evening was the second contribution relating to ISEP, which came from the Depute Head of the school, who had been the most critical person some four years earlier when I had fed back evidence from the initial round of data collection. Thanking me for my speech, he told his audience that not everyone in the school had been as open to evidence as I had suggested. Indeed, he himself had been very resistant to the picture of the school painted by the data, to the extent of thinking that it portrayed a different school from that which he had grown to know and to love over the years. For him, it has been a hard learning experience over the years of the project to gradually begin to appreciate the value for the school of openly and honestly dealing with such feedback, even when the evidence didn't always match one's own self-perceptions.'

The evidence from three sources – the critical friend himself, the head and depute, and the three questionnaire sets – points to improvement in Gray *et al.*'s capacity-building terms (see Chapter 1). This was a school, a year after the end of the project, feeling a renewed self-confidence and with a new strength in honest self-appraisal.

It cannot be assumed that improvement of this nature was uniquely and directly as the result of involvement with ISEP. There are often references to change having been initiated before that. However, schools readily accepted that their involvement with ISEP had been in order to advance the change process in some way or other and claimed that ISEP had been a catalyst for change, although not always in the ways that they had anticipated.

● Critical friends 'as ithers see them'

The basis for most of the comments that follow are from the review interviews. Selections from the comments have been chosen to illustrate the range and depth of the work in schools, as well as to attempt to gauge the overall reaction of schools.

In general, comments were very favourable. While no interviews were conducted in advance of the involvement, retrospective accounts reveal an element of suspicion, fear and apprehension about what the project might bring. References to 'people from ivory towers', 'so-called experts telling us how to do our job' were evident in some schools at the outset. In virtually all cases where critical friends had been allowed to operate effectively, respondents spoke of them warmly. They described the professionalism of critical friends, the atmosphere of trust that had been built up, good working relationships that had been established, practical interventions that had been effective. References were made also to the breadth and depth of their knowledge, their understanding and empathic qualities, their wide range of contacts and their access to materials, literature and other sources. Schools seemed appreciative of the difficulties critical friends faced (not least in terms of time) and the constraints of the project itself, which placed certain restrictions on their activities. There were frequent favourable references to the style and personal qualities of the critical friends – always supportive and positive, yet critical, constructive and sometimes challenging and confronting.

What follows is a series of extracts from some of the review interviews which illustrate these points further. (In each case, critical friends are simply identified as 'CF'.)

From a school where CF was absorbed:

'We wanted to change and CF knew her stuff so that was one of the important things that made it work . . . the fact that CF was coming in regularly kept us focused and kept ideas going longer knowing that she'd be discussing it . . . Our school is behind and we know that. At the last discussion I felt that it was all good that we knew we were behind and were prepared to admit there was a problem. We did feel that we did not need the children to be put through the worry and upset of that test to prove that. We could have told the researcher . . . The improvement will only be seen if the researchers look at the tests and acknowledge that they have tried it – it may be total rubbish but at least they have tried.'

From a primary school where reaction was mixed:

'CF made a great impact on staff as an astute evaluator and a 'nice guy'. His reputation went ahead of him and many were in awe until they got to know him better . . . Several staff were, and still are, sceptical of the approach taken through questionnaires and the value of the statistical information obtained. Many teachers were concerned by the implications of the questions on the 'added value', especially those to be completed by the pupils.'

From a primary school generally representative of wider views:

'Contact was good and worthwhile. Assessment was fair and friendly. I felt that I was able to be completely honest and that confidentiality was assured. CF was able to be used as a sounding board. We were not given the answers but were able to talk through the problems and come to conclusions ourselves. INSET (0.5 day) helped spark off discussion, then she withdrew to let school begin to 'sort itself'. CF had access to information not readily available to schools.'

And from one unreservedly positive primary school:

'CF was not critical. He appeared to value each individual situation and what each person had to offer to that situation so you felt at ease in his company. He helped us to keep focused and positive about the situation here. After the initial results the staff morale in the school sank and the staff were zonked. CF came quickly back to looking at the positives and look at what we were actually doing and not at what we were not doing . . . He helped us to be reflective, to see how we could improve our own practice . . . He was not judgemental . . . He respected people's point of view. Much of the development here has come from within the staff. People have not rushed outside for solutions. That is the way the change in development has taken place.'

By contrast, in a secondary school where the same critical friend found engagement difficult, the headteacher described the contact with the critical friend as 'limited but supportive' and continued:

'The school was, in the main, self-sufficient in its development. The "status" of the project was not seen as an integral part of the life of the school. My view of the project was that the school would continue along its chosen path with its targets and tasks to be achieved . . . Staff have misgivings about people in "ivory towers" but are very welcoming of sound professional advice to assist them in their teaching or management. Critical friends must be able to bridge that gap. Fortunately our CF is capable of meeting this challenge.'

In another secondary school, when asked if the critical friend had made a difference, the headteacher replied, 'I don't think so.' (This, however, in a school where the critical friend had worked extensively with a number of departments.) However, the same headteacher said of the school's involvement with ISEP (and the critical friend):

'It has given the school very useful audit information which has confirmed progress in a number of areas while at the same time helping to focus attention on a number of other areas. It has been a means of encouraging certain development opportunities both across the school and in particular departments. As CF is a respected figure, his own input to certain departments has been helpful.'

Another typical view from a secondary school:

'CF was a sounding board who visited as frequently as we wanted. He was helpful, informative, supportive in a tangible way with materials and information. He took the lead in a parents' evening . . . From day one the relationship was fine. He brought his own credibility and background with him. It grew stronger as time passed and confidence and respect in each other grew.'

When asked if the critical friend made a difference:

'Very much so. He was a source of ideas and help in finding the right direction. It was valuable to have him for discussion and confirmation. He was an external voice of reassurance. He was honest and practical and willing to speak his mind.'

The major, indeed the only, serious criticism offered of the work of critical friends with schools concerned time. Schools most certainly would have welcomed much more of the critical friends' time, although they appreciated that this was one of the constraints of the project. They also recognized the considerable difficulties of matching available times of critical friends with times when school staff were also available. Whereas this had not prevented the work of ISEP proceeding, it had been, in many cases, an inhibiting factor identified by schools and, to be fair, by critical friends themselves.

The preceding comments have served to give a flavour of what others thought of the work of critical friends in their schools. There have, in fact, been few comments from class teachers and that is unfortunate. The views of headteachers do not necessarily always reflect staffroom opinions!

Another 'critical friend', writing in another time and with different circumstances in mind, perhaps offered our schools and critical friends a kind of rationale for 'critical friendship':

Oh wad some pow'r the giftie gie us
tae see oorsels as ithers see us.

9

A profile of change

John MacBeath and Louise Stoll

Researchers have devoted half a lifetime to identifying the processes by which teachers develop, practices change, and schools improve. Our understanding seems to grow in small incremental stages, each study bringing insights and challenging old beliefs. In the ISE project one of the tools we used was called the change profile. Its purpose was to chart how staff evaluated their school over time. Although this was also the purpose of the questionnaires, the change profile provided the stimulus for a deeper probing into attitudes and values. Built into the process was a press for evidence in order to bolster, or challenge, off-the-cuff judgements of a school's strengths and weaknesses, its effectiveness and direction of change.

● The change profile

The change profile consists of 10 items (Table 9.1) on which members of staff are asked to give their school a rating on a four-point scale (where one is negative and four is positive) similar to that used by HM Inspectors in Scotland. Each of these 10 items is amplified by a short explanatory paragraph, suggesting a key principle of school effectiveness and improvement (see Figure 9.1).

The change profile was completed by a small group of five or six representative staff, first on an individual basis with staff then being asked to work as a whole group to try and arrive at a consensus rating for all 10 items. The headteacher completed the same profile independently of this, as did the researcher and critical friend. Typically, both researcher and critical friend joined the discussion with the small staff group, with one of the two 'neutrals' in the chair to steer, mediate, manage time and consistently return to the evidence questions – 'How do you know?', 'What is the evidence for that judgement?', while the other took notes. While the outcome of the exercise

Table 9.1   The ISEP change profile

Characteristic	Rating			
	1	*2*	*3*	*4*
1 A learning school				
2 High expectations of achievement				
3 Ownership of change				
4 Shared goals and values				
5 Effective communication				
6 Focus on pupil learning				
7 Effective leadership				
8 Home–school partnership				
9 Positive relationships				
10 Collaboration				
11 *				

* Please use this space to add any other condition or characteristic that you think is important for school improvement.

was a set of scores and a baseline position on schools at the beginning of the project, it was the process of scoring itself that generated deep insights into the school as an organization, its ability to be self-reflective and its readiness for change. As a sole source of evidence the change profile has obvious limitations but, taken together with other tools of inquiry, it proved to be a valuable instrument that could be used by schools as a starting point for a quality audit.

One of the most immediate pieces of evidence to emerge from the analysis of the change profile was the disparity of judgements from the three perspectives – teachers, headteachers, and researcher/critical friends. As Table 9.2 shows (providing an aggregate score across the 10 items for each of the 12 schools), there was a consistent tendency for headteachers to be more optimistic than their staff and for us 'outsiders' to be more pessimistic in our judgements. School M, for example, shows a sizeable discrepancy between headteacher and staff and suggests a head who seriously misread the temperature of the organization, in this case most conspicuously in relation to the item on 'effective leadership'.

This is a significant starting point for exploring growth and change, not only for us as researchers but for the school itself in confronting this apparent gap in its communal self-knowledge. Without this how could school M enter seriously into development planning or improvement initiatives?

The story is perhaps best told by a closer examination of one of these 12 schools. What did the change profile reveal and how much did it add to our understanding of change when taken together with other sources of evidence? The school in question is school L (which we shall call St Leopold's, to give it a more human face). Table 9.3 shows how the profile looked when broken down by the 10 individual items.

Pupil learning is likely to be enhanced when the following statements apply:

1 *This is a learning school*
   There is a commitment by staff to reflect, to adapt and to learn. This expresses itself in staff dealings with one another, with pupils and parents. People are not afraid to try something new and are encouraged to experiment.

2 *There are high expectations of pupil achievement*
   There is a widely shared commitment to high achievement. Staff believe that all children can surpass their own, teachers' and parents' expectations. Efforts are made to share that conviction with the pupil and parent body and to realize it in a range of practical ways. There is a belief that all teachers can and must make a difference to children's learning.

3 *There is ownership of change*
   People behave proactively rather than reactively. They initiate change in a way designed to further the main purpose of the school rather than simply responding to imposed change from the outside. It is a common assumption that no matter how effective the school is, more can always be achieved.

4 *There are widely shared goals and values*
   There is shared understanding of the school's values and priorities and shared commitment to its core values. This is important at the level of teaching staff but should be extended to support staff and, as far as possible, to parents and pupils and other key players. There is talk about 'what is important in this school' as part of an ongoing process of self-evaluation and development.

5 *There is effective communication*
   Members of the immediate school community (plus parents and others in the wider community) are kept informed; are confident that their information is acted upon and that their views are heard by the school. People feel free to speak their mind.

6 *Pupil learning is a major focus of attention*
   In the forefront of the school's planning, innovation and change is a concern for pupil learning. It is manifested in day-to-day dialogue among staff and in pupil–staff and staff–parent relationships.

7 *Leadership is effective*
   There is confidence in those who make key decisions about the vision and direction of the school. They are able to recruit and motivate people and foster a culture open to change and learning.

8 *There is real home–school partnership*
   Staff believe that parents have a key role to play in supporting pupil learning; and in the school in general. Staff and management make efforts to inform and involve parents on a collaborative basis.

9 *Relationships are based on respect for individuals*
   There is a high level of mutual respect among staff for one another's professionality and for the integrity of the individual. All are seen as having something to offer. Respect for the individual is also demonstrated in staff dealings with pupils and parents. Recognition and celebration of differences and different achievements are highlighted. Diversity is seen as a strength. There are high levels of mutual trust.

10 *Collaboration and partnership are a way of life*
    People work together. There is a consistent approach which is supportive. People are not left to sink or swim. People are available to help each other. Team teaching, mentoring, peer coaching, joint planning and mutual observation and feedback are a normal part of the everyday life of the school.

Figure 9.1   Change profile: conditions for school improvement

Table 9.2 Comparison of mean change profile scores by headteacher, teaching staff and critical friend/researcher

School	Friend/Researcher Total n = 24	Head Total n = 9	Staff Total n = 64
School A	3.0	3.6	2.9
School B	3.0	3.2	3.2
School C	2.7	2.9	2.8
School D	2.5	n/a	3.4
School E	2.6	n/a	3.0
School F	2.5	2.9	2.7
School G	2.4	3.0	3.1
School H	2.0	2.9	2.7
School J	2.6	n/a	2.6
School K	2.1	2.9	2.3
School L	2.0	2.6	2.4
School M	1.3	3.1	2.3

Note: n = staff 64, headteacher = 9, critical friend/researcher = 24.

We see in Table 9.3 the same tendency for there to be a disparity among qualitative judgements from the different perspectives of the outsiders (critical friend and researcher), the main players (the teachers) and management (the head). It raises as many questions for the research team as for the school itself. For example, is the research team out of touch with the reality of school life? Does it not understand the nuances, given that the rating has been made after only two days in the school? Or does it benefit from a perspective not available to the staff or the headteacher? Alternatively, perhaps, are the criteria

Table 9.3 St Leopold's: comparison of consensus change profile scores by headteacher, teaching staff and critical friend/researcher in 1995

St Leopold's	Friend/Researcher n = 2	Head n = 1	Staff n = 5
A learning school	2	2	3
High expectations	2	2	2
Ownership of change	2	3	2
Shared goals	2	2	2
Effective communication	3	3	2
Focus on pupil learning	2	3	3
Effective leadership	2	3	1
Home–school partnership	2	2	3
Positive relationships	2	3	2
Staff collaboration	2	3	1

being understood and applied differently by the research team? Similarly, is the head out of touch with his/her staff or seeing things that staff don't see? On the question of effective leadership, for example, what set of assumptions, experience and sources of evidence are being brought to bear on that judgement? Are those who lead, or those who are led, in the best position to make such a judgement? From the bird's-eye perspective, the head judges there to be good staff collaboration. From their perspective in the thick of things, staff have a markedly different view.

These data, intuitive and ambiguous as they are, provide an excellent take-off point for the school to reflect on itself, to monitor its own process of change and to use the help of the critical friend to address its inherent tensions and move on. The following narrative hopefully gives some of the richer flavour of St Leopold's as a school in the process of change.

● We wouldn't have started from here

'If we wanted to become a really effective school we wouldn't have started from here', said one member of staff who was struggling simultaneously with the change profile and the concept of the effective school. St Leopold's could not by any definition be called an effective school, but it had enough self-knowledge to recognize how far it would have to travel and that improvement has to start somewhere.

The Scottish Office's nationally published performance tables showed St Leopold's near the bottom of the heap, with less than one in three pupils achieving Standard Grades (1–4) against a national average of 70 per cent. The poor performance of the school nationally, together with unhelpful headlines ('The worst school in Scotland?') was seen as unsurprising but, nonetheless, a source of considerable irritation to staff. It was not in anyone's judgement – teachers, management team, or from the research team's viewpoint – a 'bad' school, but clearly one dealing with adversity.

The school sits in the open wasteland of one of Scotland's most disadvantaged inner city areas, blighted by unemployment, ageing housing stock and a legacy of low achievement passed on from generation to generation. The second-year cohort whom we chose to follow for the two years of the project was described by more than one teacher as 'the class from hell'. This class was, even for St Leopold's, atypically low achieving, a 'rump' that had been left behind after a recent school amalgamation, their more ambitious classmates (or more aspiring parents) having opted for another nearby school.

Although described fairly consistently as a 'happy school' with amicable staff relationships, there were tensions that revealed themselves even before the beginning of the project and before the completion of a change profile whose results belied that all-too-easy characterization of the school as a harmonious place.

St Leopold's was one of the schools whose name had been randomly generated by the Scottish Office computer and, along with 200 other schools, invited to a half-day introductory seminar to hear about the project and decide whether or not to consider participating in the study. The senior management of St Leopold's were keen to be involved in the ISE project because they saw in it an opportunity to revitalize the school, to challenge the inertia and underachievement that are all too commonly endemic features of an inner city school.

The assistant head who attended the invitational briefing was immediately keen for the school to be involved then and there but, in common with all schools, was asked to consult with staff before committing the school to a decision. A few days later he phoned to ask if one of the research team could come to speak to the whole staff at 4 o'clock in order to brief them on the project and answer the difficult questions – workload issues, confidentiality, the voluntary nature of staff participation, and what was going to be in it for St Leopold's. In the event, the meeting was fairly cordial and a week later the assistant head called to say that the staff had agreed to be involved. The call had, however, been preceded by a long, and in places vitriolic, letter from the union representative, alerting the critical friend to the existence of a 'significant' body of dissent among the staff and pointing out that he personally as spokesperson had made his dissent known but was, 'typically', ignored by the senior management team.

When the issue was raised with members of the SMT, their response was one of resigned indulgence, pointing to a regular and voluminous flow of correspondence from the union representative, whose dissatisfaction with management was a running theme. From their perspective this was one of the reasons why they wished to be involved in the project. They felt themselves constantly being dragged back by this kind of reflex reaction to innovation and change. The school, they said, needed the challenge of an outsider to work with them, to move on St Leopold's which, by their own assessment, could justifiably be described as a 'struggling' school (Stoll and Fink 1996).

So when it came to the data collection phase and the completion of the change profile, these prior experiences served as a backdrop for the researcher and critical friend in making their assessment of the school. These responses constituted data of a sort, anecdotal, impressionistic, but none the less powerful in telling part of the story of St Leopold's. Informal and off-the-cuff assessments such as these were only a surface reflection of school life but they did generate an animated dialogue around the 10 change profile items. Staff's experience of the school had deeper roots, and the judgements they brought to the exercise illuminated other facets, other versions of the 'truth' about St Leopold's.

An incident on the same day as the change profile exercise offered a further glimpse into the ethos of the school. It revealed a dark corner of school life, atypical of the wider ethos but highly significant in terms of its effect on staff, on pupil attitudes, on the school as whole and on its capacity for improvement.

On our second day in the school we made the conscious decision to make an uninvited visit to the 'top staffroom'. The dead tea bags in the sink, the congealed sugar, and the archaeological layers of caffeine on the glass cups told their own story. One member of staff was asleep with his feet on the mantelpiece, apparently oblivious to our presence, but his occasional smiles betrayed his careful monitoring of the conversation. The conversation (no dialogue here) was the 'top staffroom' perspective on the school, on school effectiveness and on the value of researchers in particular. Making friends with this group of staff might, with a little ingratiation, have been easy, but attempting to engage in a productive critical dialogue might not have been so easy, nor the wisest investment of time and energy. The aphorism 'don't water the rocks' sprang simultaneously to the lips of researcher and critical friend.

(MacBeath 1998: 120)

This is a classic example of 'balkanization' (Hargreaves 1994) – segregated islands within one organization which breed rumour and allow antagonisms to take root. The brief visit to the upper staffroom, a social system in miniature, helped to explain some of the contradictions in the data we were gathering. The data suggested, on the one hand, a friendly ethos, good staff relationships (themes emerging consistently through interviews and informal conversation) but at the same time a low grading by staff for 'collaboration' on the change profile.

The top staffroom was an issue that, as researcher and critical friend, we felt should be addressed sooner rather than later by senior management. The two alternatives we considered were, one, to suggest to the management team that the top staffroom be summarily closed; the second option, taking a longer term view, to hope that the process of school improvement would lead towards its demise and the reintegration of the half-dozen self-exiled staff. In a sense the closure of the top staffroom might be taken as one measure of school improvement.

● Term of trial

The data gathering involving researcher and critical friend took place over two days, conducting interviews with the head, individual members of staff and groups of pupils. The development analysis interview, as described in Chapter 7, was conducted with the head and depute head while a group of five staff (including the longest serving and the newest teacher) completed the change profile. In addition to this, as a separate exercise, second year pupils, teachers and a sample of parents completed questionnaires and returned them to the Quality in Education Centre.

The following is a brief summary sketch of the school emerging from these quantitative and qualitative data.

● St Leopold's – the school

Judgements about the ethos of the school are affected by first impressions. The unprepossessing exterior of St Leopold's is reflected in a bleak interior, with evidence of crumbling plaster in stairwells and little relief by way of posters or images in corridors and other public spaces. It is a school too physically big for its pupil population of around 300 who often seem lost in its endless corridors and broad staircases. A progressively falling roll has led to deflated staff morale, concern over possible closure and the unsettled feeling that such uncertain futures generate. ('What's the point of trying?' as one member of staff puts it.) While the depute head, reflecting the views of his colleagues, described the strengths of the school as 'positive ethos' and 'community spirit' he also described a 'them and us' attitude among staff. This was explained further by one of the assistant heads: 'There is a core of committed hard working staff, but there's also a small group who are cynical and dismissive of children's ability, some of whom have lost out on early retirement.'

Discipline problems, in the view of a number of staff, stemmed from members of this disaffected group, not because they weren't strict, but often because they *were*. The research team heard that these children, often with low self-esteem, responded much better to a calm supportive approach. (One classroom observation, in which the headteacher took over from another teacher who had clearly lost control, provided a dramatic illustration of the immediate calming effect of a warm personal touch.)

The emphasis on caring and the overall policy of support and praise was attested to by pupils who commented positively on the majority of teachers as good at praise. Interviews with pupils confirmed the quantitative data. Most reported they like school (70 per cent always or usually). Most felt they usually got on well with teachers (68 per cent), while 83 per cent saw their teachers as always or usually fair.

Parents were, as seen by staff, passively supportive. Data from the parents' questionnaire shows a consistently higher than average rating for the school,

Table 9.4   Parents' perceptions of their children's school in 1995: comparison between St Leopold's and total secondary parent sample

	% agreement	
	St Leopold's	All schools
My child finds school work stimulating and challenging	95	85
The school has explained to me how I can help my child's learning at home	90	58
Teachers are good at letting me know about my child's strengths and weaknesses	95	77
Teachers deal effectively with bad behaviour	92	79
Pupils respect teachers	85	65

confirming the support of parents but perhaps also suggesting a generally uncritical affirmation.

Parents, despite this strong endorsement, were seen by teachers as disinclined to become involved, carrying a legacy of their own unhappy school days. The school knew its community well through strong links with other agencies – housing, health, social work, police – and because it was a relatively small and tightly bounded geographical area.

The foremost priorities for the school were generally seen as staff development, improvement of learning and teaching, and raising the sights and expectations of pupils, parents and teachers.

● Feedback

Evidence collected by researcher and critical friend – subjective and impressionistic, qualitative and quantitative, data from the change profile, development analysis, and more detailed comments from staff and pupil interviews – was fed back to the staff of St Leopold's. The first round of feedback was given to the senior management team as they were most easy to identify from the data and needed time to consider where they would go with it next. The next visit to the school by the critical friend was to sift through the qualitative data with the SMT, examining the change profile, trying to untangle the strands and to make sense of the themes from the pupil and staff interviews. The quantitative data, still being processed along with 79 other schools, were kept for a subsequent visit.

While, from the outset, the critical friend reiterated the importance of being open and non-defensive, most members of the management team appeared to need no such ground rules. They were quick to acknowledge their weaknesses, recognized areas for improvement, and only occasionally sought to explain away the less palatable findings. This attitude to the data was helped by some very positive results, such as the response of pupils, particularly in respect of being praised by teachers, which was, for the SMT, a welcome affirmation of school policy.

Among the less palatable findings was a staff ranking in the change profile of 1 for leadership. The critical friend, who had given a ranking of 2, found himself in the delicate position of having to justify these judgements. While the long and recent absence of the headteacher through illness was an explanatory factor, it also served to highlight the issue of shared leadership and the degree to which this extended beyond the head and beyond the management team.

Many of these themes were revisited on the next meeting with the management team, the purpose of which was to discuss the quantitative data on pupil attainment, in conjunction with pupil, teacher and parent attitude data. The job was made easier by a summary digest of the questionnaire and attainment outcomes, drawing out some of the main messages from the data, highlighting strengths and weaknesses and including normative data which showed where the school stood in relation to the other 35 secondary schools in the study.

The following are some examples from that digest.

Of the 54 teacher questionnaire items, 13 fitted the ISEP normative definition of perceived strengths in secondary schools (that is, 66 per cent or more staff agreeing that the given statement was true of their school). Of these 13 strengths, three were significantly above the whole-school sample:

- Teachers have a say in topics selected for the school staff development programme.
- Teachers have a say in the school development plan.
- The plan includes practical ways of evaluating success in achieving goals and targets.

These data seem, at first sight, to lend further ambiguity to the low ranking for collaboration on the change profile, but on the 17 items in which the school fared less well (33 per cent or less saying it was true of the school) it was often to do with collaboration and shared values about learning and teaching. For example:

- Teachers regularly collaborate to plan their teaching.
- Teachers share similar attitudes and beliefs about effective teaching/ learning.
- Standards for pupils are consistently upheld across the school.

This seemed to suggest a disjunction between development planning and learning and teaching. However much staff were consulted on the development plan itself, it did not appear that it reached into those critical arenas for change – the classrooms. The clearest and most singular message from the data pointed to the need to focus planning squarely on the quality of learning and teaching across the school. It was a priority to which senior management gave immediate consent as it reaffirmed their own concern for a more concerted whole-school approach to these issues.

Two further responses to the questionnaire shed further light on this. On the statement, 'Staff have a commitment to the whole school and not just their class or department', there was only a 13 per cent agreement (48 per cent for all ISEP secondary schools); and on the highly significant indicator, 'Teachers like working in this school', there was only 19 per cent agreement (62 per cent for all ISEP secondaries).

It has to be borne in mind that, in response to any of the questionnaire items, teachers were not stating their own personal view but making a judgement about their colleagues' views. This is a quite different measure from stating one's own view (which would probably have yielded a higher positive percentage) but it is an equally, or even more, valid measure of school morale or ethos because it reveals teachers' perceptions, and sometimes lack of knowledge, of the collective. Across all our case study schools it provided rich insights into the school's readiness for change.

These data provided the senior management team with a challenging view of their school and, at their second meeting with the critical friend, two hours were spent sifting through these data, commenting, raising questions, seeking different interpretations and exploring implications. As well as the window it opened on their school, the crunch question was how to replicate this reflective self-evaluative process with the staff as a whole and how to turn the data to use for school improvement. How should the data be fed back to staff most effectively and where could that lead?

It was agreed that the next professional development day would be given over to working with the data as a whole staff and that, on the next visit, the critical friend should sit down with the depute head to plan a day of intensive interactive work with staff. The focus would be on systematic perusal of the data, interpreting, discussing implications and applications and agreeing whole-school priorities for future action.

In the event, the day was managed by the depute head and the critical friend working together as a pair, taking it in turns to introduce and debrief each session. The opening ten minutes of the session could have set the tone for the day, moving it in one direction or another. Before the depute head had finished his introduction, outlining the purpose and structure of the day, the union representative jumped to his feet to contest the statement that the school had 'agreed to be involved'. He personally had not given his assent and he believed he could also speak on behalf of many of his colleagues. For a moment the challenge was left hanging in the air, then without demur the depute head went on to introduce the critical friend, asking him to present a summary of the data, from staff themselves, from pupils and parents. His presentation was interrupted at frequent intervals by the union representative whose issues were on reliability and validity, including: 'How many of the staff completed the questionnaire?' 'How valid are people's perceptions?' 'How valid are people's perceptions of other people's perceptions?' 'Aren't many of the items highly ambiguous? For example, "Staff believe all pupils can be successful" – doesn't it depend on your measure of "success"?'

Whatever the motive of the interrogator, treating these as serious and useful questions helped both to defuse the hostility and to put on to the agenda some key issues for teachers themselves to resolve. What did *they* understand as 'success' and how did that, in turn, relate to issues such as 'Teachers share similar attitudes and beliefs about effective teaching/learning' and 'Staff have a commitment to the whole school and not just their class or department'?

It provided an important and helpful entrée to the deep-lying issues of shared values and common language among staff. The questionnaire item 'Teachers in this school believe all children can be successful' set in train a rich and penetrating discussion on what 'success' meant, not only to different teachers, but to different subject disciplines – to art, to maths, to PE and to English teachers. The ensuing discussion touched on essential values and untested assumptions that, as the union representative was later to say, had never before been discussed as a staff.

The fact that these early interventions were sidestepped, pre-empting a peripheral debate about what did or didn't happen in the past, helped to set the tone for the day. The lack of defensive response from either the depute head or critical friend was both a promising beginning and a valuable lesson for all of us. The swift move out of plenary to the first group activity also helped to focus attention on the task and there was an immediate buzz of animated conversation, including the easily overheard comment from the top staffroom sleeper, 'F***ing American crap'.

The ultimate wide-awake participation of the sleeper and a high level of involvement by the union representative over the course of the day reflected the generative power of the data. The personal vote of thanks by the union representative at the end, together with the generally relaxed, purposeful and good humoured atmosphere, could be ascribed in some measure to the approach of the depute head and the critical friend in handling, welcoming and using conflict. This sharing of common and varied perspectives encouraged one member of staff spontaneously to query the continued existence of separate staffrooms and to argue the case for provision that would bring them more closely and continuously into contact with one another. Although it was to take a year to happen, the top staffroom was eventually closed.

At management level, the staff development day fed back directly into school development planning, targeting areas where teaching was weak, with members of the management team themselves taking some of the most difficult and low-achieving classes. While the critical friend continued to work with the management team, it was the level of the classroom with one individual teacher that was to bear most fruit.

The newest teacher in the school, who shall be called Mark, taught physics. One wall of his classroom bore the banner with a message in large letters: 'STUCK? GOOD. NOW IS YOUR OPPORTUNITY TO LEARN SOMETHING'. He had worked hard, and to a large extent succeeded, in creating a mastery learning ethic (Dweck and Licht 1980) in his classroom. With young people used to giving up and giving in when confronted with an obstacle, he had worked assiduously to persuade them that difficulties are challenges to be enjoyed and overcome. This was a teacher who needed no persuading to research further into his pupils' learning, to evaluate the effectiveness of their learning and to experiment with innovative approaches to thinking skills. With encouragement and some guidance on the literature, and a great deal of self-motivation, Mark began to develop a course on thinking and memory techniques, generating enough material to fill a ten-week block of PSE time.

Together with the critical friend, an evaluation approach was devised to measure change in pupils' attitudes to learning, to school, and themselves. The first trial, comparing pupils in the programme with a non-participating 'control' group, produced significant results that exceeded expectations. While subsequent evaluations of the next two cohorts were less positive, there was clear evidence that pupils responded well to this initiative and were using and profiting from techniques such as mind-mapping, relaxation and visualization. Pupils' work began to overflow into the corridors – models, diagrams, mind maps, experiments bearing labels such as 'I tried this experiment fourteen times before I got this to work!'

Similarly high levels of enthusiasm and positive results were obtained when the depute head taught the course, and teachers from other departments began to show an interest in the approach, which Mark had named *Learnu-copia* and had put together as a set of around one hundred coloured and densely-packed overhead transparencies.

In the second year of ISEP, Mark ran a session for members of St Leopold's staff, a voluntary activity that attracted a dozen teachers over two sessions. Mark's approach to learning skills not only attracted other staff within the school, but stimulated wider interest – from other schools, from the media, from the education authority and from the Scottish Office. A workshop session at a national conference, run by an assistant head and Mark together, was attended by a number of civil servants, HMI and headteachers, increasing the already growing demand for in-service workshops and copies of the *Learnu-copia* materials.

Over the following months the headteacher of St Leopold's allowed his young member of staff a great deal of latitude to run courses for other schools, a level of demand which could not be met without serious disruption to Mark's own teaching. Two years on, the demand has grown and both Mark and the depute head, both now teaching in other schools, continue to run courses for other schools and authorities when time allows.

This is simply one strand of what happened in St Leopold's, but of particular interest because it illustrates a process of improvement which is exemplary bottom-up/top-down – that is, a movement of ideas and practices at classroom level, endorsed and supported from school senior management. It illustrates 'the rule of the vital few' (Koch 1998) – the power of a significant minority to create a disturbance and to begin to make a difference.

The improvement process in St Leopold's may be tested against Gray *et al.*'s (1999a) three categories of school improvement – tactical, strategic and capacity-building. The tactical approach, to push up examination attainment, was subsidiary to a more strategic approach to the raising of standards over time and to building in resilience and conviction to the school's capacity for change. The developments that started in one physics classroom not only sowed the seeds of better learning and teaching in the school but in the wider system too. Learning skills materials developed in St Leopold's (and financed by the London-based charity Highest Common Denominator (HCD)) have been purchased in large quantities by Scottish authorities and individual schools. Many of the ideas and practices seeded in St Leopold's are now taking root and germinating in other soil.

Improvement may be measured by standards of attainment in St Leopold's. This would show a 12 per cent rise on the previous year but comparable results to the year before that, illustrative of Gray and colleagues' findings that year-on-year results can be very misleading and that we need to look to trends over time. The 1995 and 1997 results were the best the school had achieved in many years and, given the starting point of the 'class from hell', the results had surpassed staff's expectations. ISEP's own value-added analysis showed a modest residual in English and mathematics, just below the level of significance.

If this were to be our measure of school improvement, it would hardly repay the effort, goodwill and commitment of St Leopold's staff, nor the investment of time by a researcher and critical friend. What we witnessed in this school was a process of regeneration. By the end of the two years it was a brighter, more attractive environment. The school was cleaner, more colourful, with more displays of pupils' work in corridors and entrance hall. Pupils themselves were more positive in their evaluation of the school, their teachers and themselves. In terms of value-added attitudes, St Leopold's not only showed significant improvement in pupil attitudes between second and fourth year, but also in comparison with the other secondary schools in the study. Table 9.5 shows a few illustrative examples.

Of the 40 items, on only four did St Leopold pupils score more negatively than the whole secondary school sample. These were on self-report of behaviour at home, adults' views of behaviour at home, teachers marking homework and, perhaps most significantly, perceptions of all-round ability ('I can do most things well') – 52 per cent positive in St Leopold's compared to 78 per cent in the all-schools sample.

At staff level there was also a higher level of satisfaction, morale and confidence and the beginning of more shared teaching and in-house professional development. The dissident rump had all but disappeared and there were new staff breathing life into tired departments. It was the consensus view of the senior management team that the dynamics of the school had changed. Where once the teachers in the middle ground would have been pulled down by the negative forces of the disaffected few, there was now a pull from the opposite magnetic pole. It was a view also shared by staff. As one teacher put it, 'There was a definite change in the atmosphere of the school. The staff who had given up and just become a dead weight were more and more marginalized. The self-help group of four or five teachers began to have a much bigger influence, taking on the moaners at staff meetings, not letting people away with things, sending out more positive signals.'

Table 9.5 Changes in pupil perceptions of their school over time

Questionnaire item	% positive St Leopold's 1995	% positive St Leopold's 1997	Mean St Leopold's	Mean all secondary schools
Liking school	70	87	3.04	2.71*
Fairness of teachers	83	96	3.09	2.87
Teachers listening to what I say	74	91	3.26	2.88*
Teachers telling me how I'm getting on with my work	57	91	3.30	2.74*
The friendliness of teachers	53	87	3.35	2.88*
The behaviour of other pupils in my classes	27	69	2.74	2.19*

Notes:
The mean is calculated on a four-point scale, 4 being a perfect positive score.
* means these are at a level of statistical significance.

It is a confirmation of the power of 'the vital few', of vitality for change that can come from the grass roots. Just as there is a critical mass of pro- and anti-school pupils (described in Chapters 1 and 4 as the compositional effect) so a teaching group can exert its own powerful compositional effect – a challenging and rewarding area for future research.

The second round of the staff questionnaire included six questions on 'change in your school in the last two years'. Table 9.6 shows the results from St Leopold's compared to all secondary schools in the study.

In the estimation of staff, St Leopold's had made significant improvements on a number of fronts. The improved ethos and morale is reflected in the 61 per cent who now saw the school as a better place to be, significantly higher than in other ISEP schools. There is a quite dramatic, 38 per cent difference, between St Leopold's and other schools in respect of raising expectations, together with 71 per cent who saw teaching and learning as having improved – a testament to the achievement of one of their primary goals from the outset of the project. On management, development planning and monitoring, St Leopold's results, although more positive than negative, are closer to those of other schools with one notable negative – 28 per cent seeing developmental planning as being less positive.

These data are given more meaning by the change profile, revisited again by the same five staff who had completed it two years previously. Overall there was a more positive response, although less so in respect of leadership and communication.

Discussion of the change profile helped to probe some of the ambiguities in the questionnaire data. The two weakest areas, from the staff viewpoint, were with respect to communication and leadership. Their experience, to which neither the head nor critical friend had access, was the impact on staff of con-

Table 9.6   Change in teachers' perceptions in the last two years

		% Better	% Same	% Worse
The school as a place to be	St Leopold's	61	17	22
	All schools	44	27	29
Expectations of pupils by staff	St Leopold's	67	28	6
	All schools	38	48	14
Learning and teaching	St Leopold's	71	29	0
	All schools	52	43	6
The quality of management and leadership	St Leopold's	44	39	17
	All schools	48	34	19
The process of development planning	St Leopold's	50	22	28
	All schools	50	40	10
Monitoring school progress towards goals	St Leopold's	59	29	12
	All schools	50	43	7

Notes: St Leopold's: n = 20. All secondary teachers: n = 1406.

Table 9.7 School L: comparison of consensus change profile scores by headteacher, teaching staff and critical friend in 1997

St Leopold's	*Critical staff* *n = 1*	*Head* *n = 1*	*Staff* *n = 5*
A learning school	3	3	3
High expectations	3	3	3
Ownership of change	2	3	2
Shared goals	2	3	3
Effective communication	3	3	2
Focus on pupil learning	3	3	3
Effective leadership	2	3	1
Home–school partnership	2	2	3
Positive relationships	3	3	3
Staff collaboration	2	3	3

tinuing uncertainty over the future of the school. Additionally, they saw a failure of the leadership forcibly to address this issue, to lead from the front and keep staff informed over developments. In this climate, development planning had also suffered. Where formerly it had been participative, and increasingly so in the first year of ISEP, in the final year of ISEP it had become 'a whipped process', as one member of staff described it, reflecting a lack of desire to invest a lot of time in planning when the future of the school was increasingly in doubt.

These concerns loomed large for staff and tended to be seen as a failure of management and leadership. On the other hand, what the critical friend was aware of, and not all staff perceived so clearly, was a leadership which appointed key members of staff and gave them a great deal of scope to exercise leadership and affect change. It is, said one member of staff 'a school of extremes', difficult to categorize easily – a management team with many qualities and some conspicuous weak points; a staff ranging from the outstandingly good to the outstandingly poor; responsive and appreciative pupils struggling to compensate for a bad beginning in many areas of their learning; an ebb and flow of energy and entropy over time; an alternation of optimism and pessimism about the future. In other words, a real school, but on most important capacity-building measures, an improving one.

● In conclusion

'All improvement is change but not all change is improvement' (Fullan with Stiegebauer 1991). Most, but not all, of the change in St Leopold's appears to have been in a positive direction. While an improving school may be judged in terms of the attainments or attitudes of its pupils (tactical and strategic improvement), staff achievements and attitudes are a highly significant measure because they continue after a cohort of pupils have moved on. Each individual member of staff in a secondary school holds a key to the success of thousands of pupils still to pass through his or her hands. As a whole staff they will be responsible for tens of thousands of pupils still to come. When they are able to have an impact on their colleagues in a wider system, as happened in St Leopold's, the outcomes may be far-reaching and profound. This is capacity building – on a larger stage.

10

The change equation: capacity for improvement

Louise Stoll, John MacBeath, Iain Smith and
Pamela Robertson

In the last few years the steady drip feed of change has been overtaken by a tidal wave of new initiatives: demands for higher standards, pressure for greater accountability and, in some countries, increasing prescription on what and how to teach. All of this has been advocated in the interest of improving schooling and preparing pupils for the future. The imperative of change cannot be denied and pupils at schools today are already living in a very different world from the one which their teachers and parents inhabited – experiencing changes to the working day and week, changes in the nature of access to information, changes in the structure of families and in their communities. Yet, despite the turbulence around them, schools have remained remarkably unchanged over the years.

As we know from more than 20 years of school effectiveness research, schools can make an important difference to pupil attainment and, consequently, to their continued formal education beyond school. We also know from studies of school improvement that some schools have been extremely successful in their attempts at improvement. However, as we discuss in Chapter 1, few studies have looked at schools that were less successful. This is, perhaps, underpinned by the belief that 'good practice' is the source of better practice, and we can learn more from other people's success stories than from their failures. In the mid- and late 1990s, however, two particularly striking phenomena have become apparent. The first is the increase in the number of 'designer' programmes for improvement (for example, the New American Schools designs; Stringfield *et al.* 1996). Schools in many areas are strongly encouraged to 'sign up', and in some places virtually instructed, to participate in a preferred programme. Given that many of the well-known design programmes have been piloted and evaluated, it may seem like carping to question whether schools should become involved in them, but the problem is that even when a programme has been evaluated and has 'passed the test', there are always schools for whom 'the pill didn't work'. When it comes to wider dissemination, less successful pilot schools are usually forgotten and insufficient attention is paid to determining whether the right programme has been selected by, or for, a school. Indeed, schools do not always know their needs, nor how to choose the most appropriate design (Datnow 1998). This is where the second phenomenon comes in – contextual differences between schools and their implications for school improvement.

In the 1980s and early 1990s a small number of school effectiveness studies examined contextual differences between schools. They found, for example, that leadership strategies in effective schools serving areas of greater advantage are different from those in effective schools serving disadvantaged areas (Hallinger and Murphy 1986; Teddlie and Stringfield 1993). Yet, in some countries, we still appear to be doing what House warned against more than a quarter of a century ago:

> *Avoid the primary pursuit of transferable innovations.* Distributed problems cannot be solved by a single innovation that will work in all local settings, for those settings are not only different and unpredictable in specifics, but they are also constantly changing . . . Different innovations will be more or less useful under widely different specific circumstances of their appli- cation. There is no Golden Fleece.
>
> (1973: 245)

House concluded that behaviour is determined more by the 'complex nature of the school as a social system' (p. 235) than by staff development in which new teaching strategies are demonstrated. While there has been increasing disquiet about a one-size-fits-all school improvement strategy, it is only recently that researchers have looked at different types of schools and tried to follow through the implications of different school improvement strategies. It appears that different change strategies, leadership styles and communication networks may be required to effect change (Stoll and Fink 1996; Hopkins and Harris 1997; Gray *et al.* 1999). Furthermore, it seems that while some schools seem to embrace opportunities offered by change, whether it is externally pre- scribed or internally inspired, others do not even appear able to get off the starting-block. Others still get started then run out of steam shortly afterwards. In revisiting the Rand Change Agent Study of the 1970s in the United States, McLaughlin concluded that 'the net return to the general investment was the adoption of many innovations, the successful implementation of a few, and the long-run continuation of still fewer' (1990: 12).

● Internal capacity and its influences

While most would agree that the ultimate goal of school improvement is preparing pupils to deal with the changing world, Fullan (1993) adds a sharper edge to that with his claim that 'the secret of growth and develop- ment is learning how to contend with the forces of change' (p.vii). Our own work leads us to a similar conclusion: that the learning opportunities for generations of pupils are determined by the extent to which their schools are themselves able to learn and grow. Successful schools are, therefore, those which provide conditions for their pupils to learn more successfully, and our explorations have led us to conclude that vital clues lie in the school's internal capacity.

While other writers have described sets of improvement-related capacities, we see it as a more generic concept. 'Internal capacity is the power to engage in and sustain continuous learning of teachers and the school itself for the purpose of enhancing pupil learning' (Stoll 1999). Determining internal capacity and readiness for change is therefore vitally important for internal and external change agents (Fullan 1993).

Our involvement in ISEP from 1995 to 1997 (Stoll and MacBeath 1997; Robertson 1998a) provided us with an opportunity to investigate schools' initial capacity for change and its relationship with later capacity and links with pupil outcome data.

● Two schools

In this chapter we focus our attention on two primary schools and what they can tell us about internal capacity and its relationship to school improvement and effectiveness. In these two schools interviews were carried out in 1995 with the headteacher, a teacher with responsibility for staff development, an experienced and an inexperienced teacher, as well as with groups of pupils in P2 and P6. The headteacher was also interviewed in 1995 and 1997, together with a colleague, about the strategy and process of a specific development in the last few years. Teacher questionnaires were distributed to all staff at the start and end of the project. In addition, a group of staff were taken through a 'change profile' (see Chapter 9) in which they individually rated their school against 10 items and then came together to agree on a joint rating. This formed the basis of a discussion with the critical friend and researcher, both of whom also completed the change profile. An 'ethos observation' form was completed by the researcher and critical friend at the end of data collection periods; the critical friend completed notes on each visit; and a 'support review' form was completed at the end of the project, eliciting schools' perceptions of support provided by critical friends.[1]

The two schools, in different parts of Scotland, serve similar deprived areas. Both performed poorly in terms of their raw score results in the English and mathematics tests in the baseline project assessments in 1995 (see Table 10.1).

Glendale Primary School

Located in a 'battleship grey' concrete building, likened by the headteacher to 'a fortress' and by the pupils to 'a prison', this 330-pupil primary school was once a secondary school. Project team members found it hard to get into the

Table 10.1 Schools' mean baseline scores on cognitive assessments in 1995

	Maths %	Reading %
Glendale	45.7	38.1
St Aubrey's	52.1	44.3
All ISEP primaries	63.2	55.1

school because of locked doors and, once inside, found it hard to see out of windows. Long corridors made it difficult to move from one part of the school to another. While the school was clean and well kept, there was a feeling of sterility, and wall displays were hard to maintain because of vandalism. The infant (P1–P3) and junior (P4–P7) departments were separated physically, with two different staffrooms, echoed in the way staff in the two departments spoke about the school. The school served an area of extreme disadvantage, with 61 per cent of its pupils eligible for free school meals. Drug problems and violence were also rife in the locality.

The headteacher had been in post for nine years at the start of the project. Her senior management team (SMT) consisted of a new depute head (DHT) and an assistant headteacher (AHT), a dominant force in the school for the last 17 years. There were 17 teachers on the staff at the start of the project, but by 1997 this number had dropped to 15. The school's chosen focus for the project was increasing parental involvement in learning.

Interviews at this school were difficult. The assistant head would not consent to the interview being recorded, and asked, 'Why are you doing this project?' Another staff member, a smoker, blew smoke in the interviewer's face. It seemed that every visit from the critical friend coincided with an emergency. Meetings were cut short and the critical friend was left waiting for long periods while crises were being averted or sorted out. On one visit a fire engine was called because a boy's head was stuck in the railings outside the school. With constant disruption as a backdrop, it was hard to get staff to focus on sustained development activities. They were on the defence and both critical friend and researcher found it difficult to create a positive climate for discussion of the issues the school was facing.

By contrast, pupil interviews were open and friendly. However, much of their discussion accepted the inevitability of violence in the playground and pupils saw shouting by teachers as a natural response to disruptive pupils' behaviour. Pupils appreciated their teachers and saw them as there to help them. Nevertheless, despite generally positive pupil feedback in this first round of data collection, staff were unwilling to accept the negatives, some even claiming that pupils were 'liars'. Teachers' own responses to the questionnaire showed that Glendale was one of the four lowest scoring schools on the items that made up Factor 3: items related to pupils' respect for teachers, pupil and parental clarity about behaviour standards, and prompt action to deal with disruption in classes.[2]

At the end of the project, Glendale pupils' raw scores were still very low: contextualized value-added analysis showed some positive growth (not significant) in the area of maths but negative movement (not significant) in the English assessments. In terms of attitudes, the value-added analyses showed positive, although not significant, progress on self-rated perceptions of behaviour, engagement and pupil culture, and negative (not significant) ratings on self-efficacy. It was, therefore, a school that performed poorly at the start and the finish of the project.

St Aubrey's

This school is situated in the east end of a large city in one of the most disadvantaged parts of Scotland and, indeed, Europe. The housing is mainly from the immediate pre- and postwar period and the local area is renowned for its drug and alcohol problems. Many children came from broken homes, with many young mothers and fourth generation unemployment. With 80 per cent of its pupils eligible for free school meals, St Aubrey's was the most deprived of the 24 case study schools.

The school is a one-storey building at the end of a long road, butting on to derelict land. Despite its bleak exterior, the entrance and reception area are welcoming, as are interior decorations for the most part, giving it a 'homely' and 'well cared-for' feel, noted by a member of the research team as 'a quality indicator in this school'. Litter monitors keep the playground tidy and 'the school is spotless and a credit to the cleaning staff'. Six years ago, the school was burnt down in a suspected arson attack. While the plant was being rebuilt, the school moved in to the local secondary school. From all accounts, the fire proved a defining moment for the school, with everyone – staff, the local community and the local authority – pulling together to help the school through the crisis.

The school's denomination is Roman Catholic, and a strong consciousness of its pastoral, moral and spiritual role was shared by all staff. At the start of the project the headteacher had been at the school for 16 years, six of them as AHT and 10 as headteacher. She was an imposing physical and emotional presence, and appeared deeply conscious of her role as an educational leader.

The baseline data-gathering experience was very positive, with researcher and critical friend being welcomed into the school. While pupil attainment levels were low and the school was ranked seventh out of 12 case study primary schools in terms of pupil questionnaire results, it was ranked first on both teacher and parent survey results. Indeed, on all three teacher questionnaire factors, the school scored in the top six or seven of all 44 primary schools, with 85 per cent or more of the teachers agreeing with 40 of the 54 items (for the primary teacher sample as a whole this was only true of 10 items). The school was welcoming of the feedback from the baseline data-gathering exercise. Its chosen project was language development and, in particular, functional writing.

Over the period of the project, the school became increasingly critical of tests being used to determine school effectiveness because of the perceived irrelevance of these assessments, although the concept of value-added continued to appeal to and intrigue the staff. They were disappointed when, due to a change in critical friend, the support they received was oriented more towards the process of change rather than specific help with functional writing. They maintained their involvement throughout, however, and the head, while critical of the tests being used, nonetheless expressed herself as 'really looking forward to the results'.

At the end of the project, St Aubrey's pupils' raw scores were still very low: contextualized value-added analysis showed some positive growth (not significant) in the area of maths but negative movement (not significant) in the English assessments. In terms of attitudes, the value-added analyses showed significantly positive progress on self-ratings of self-efficacy and positive, although not significant, progress on self-rated perceptions of behaviour, engagement and pupil culture.

● **Comparing outcomes and improvement**

At the end of the project, when the pupil assessments and attitude questionnaires were repeated, neither of these two schools made significant gains in pupil attainment, but in relation to pupil attitudes St Aubrey's showed a significant boost in pupils' self-esteem. This result is particularly interesting, because only two of 44 primary schools added value to their pupils' attitudes in this area. Given that as pupils grow older their attitudes tend to become less favourable (MacBeath *et al.* 1998), this is an important result. In addition, the headteacher had argued passionately at the start of the project that the most important thing the school was trying to achieve was 'to make children feel valued; to build their self-esteem'. Another teacher at the school said, 'When ISEP tries to take a snapshot of a class at a certain time there is no magic wand we can wave to make these children's lives better which in turn would affect their learning. Firstly we have to boost their self-esteem.' It appeared that what they had set out to do had been achieved. The results in these two very different schools, both starting from such adversity, raise the question 'capacity for what?' Are the outcomes selected by many school effectiveness projects, and by governments and state departments, the appropriate outcomes for all schools? If so, should pupils in all schools be expected to achieve them over the same time period?

Given that the project had dual foci – to look at effectiveness and improvement – the research team decided from the outset to analyse the qualitative data and teacher questionnaire data separately from the pupil outcome data, so that improvement could be viewed from different perspectives. After the initial data collection, a variety of techniques were used to examine separate pieces of qualitative evidence, together with survey data, in order to inform predictions about possibilities and directions of improvement (Robertson and Sammons 1997a). Schools were rated on a five-point scale based on their perceived potential for improvement, as well as their approach to school development planning (Reeves and MacGilchrist 1997):

1 = no likelihood of improvement
2 = little likelihood of improvement
3 = on present evidence it is very difficult to tell whether there will be any
    improvements in this school
4 = considerable likelihood of improvement
5 = every likelihood of improvement

On the basis of available evidence, Glendale was assigned a score of 1 and St Aubrey's a score of 4.

Thirty-five subthemes had been revealed in the analysis of the initial teacher interviews.[3] Each subtheme was associated with one or more of the main project themes – ethos; learning and teaching; and development planning. At this stage, the evidence spoke so strongly about the importance of leadership that this became a new central theme of the project.

In 1997, each fragment of evidence from the data gathering at the end of the project was coded against each of these subthemes and rated on three scales in terms of what it revealed about the current quality of the school and about its potential for improvement. A five-point scale was used (from –2 to +2) to take account of the negative or positive contribution of each cluster of evidence. Ratings were cross-checked. A database was created to hold this categorical information (Robertson 1998a). Each school could therefore have a report based on the main themes and subthemes of the project, with associated scores for *current quality, potential for improvement* and *improvement perceived by the respondents.*

Across the 12 case study primary schools, the range of 'ethos' values derived from teacher interviews was from –23 to +32. In Glendale, it was possible to see from database reporting that the major negative components of the score were:

- pupil behaviour and discipline;
- teacher responses to challenges in the socio-economic circumstances of pupils;
- pupil–pupil relationships;
- pupil self-esteem and self-efficacy;
- parent liaison and involvement.

In contrast, in St Aubrey's, the major components of the relatively high 'ethos score' were:

- perceptions of teacher expectations of pupils;
- teacher morale and engagement with the school;
- teacher responses to challenges in the socio-economic circumstances of pupils;
- the influence of historical events on present activity;
- pupil relationships with teachers.

Tables 10.2, 10.3 and 10.4 show an example of categorization and scoring of the teacher interviews on the three scales.

Table 10.2   Current quality (1997)

	Glendale	St Aubrey's
Ethos	−39	44
Development planning	3	18
Learning and teaching	−2	53
Leadership	−10	19
Total	−48	134

Note: See Chapter 6 for an explanation of current quality score.

Table 10.3   Potential for improvement (1997)

	Glendale	St Aubrey's
Ethos	−23	32
Development planning	3	18
Learning and teaching	−3	46
Leadership	−10	17
Total	−33	113

Note: See Chapter 6 for an explanation of current quality score.

Table 10.4   Perceived improvement (1997)

	Glendale	St Aubrey's
Ethos	0	14
Development planning	12	9
Learning and teaching	5	34
Leadership	−13	3
Total	4	60

Note: See Chapter 6 for an explanation of current quality score.

Figures in these tables suggest that while initial indications of potential for improvement may not differentiate between the two schools in terms of their final pupil attainments as measured by mathematics and English tests, strong differences exist in relation to processes and themes of improvement. Not only is St Aubrey's rated as far exceeding Glendale in terms of its current quality (Table 10.2) and its own teachers' perceptions of their school's improvement (Table 10.4) but the research team anticipates further potential for improvement (Table 10.3). One question this raises is whether, with a little more time, gains in pupil outcomes might be observed. It has also led us to consider how we might further explore schools' internal capacity for improvement.

● A model of influences on internal capacity

Many of the contrasting features analysed in these two schools are illustrative of features of a model of influences on schools' internal capacity (Stoll 1999). Internal capacity is influenced by the individual teachers within the school, the school's social and structural learning context, and the external context (see Figure 10.1). In Figure 10.1, the school is depicted by an amoeba-like shape. This emphasizes the dynamic and adaptive nature of schools; in many ways they could be seen as organisms (Morgan 1996). The breaks in the lines indicate that influences at each level (individual, school and external context) are not discrete and self-contained: rather, they blend in complex ways to create different patterns of relationships.

The nature of ISEP did not permit detailed analysis at the level of the individual teacher. For the purposes of this chapter, therefore, we have restricted ourselves to examining the school and external levels, although we acknowledge, as the model does, that individual teachers as learners influence the school's learning context, and are given their place right at the centre of school change. Eight interacting influences are particularly important to the teacher's capacity to engage in and sustain continuous learning: life and career experience; beliefs; emotional well-being; knowledge; skills; motivation to learn; confidence that (s)he can make a real difference; and sense of interdependence

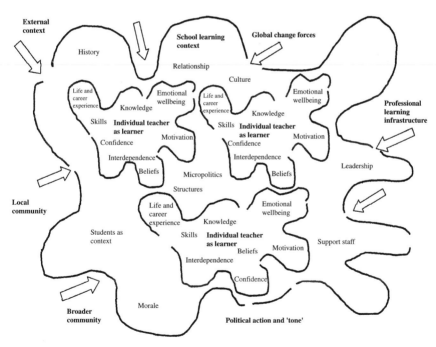

Figure 10.1   The influences on internal capacity
Source: Stoll (1999).

(Stoll 1999). From these schools' accounts, it is clear that if significant change was going to occur it would have to have an impact on people's belief systems, their sense of interdependence, and the confidence that working together they really could make a difference to the lives of these children, however deprived their community. The particular focus of the interviews, however, generally emphasized school-level and external influences, rather than individual teacher influences, and the remainder of this chapter will focus on those two levels, although the following example is worthy of comment at teacher level.

'Can do' beliefs at St Aubrey's came through clearly from everyone interviewed. In one teacher's criticism of the Quality Assurance inspection of her school recently, she commented:

> 'We want the best, but we have to give children tasks they can achieve, an appropriate curriculum. One of our problems with QA was that they came in to the school and saw well-mannered children, speaking politely and they thought we weren't pushing them enough. They didn't realize that our children can't take a lot of pressure. They are vulnerable and they have to be able to cope with what they are doing so you can praise them. It doesn't mean that you don't push them further the next time.'

She added emphatically: 'If they are going to learn . . . they will learn here'. Another colleague displayed the same firm beliefs: 'Everyone wants the children to achieve great things', and 86 per cent of the teachers at St Aubrey's felt that 'teachers in school believe all pupils can be successful' (in comparison with 60 per cent for the whole primary teacher sample).

● The school learning context

Teachers as learners do not operate in isolation. Their experiences, emotions, knowledge, skills, motivation, confidence and interdependence interact with the learning context in which they are located (as the spaces in the model outline denote). This context, the other fundamental part of a school's internal capacity, is influenced by a set of social forces:

The particular mix of pupils

Size and age of the pupil body; their ethnic, social class or cultural background; whether they are all girls, all boys or a mixed group; whether they are of a particular religious denomination; and the number with special educational needs all play a role. McLaughlin and Talbert (1993) note:

> Contemporary pupils bring different cultures and languages to school, different attitudes and support to the classroom and learning. They themselves are required to navigate difficult and competing pressures of family, peers, and community at the same time that they are expected to function as pupils.
> (1993: 6)

The social mix of the school influences a school's functioning, largely because of the cumulative effect of the peer group processes: how pupils relate and act as a group (Thrupp 1999). Thus, the very pupils who attend a school flavour it in a particular way through their own pupil culture.

In St Aubrey's one teacher described pupils as: 'friendly, loveable. They can be difficult. They take a lot of teaching but they respond well. They are well behaved in the classroom.' Another explained: 'On the whole they are very caring. They are streetwise; they possess knowledge outwith that of the teacher, but lack maturity. They behave well in the classroom, less well in the playground.' She also noted they 'can't take pressure. If you "push on" and "up" the pace, then they complain of illness.' One respondent described some of the children's home lives as 'emotional turmoil', saying they were often exhausted when they arrived or 'have so many things on their mind that reading and number work is very hard'. Researchers' field notes and teacher interviews confirmed that pupils' language outside the classroom was different from that inside. A researcher also commented that sometimes there was a feeling that aggression was being kept in check, and could explode if supervision was withdrawn. In contrast, however, she observed an unattended class of pupils working quietly.

Glendale staff appeared to view their pupils very differently. In the staff survey, no teacher agreed with the statement 'pupils in this school are enthusiastic about learning' (compared with 65 per cent for primary teachers in all project schools), and only 30 per cent thought that 'pupils respect teachers' (compared with 68 per cent for all project teachers). The headteacher felt most children were reasonably well behaved and motivated but noted that higher than average numbers of slow, poor learners and more children with social and behavioural problems affected the peer group as well as themselves: 'Much time is given to the aggressive, disruptive children.' The assistant head felt there were split priorities in the school: 'You are not able to do your job because of the concentration on discipline and the amount of time you have to spend on it.' She also believed: 'The children are out of control.' This contrasts with the view of a new teacher who found the pupils 'mannerly and courteous'. This split of opinion was characteristic of many responses to interview questions and tells us that the situations teachers describe are ones which they may also be creating.

Relationships

Working together productively in schools depends on positive relationships. When teachers come together as a whole staff or in departments, a dynamic of relationships is created. In some ways, successful schools share many attributes of caring families (Stoll and Fink 1996), but in some relationships are dysfunctional (Reynolds and Farrell 1996), severely inhibiting capacity for improvement. Such difficulties are picked up quickly, for example, by this new teacher in Glendale: 'I was aware straight away about ripples between the staff.' The relationship between the headteacher and assistant head in Glendale could be described as strained. An outside observer noted: 'The assistant head is an obstacle to every good thing happening in the school', while the head merely commented, 'We agree to differ.'

At St Aubrey's, relationships between teachers were described in researchers' ethos observation forms as supportive: 'A good team spirit is a feature. Staff talk about the school as a family . . . staff also respect each other's strengths.' Communications and relationships were viewed by staff interviewed as a strength: 'People are willing to share and discuss problems'; 'Staff are very caring.' Researchers also commented on the apparent high staff morale, displaying 'a positive attitude towards work and helping the pupils. All staff appear to work beyond normal school hours' and were 'united by care for their pupils'.

Morale

While morale is often associated with external conditions, it can vary from school to school (Evans 1998). Satisfaction and morale is higher in some schools than in others. Stark contrasts were seen between the two schools, when we compared teachers' reactions to the questionnaire item 'Teachers like working in this school.' In St Aubrey's, 100 per cent agreed with the statement, while in Glendale, only 13 per cent agreed (with an agreement rate of 76 per cent across the total primary teacher sample). Moreover, in 1997 almost a third of Glendale teachers (30 per cent) felt that the school had got worse 'as a place to be' over the previous two years, in comparison with none of the St Aubrey's teachers (and 11 per cent across the entire primary teacher sample).

History

Schools, like other organizations, go through life cycles (Schein 1985). During some periods they are 'ripe for improvement'. At other times there may be institutional 'inertia', often dependent on the staff at the time, the leadership, and whether previous efforts at innovation have been successful or otherwise. Some schools may have experienced a significant event – an amalgamation, threatened closure, or a fire. In others, teacher mobility is high or they have a history of appointing large numbers of recently qualified teachers. Over the years, certain schools also build particular traditions and reputations. All these can influence internal capacity.

History appears to have been significant for St Aubrey's, the fire exerting both positive and negative effects but, on balance, the positive outweighed the negative. While there was clearly devastation at the loss of resources built up by teachers over the years, there was an immediate marshalling of significant support from the local authority, new resources, and 'rallying around' of staff as a single unit in the aftermath of the event. This was achieved in the face of loss of pupils' work into which they had put much effort, upheaval involved in relocation into temporary accommodation, and immediate effect on staff morale. Relocation in part of the local high school also helped to build new connections. Perhaps something symbolic in the fire marked the end of the old and the beginning of the new. Added to this, the following year the school received a Curriculum Award in London. It had promoted great pride among teachers and parents, and had provided an important boost after the fire tragedy. Threat of closure prior to the fire had also seen mobilization of parental support, and closure was happily averted.

Specific historical events did not appear to have played a major role at Glendale, although staff changes seemed significant, with some new teachers attempting to introduce changes and bring together a split staff. Notably, the depute head, new just before the start of the project, tried to bring in team teaching, although by the end of the project, researchers noted that she seemed to have given up, and was looking to move to another school.

Culture

Improvement attempts that do not address school culture can be seen as 'doomed to tinkering' (Fullan 1993) because school culture influences readiness for change. The essence of a school's culture is the deeper level of basic assumptions and beliefs shared by members, operating unconsciously, and defining the organization's view of itself and its environment (Schein 1995). Each school has a different reality of school life, how to go about its work, and its orientation to learning. The views of teachers in the two schools highlight differences in expectations. In Glendale, when asked about the most significant factors affecting pupils' ability to learn, replies included: 'Home background, deprivation, parental views on education. Often survival is more important than taking on board educational opportunities', and: 'Some children are never going to achieve very much.' An aura of powerlessness was emitted, a feeling that it was impossible to overcome the forces ranged against the school, most notably social factors and deprivation. Feedback of data was resisted and the increased accountability that the school was facing was viewed as creating 'quite a burden'. While each person interviewed offered a broadly similar vision of what the school was trying to achieve ('a good, wide education'), their perceptions of how this might be achieved, and barriers to achieving it, varied.

In contrast, in St Aubrey's, a teacher commented: '. . . there are no limitations. You can come in this door and the world is your oyster . . . the children will be encouraged. Nothing is holding us back', while another told of how 'the school is always trying to better itself'. The headteacher was clear: 'Children come first . . . Pupils expect to be taught and taught appropriately and stretched.' This was reinforced by all teachers interviewed, including a new member of staff, who felt the most important thing she was trying to achieve was: 'To take the child from where they were when I got them and to take them forward . . . I try to build confidence.' And when she was asked what she expected from teaching, she replied: 'A feeling that I am doing something for every child in my class. Not only knowledge, but standards.'

St Aubrey's also displayed norms of continuous improvement and collegial-ity (Rosenholtz 1989; Stoll and Fink 1996). The headteacher remarked: 'Learn-ing and teaching is part and parcel of the conversation of this school', confirmed by 100 per cent agreement to the teacher survey item 'teachers regularly discuss ways of improving pupils' learning' (compared with 74 per cent for the primary teacher sample as a whole), 93 per cent agreement to 'teachers regularly collaborate to plan their teaching' (57 per cent for the pri-mary sample), and 100 per cent agreement to 'staff have a commitment to the whole school and not just their class or department' (72 per cent for the primary sample). Teachers told interviewers people were willing to share and discuss problems; a new teacher found teachers planned in pairs: 'You bounce things off each other . . . I find that excellent.' The school had also chosen to participate in the project for feedback on how it was progressing and a 'fresh' perspective on the school.

Micro politics

Schools are full of internal politics (Ball 1987); they are places in which con-trol is a key issue. Teachers make strategic decisions daily as to what is ideal and possible in their context. Some are ambitious, some want to influence school decisions, others want to be left alone. Some schools, however, pro-mote positive politics (Blase 1988), such that natural political activities of staff contribute to school goals.

The two staffrooms at Glendale symbolized the rift between the staff. In the assistant head's opinion: 'The smokers were thrown out, and this has caused a split in the staff.' Teacher responses to the survey highlighted disagreements. Only 36 per cent thought 'decision-making processes are fair' (in comparison with 62 per cent for the whole sample), and even fewer (29 per cent) that 'staff participate in important decision making' (compared with 59 per cent for the whole sample). The staff development coordinator, new to the school, mused, 'Where there has been consultation with staff, I do not know how deep it has gone.'

In contrast, at St Aubrey's teachers felt their opinions mattered and they were encouraged to give their views on school policies. The headteacher com-mented there was so much ongoing talk in the staffroom about issues that, once a decision had to be made in a meeting, there was seldom disagreement and if there was, 'we disagree without falling out'. She reflected back on what the school had been like when she arrived. The previous headteacher 'did divide and rule. One set would be cast up to the other. There has been a major shift, but it took a long time. Everyone is now treated with mutual respect and we can talk to each other. The community now knows that this is what the school stands for.' Indeed, all teachers agreed with the survey item 'there is mutual respect between the staff and the senior management team', while 87 per cent agreed that 'decision-making processes are fair' and 'staff participate in important decision making' (the remaining 13 per cent were uncertain). The several new staff at St Aubrey's were viewed as bringing a counterbalancing influence, as exemplified in a comment by a teacher at the school for 16 years: 'New people bring new outlooks, yet we have stability with the head and deputy head.'

Support staff

Support staff can play a significant role in the lives of a school. Many live in the local area and are connected to the local community. Their involvement and interest in the school as a whole, and the ways in which they facilitate learning, are all potential influences on a school's internal capacity (Mortimore *et al.* 1992). Support staff in both schools were viewed as friendly by the research team on their initial visit. Those at St Aubrey's were also perceived as particularly helpful. In this school, all of the teachers agreed that 'non-teaching staff feel involved in the life of the school' (compared with 76 per cent for the entire primary teacher sample). The head, reflecting on what she described as a participative management style, observed: 'The buck does stop here, but I do not see myself being separate in any way from any of the staff. From the cleaner right up we are all in this together and everybody's role is important.'

In Glendale, only half of the teachers thought 'non-teaching staff feel involved in the life of the school'; the other half were unsure, and the role and participation of support staff was not discussed by any teachers interviewed.

Structures

Schools are bounded by structures that can shape their capacity to learn and respond to change. For example, traditional egg carton, compartmentalized school designs inhibit collaboration, whereas more flexible architectural designs are more likely to support collaborative cultures. The size of the school and classes within it, the physical plant, and how the school day is divided are other examples of structural aspects of a school's capacity. These types of structure could be viewed as 'givens', over which staff members may have limited if any control (Mortimore *et al.* 1988), but even within such structures decisions can be made concerning location of different departments or classes. While structural conditions appear to be less powerful influences on developing school-based professional communities than social conditions (Louis *et al.* 1995), they can influence internal capacity.

Glendale staff's descriptions of their school building were stark: 'The outside . . . was horrific looking'; 'One of the things that struck me to begin with was that there was not that welcoming atmosphere about the school. It is badly signposted and I think the building has lost its humph: when you enter a department it should meet you and I don't think ours does.' Glendale parents, while generally positive about the school in survey responses, were less impressed than other parents that 'school buildings are kept clean and in good order' (37 per cent disagreed, versus 7 per cent for the total primary parent sample).

In St Aubrey's, by contrast, bright and interesting displays of pupils' work adorned the walls. The rebuilding after the fire enabled minor adaptations: 'This improved the educational environment of the school, for example resource areas and storage facilities', and gave 'a facelift' providing 'a welcoming atmosphere'. The school is open plan and, in the headteacher's words, this 'forces cooperation. It can be threatening, but it also provides support. Teachers watch and learn from each other.' A new teacher agreed: 'I was glad to have come in to an open plan school. I like people being able to move in and out of my class.' It had also been arranged for everyone to get together each morning from 8.30 until 9.00 for consultation and planning sessions.

Leadership

Countless studies have found positive leadership to be a powerful force for school effectiveness, school improvement and organizational learning (for example, Hallinger and Heck 1996; MacBeath 1998; Mortimore 1998; Leithwood *et al.* 1999). St Aubrey's leaders appeared to present a picture of clarity about their vision and focus. In both 1995 and 1997, all teachers agreed that 'the SMT communicates a clear vision of where the school is going', and 93 per cent and 100 per cent respectively (in 1995 and 1997) agreed that 'the primary concern of everyone in the school is pupil learning'. There was also a high level of satisfaction with what one teacher described as the school's 'open management'. When asked about her headteacher's leadership and management, a teacher responded: 'Superb. She knows everything that goes on. She knows the curriculum, the children, the staff inside out, she picks up on your attributes. She brings out the best in everybody. She knows how her school wants to be.' The head was extremely clear about her role: 'I know what I want and I will get it.' She acknowledged she was occasionally manipulative or devious but this was done 'with good humour and also with respect for teachers', whom she believed often knew much more than she did about classroom practice. She, therefore, viewed criticism as inappropriate. Others saw her as leading by example, and some explained how in the previous two years a larger senior management team (SMT) had evolved as she had brought in new people to work with her. While the SMT was seen as making a lot of the decisions, everyone felt they were consulted. Hiring decisions were also viewed by the head as critical, so the school could 'capitalize on what they brought with them'. In contrast, a teacher in Glendale commented: 'I would describe the management style as autocratic to a certain extent and not approachable enough.' Results of the teacher questionnaires in both 1995 and 1997 showed teachers responding negatively to many items within the leadership and management factor. In 1995 the school was one of the four lowest scoring primary schools on this factor, and one of the six lowest scoring schools in 1997. Furthermore, when asked about change in leadership and management in the school over the previous two years, 30 per cent of the teachers felt it had become worse (compared with 9 per cent for the total primary teacher sample).

● External contextual influences on internal capacity

While the school's capacity and its readiness or orientation for change is internally driven, the external contextual influences on a school's internal capacity cannot be ignored. Central among these are the following.

The local community

Schools are located in and serve very different communities. School effectiveness researchers have consistently demonstrated the impact of pupils' background characteristics on their school achievement. Parental expectations and aspirations may also vary according to location and type of school. The demography of a school's community can not only affect attainment outcomes but a school's internal capacity for improvement. Disadvantage, however, does not automatically inhibit its internal capacity. Schools in disadvantaged areas can boost their pupils' progress more than those in advantaged areas as our own study and previous research (Mortimore *et al.* 1988) has shown.

Both in Glendale and in St Aubrey's, pupils brought with them into the school their experience of multiple disadvantage – a key factor affecting school ethos, pedagogy, management style, pupil–teacher relationships and relationships between home and school. While social background factors are key constraining influences on overall school attainment, they do not diminish the school's internal capacity nor need they necessarily inhibit the process of sustainable improvement. It need not imply that the teachers cannot prepare their pupils for challenges they will face in the changing world beyond the school gate. Comments of teachers in the two different schools, however, reveal significant differences in how they viewed their local communities and their impact. At Glendale, the community's influence was described as the main limitation of the school: 'The community influence anything we try to do.' More than a third of the parents responding to the survey (37 per cent) disagreed that 'the school has a good reputation in the community', significantly more critical than ISEP primary parents as a whole (6 per cent).

Although the St Aubrey's catchment area was similar to Glendale's, and the academic starting point of its pupil intake generally 18 months below the average ('colours, number, recognition of shape cannot be taken for granted'), parents were seen as a strength: 'They are loyal and supportive', and teachers commented that the headteacher 'knows them as a friend'. The head explained how it was necessary to offer a very safe and caring environment, for parents as well as pupils: 'A lot of the parents, if it is a first child coming to the school, come to us with the baggage of their own experiences of school and they do not always have pleasant experiences.'

The broader community

The broader community can include many different groups. Universities' and businesses' requirements of those leaving schools influence curricula and assessments. Similarly, unions' policy and practices influence how at least some of their members respond to changes in school. Attitudes of the broader community to schooling, particularly the media, can also affect teachers' motivation and belief that what they are doing is worthwhile. Other key stakeholders include local authorities. In Scotland these have not faced the same threat as their counterparts in England. 'Devolved School Management' has given more autonomy to schools but authorities, nonetheless, continue to play a significant role.

For St Aubrey's, local authority support was high at the time of the school fire, both in terms of people and finance. As one staff member commented in 1995, 'I have nothing but praise for the local authority.' Concerns were being noted, however, that 'support is now crumbling', and by 1997 staff talked of a lack of support for an increasing number of children with emotional, behavioural and learning problems: 'and there is no one there to answer your cry for help'. In Glendale, the picture was somewhat reversed. In 1997, the headteacher felt the school and local authority had moved closer together since 1995, and described various authority initiatives. A new teacher commented however, in a somewhat strained interview, that learning support had been lost.

Political action and 'tone'

Policies and beliefs about the purpose of education that underpin them are critical influences on schools. The sheer amount of policy-oriented change is particularly significant. Overload is a dilemma and, with the best will in the world, teachers bombarded by unrelenting changes over a short time period tend to be exhausted. They find it hard to maintain energy, enthusiasm and, ultimately, willingness for change (Helsby and McCulloch 1996). It is not necessarily teachers' characteristics that cause resistance, but pressures on them and limitations to their involvement in making change happen (Fink and Stoll 1998). With increasing demands on them, they face intensification of their work leading, in many cases, to feelings of guilt (Hargreaves 1994). While, for some, these present fairly easy-to-resolve dilemmas, for others there are uncomfortable tensions or constraints that can lead to stress (Woods *et al.* 1997). The very language and labelling of schools as 'failing' contributes to low teacher morale and feelings of impotence, and encourages the general public to believe that standards are low and that a significant minority of schools are in a state of perpetual crisis (Stoll and Myers 1998).

Glendale teachers described an increase in paperwork ('it tends to take up so much of your time that you really can't think straight with specific ideas that you want to teach . . . it's way over the top'). In 1995 the headteacher commented that the Scottish Office supported schools 'through the volume of manuals and guidelines received. The 5–14 documents are leading the way with the curriculum', and their ethos documents were 'fine, if you concentrated on that alone'. By 1997 she concluded: 'Information is sent to be read, but it doesn't really affect teachers or classrooms', while another teacher's view was 'This 5–14 with its 10,000 strands. There's too much curriculum change, too much jargon . . . 5–14 has affected terminology rather than practice . . . the burdens of 5–14 are too great.' In contrast, one teacher at St Aubrey's felt the 5–14 changes were 'for the better, but it involves a lot of work and you need to be organized', while another thought the 5–14 documents had 'made us more aware', although she, and other colleagues, had specific concerns about one subject document which 'made us feel deskilled'. By 1997, however, the headteacher found the documents 'much better than before . . . clearer, and quite helpful'.

Professional learning infrastructure

Some schools are located in areas or regions where the professional learning infrastructure is better developed than in other areas. Fullan and Watson (1997) argue that systems that sustain high-quality professional development have frameworks of support including elements such as appropriate policy, shared and agreed-upon priorities, time to engage in learning, access to best practice and recent research, and appropriate rewards and incentives.

Both schools were in areas where they could draw on a variety of external sources, although neither was entirely happy with the externally available support. The head of St Aubrey's described the school's experience of external staff development as 'not very positive', with some described as 'totally in-adequate, staff returning frustrated, feeling time was wasted'. She believed: 'The focus should be on what staff feel they need in relation to the school development plan and individual professional needs. Our career reviews are helpful in determining this. Staff have an informal chat with the head or depute head – where do you want to go? How can we help you get there?' The school's staff development coordinator added that staff development mainly takes place in the school: 'where the most important staff development takes place . . . courses can be valuable, but staff development is not just going on courses'. Other teachers thought within-school staff development was 'continuous' and that if they wanted anything else, it was available. Indeed, when asked how the College of Education supports the school, one teacher replied: 'It's the other way around. We help the college.' This school, therefore, appeared to have built its own infrastructure.

Although Glendale's headteacher felt that staff development was suited to the school's needs, and 'the senior management team can give greater direction from an overview of the development plan and perceived staff needs, plus being able to send several staff on the same course', she also commented on variable quality of outside courses, and problems in devising time for feedback by teachers who had attended courses. In response to a question about staff development, however, an inexperienced teacher appeared more concerned 'that staff should feel that they are not on their own; that the management should be there to back them, as part of a team'. Teacher survey responses also showed that only 32 per cent of respondents agreed 'staff development time is used effectively in the school' (compared with 100 per cent agreement at St Aubrey's and 59 per cent agreement in the total primary school sample).

Global change forces

Social, economic, technological, political and ecological forces, among others, shape our daily existence. Institutions, political, economic and social structures and, indeed, value systems worldwide appear to be changing or under pressure to do so. Such forces have major ramifications for all schools, including Glendale and St Aubrey's, making it increasingly imperative that schools have the internal capacity to respond to such forces.

● **Issues**

Preliminary analysis of the data for two Scottish schools suggests that the model of influences on school capacity may offer possibilities in helping identify schools with the internal capacity for change, but it also raises some issues:

• *The capacity model needs further testing in a range of contexts,* and in relation to what is already known about improvement in different types of schools.
• *The model is not a model of increasing pupil outcomes* per se. It is an attempt to take a closer look at a school's internal dynamics and potential: what can help or hinder it from starting and sustaining the learning process. It is based on the premise that pupils will learn best when their teachers and schools learn. This may not always have appeal in a time of increased accountability and emphasis on standards, but it raises serious issues about the meaning of school quality, as well as potential for quality.
• *The various influences at the three levels can be positive, neutral or negative,* and are a complex braid, many of which are interconnected. This needs further investigation to try to understand the way the influences connect. It also suggests that designers of improvement or restructuring programmes are likely to find it hard to identify particular actions to be taken in relation to each specific influence. There are no simple solutions.
• *The model highlights that schools can significantly differ from each other in a subtle range of ways.* This means that ongoing auditing of the influences that affect each school is essential. Furthermore, for some schools, capacity building may need to focus on helping teachers develop the motivation and confidence to be able to get started in a change process, never mind becoming experts in a particular new teaching strategy.
• *In emphasizing social dynamics and social systems, the model tries to reach a more fundamental level about human relationships and philosophies of life.* The differences in language of teachers in these two Scottish schools in areas of equal deprivation suggest a great deal more needs to be understood about differences between schools as human and dynamic systems before governments, in particular, advocate tightly controlled and regulated designs. The sharp contrasts of the two schools seem to suggest that the schools' learning context is of more significance to their internal capacity than the external context. However, these are two schools serving very similar catchment areas.

If one had been located in an area of affluence the picture might have been different, although 'cruising' schools (Stoll and Fink 1998) possess powerful norms that inhibit development.

● Research challenges

We believe it is necessary to continue working with and studying schools to develop greater understanding of their internal capacity in the following areas:

- *How the different influences work together* – How do the range of combinations interact within and between levels? How important is each in the model? For example, if a school focuses considerable energy on external forces, dealing with extended negative media attention or implementing a state or national government curriculum that does not take into account its local circumstances, needs or interests, to what extent might the learning context suffer or atrophy (Fink 1999)?
- *Are the influences the same in schools in different phases?* If not, how do they differ? Which ones are more important in secondary schools, for example, and why? What is missing?
- *Differential internal capacity of different schools* – For example, are individual teachers in a school like Glendale actually different from those in one like St Aubrey's, two schools in very comparable social areas? Are they generally less confident as individuals that they can really make a difference to the lives of pupils in disadvantaged areas? Alternatively, are the leadership, relationships, culture and within-school internal learning context holding them back?
- *How to build capacity in different types of schools* – For example, if schools like Glendale are characterized by dysfunctional staff relationships, micro politics, and underpinning beliefs that some children will never learn, are the most important actions to be taken (a) developing a continuing focus on people, (b) promoting positive politics, (c) combating low expectations? Is it even possible or appropriate to determine a time sequence for capacity-building strategies?
- *How schools with variations in their initial change capacity use different change strategies* (Stoll and Fink 1996; Hopkins and Harris 1997; Earl and Lee 1998) and how they use external support – for example, did St Aubrey's really need a process consultant or would specific help in their chosen area of writing have been more valuable? When does a school know what help it needs, and is there any school, no matter how successful, that would not benefit from a critical, external eye?

Some of these questions can be answered through statistical modelling. Many, however, depend on drawing on detailed case studies of schools and their improvement efforts (for example, Louis and Miles 1990; Mortimore *et al.* 2000) and by producing further case studies whose value as freestanding narrative should not be underestimated. As Robertson (1998b) argues, they show the way teachers understand the schools in which they work; and how they see the wider Scottish educational context. She continues: 'These studies contribute towards our understanding of schools as organisations and also to the debate about the meaning of the "good school"' (1998: 4). Certainly, this cannot be teased out in infrequent regulatory inspections. This is because the nuances of people's belief systems, interpersonal dynamics and subtle interconnections among influences are more likely to be seen over time. Only through ongoing involvement with the school and use of qualitative instruments over time could the project team see that a positive interview from the headteacher of Glendale at the start of the project was merely 'putting a front on it'. In contrast, the interview with the assistant head at the same time, while unpleasant, and difficult to carry out, was honest. This highlights the need for further carefully controlled longitudinal studies. Until more is known, through detailed case studies and specifically focused and evaluated capacity-building programmes, it is all too easy for blanket policy solutions to be advocated.

Greater attention also needs to be devoted by researchers to exploring how schools use research findings and how they could be used more beneficially. Without specific support, practitioners appear to view dissemination of research as imposed change (Wikeley 1998). The role of researchers in supporting and promoting the development of schools' internal capacity could offer great potential.

● Conclusion

Bringing about change in schools is extremely complex. School improvement and other reform strategies thrust on, or even offered to, teachers without taking account of unique differences between schools in their internal capacity are likely to lead to loss of the energy and creativity needed to take schools forward in the future. While support for real improvement involves challenge and accountability, more fundamentally, this study emphasizes it is about helping schools understand and develop their own capacity. This means focusing on individuals, their internal learning context and the external context. Without this, the chances of deep and lasting changes that can lead to improved pupil learning are slim.

● Notes

1 See Chapter 3 for further details of project design.
2 See Chapter 6 for teacher questionnaire factors.
3 See Chapter 7.

11

Beyond 2000: where next for effectiveness and improvement?

Louise Stoll, John MacBeath and Peter Mortimore

The passing from one millennium to the next may have been merely symbolic but it brings with it the opportunity to reflect on what has gone before and on what lies ahead. How well can our current system serve the needs of learners in the future? How adequate are past and present 'solutions' to the world of 2050, the world in which our school students of today will be living and working and educating the next generation? What meaning will 'effectiveness' and 'improvement' have in that context?

Even now, reflecting back on the ISE project, things have changed. We know more now than we did then and we will know still more tomorrow. The shifting landscape of education nationally and internationally, new directions in policy and the rapidity of social change mean that some issues have now assumed greater significance. From the standpoint of the present, there are things we would have done differently in ISEP were we to begin the whole process over again.

In Chapter 1 we reviewed what we have learned from the effectiveness and improvement 'movement'. In this chapter we look forward to the possibilities of the next decade and the issues it will present for educational effectiveness and improvement. Drawing on the work of ISEP, on other projects to which it gave rise, and further developments whose connections to ISEP are more tenuous, we propose ten imperatives for practitioners, policy makers, researchers, parents and other educational partners.

Develop a wider range of skills and qualities for a fast changing world

Some commentators argue that the 'revolutions' – in information, knowledge, population, globalizing and localizing, social relationships, economics, technology, ecology, aesthetics, politics and values – represent a major paradigm shift. The repercussions of these, they argue, will have a profound influence on pupils' lives (Dalin and Rust 1996). The knowledge base, it is said, is doubling every four years (Watkins *et al.* 1996). Technological advances have made information accessible in a way we could not have dreamed of only a few years ago and which is unimaginable in the social world ten years from now. With homes and classrooms connected to the Internet, young people's learning opportunities have dramatically expanded. In one sense there is a more intimate connection between home and school, while in another sense the gap between them widens. Family structures are changing dramatically. There are higher proportions of parents remarrying and a significantly larger number of children living with half brothers and sisters. Their parents and grandparents are living longer, with more leisure time and greater need for resources, healthcare and family support. They will, less and less in the future, reminisce nostalgically about a 'job for life'. We are already living in a society where people move several times in their career and often hold a career portfolio of different jobs. People are increasingly working from home or in a different town or city from their family, and employers have greater expectations that employees will be mobile and will take responsibility for their own professional development.

In such turbulent times the inescapable question is, 'What should education be for? What are its essential purposes?' Literacy and numeracy are likely to remain as important basic skills, and their significance has been underlined by school effectiveness research over the last twenty years, but it is increasingly clear that success in the future will depend on considerably more than being literate, numerate and technologically competent. Given the pace and unpredictability of change, as well as the need to maintain and, in some cases rebuild, community, other skills assume equal importance. These include flexibility, problem solving, collaboration, empathy, self-awareness, ability to deal with complexity, and a love of learning. Indeed, if young people do not have the capacity to keep on learning, their future options will be dramatically reduced.

UNESCO's International Commission on Education for the Twenty-first Century (Delors *et al.* 1996) has argued that 'Each individual must be equipped to seize learning opportunities throughout life, both to broaden her or his knowledge, skills and attitudes, and to adapt to a changing, complex and interdependent world' (p. 85). The Commission has proposed 'four fundamental types of learning which, throughout a person's life, will in a way be the pillars of knowledge' (p. 86). These appear to be an appropriate and comprehensive set of desirable learning outcomes. They are:

- *learning to know* – acquiring a broad general knowledge, the instruments of understanding, and learning to learn;
- *learning to do* – the competence to deal with many situations and to act creatively on one's environment;
- *learning to live together* – developing understanding of others and appreciation of interdependence, to participate and co-operate with others;

- *learning to be* – developing greater autonomy, judgement and personal responsibility, through attention to all aspects of a person's potential.

The Royal Society of the Arts (RSA), in a recent publication, notably titled *Opening Minds* (Bayliss 1999), suggests five categories of competence that complement those of UNESCO, but are more specific. These are: learning; citizenship; relating to people; managing situations; and managing information. Common to both the Delors Commission and the RSA Report programme is the conviction that current forms of assessment pay attention to only a small percentage of young people's abilities and competencies.

Through use of the ISEP pupil survey, we attempted to tap in to the more affective outcomes, eliciting pupils' views of their own learning and school experience (Thomas *et al.* 1998). We found correlations with attainment measures problematic, not because attitudes and achievement are not intimately connected, but because in neither sphere are we able to measure the subtleties, complexities and dynamics of deep learning in which emotions and thinking are inseparably married. In the 1980s, some of us examined pupils' speaking skills and practical maths problem solving as outcomes in a study of primary school effectiveness (Mortimore *et al.* 1988). We found that the classroom processes positively correlated with better oracy outcomes were somewhat different from those associated with improved literacy and numeracy (Mortimore *et al.* 1986).

No properly controlled school effectiveness study, however, has examined the impact of schools on arts outcomes or the link between these and better literacy and numeracy. We do not know whether the making of better musicians and artists will give us better linguists and mathematicians, although we know that maths and music are related. Nor do we know enough about how a sense of achievement in one area of school life can engage pupils' interest in other areas of learning. ISEP did, however, give us the opportunity in a limited way to explore the connections between learning skills and attainment outcomes and there is interesting case study evidence which we discuss in Chapter 10. We have as yet no 'hard', systematic, long-term evidence to show that a focus on developing pupils' understanding of their own learning will lead to improved learning outcomes. Indeed, there is evidence from the United States which finds a negative correlation between deep learning and standardized testing (Sacks 1999). In an age of reliance on numerical data, what gets assessed gets valued. The challenge for this millennium is to find the tools to evaluate deep learning.

Emphasize learners and learning and consider implications for teaching

One of ISEP's key focus areas was learning and teaching. The basis for its inclusion was strong. Apart from the Scottish Office's own emphasis on the area, there was clear evidence from school effectiveness research that the classroom was the place where pupil progress was particularly demonstrated (Hill *et al.* 1995; Scheerens and Bosker 1997; Sammons 1999). Much of the work in this area, and in teacher effectiveness research, has started with a behaviourist focus on the teacher's actions, and examined student learning as an outcome: hence the more common ordering of the phrase 'teaching and learning'. A parallel body of knowledge, however, argues that effective learning involves processes as well as outcomes, and it is necessary to understand learners, how learning takes place, and what influences learning (see Watkins *et al.* 1996, for a review).

A more positive finding of ISEP was the orientation displayed by teachers towards improving pupils' learning. This was demonstrated in the significant increase over the project period in the percentage of both primary and second-ary teachers who reported that 'teachers in this school believe that all pupils can learn', and 'teachers in this school regularly discuss ways of improving pupils' learning'. This may have less to do with the intervention of the ISEP team than with a climate of growing interest in accelerated learning, thinking skills, multiple intelligences – terms which were largely unknown to Scottish teachers five years ago but are now much more familiar.

The last decade has seen the publication of a large number of new research findings on the brain, with significant implications for educators (see McNeil 1999 for a review). Similarly, theories of multiple intelligences (Gardner 1983) and triarchic intelligence (Sternberg 1985) have now been joined by those highlighting the importance of emotional intelligence (Salovey and Mayer 1990; Goleman 1996).

In short, we concur with those who argue for a shift in orientation towards an education that is learning and learner-centred. We endorse efforts being made to broaden the concept of achievement (DfEE 1998) to encompass all learners, whatever their age. We agree with a perspective that

> couples a focus on individual learners (their heredity, experiences, per-spectives, backgrounds, talents, interests, capacities, and needs) with a focus on learning (the best available knowledge about learning and how it occurs and about teaching practices that are most effective in promot-ing the highest levels of motivation, learning, and achievement for all learners).
>
> (McCombs and Whisler 1997: 9)

Constructivist theorists suggest that learners assimilate and accommodate new information most effectively by 'reconstructing' this for themselves, turn-ing information into knowledge that is individual and 'owned'. Perkins (1995) argues that 'knowledge comes on the coat tails of thinking'. With the benefit of thermal imaging we can see in brilliant technicolour how the brain responds to different stimuli and makes its own patterns of thought. It allows highly plausible inferences about how learning takes place and how infor-mation filters its way through feeling and thinking centres into emotionally charged knowledge and memory.

When we understand more about the learner and his or her learning, we are faced with the question, 'In what places might learning occur?', and in response we come back to school as one, but only one, of many possible answers. Reviewing reports of the latest activity in school effectiveness and school improvement in 19 countries in Europe, the Americas, Asia and the Pacific, the Middle East and Africa, Townsend *et al.* (1998) pose a challenge as they muse about a possible change of focus for school effectiveness and school improvement: 'It is almost as if the advent of the third millennium has brought with it the need to reconstruct our view of the purpose of, and even the need for, schools' (p. 357).

While we do not concur with those who view schools as having outlived their usefulness (Mann 1997), there is undoubtedly a changing role for education in a changing world. Bentley argues:

> . . . education must be both broader and deeper. Broader, because it must include a wider range of learning experience, experience of roles and situations which mirror those we value in society. Deeper, because it must nurture a greater understanding in young people: understanding of themselves, their motivations and goals in life, and of the subjects and disciplines they study . . . It must be able to use human, financial, social, cultural and informational resources from the whole of society to stimulate and develop young people's ability to learn and understand for themselves.
>
> (Bentley 1998: 1)

Schools cannot be expected to undertake such a challenge alone, if pupils are to be properly prepared for their future. Bentley continues:

> This learning will not take place only inside schools and colleges, but in communities, workplaces and families. It requires a shift in our thinking about the fundamental organisational unit of education, from the school, an institution where learning is organised, defined and contained, to the learner, an intelligent agent with the potential to learn from any and all of her encounters with the world around her.
>
> (1998: 1)

In short, schools and other formal organizations for learning will just be seen as one element of learning in the future (Watkins and Mortimore 1999). The implications of this for future research are that studies comparing schools in their effectiveness or improvement will need to take much greater account of the multiplicity of learning experiences which children and young people have outside schools. We will have to take greater account of contexts, opportunities and constraints on learners. More fundamentally, if schools are only one element of a learner's potential learning encounters, detailed longitudinal case studies of learners, rather than schools, are likely to be more helpful in understanding what combinations of experiences best promote the learning of different people. Such case studies will also need to start in the earliest years of learning, given our knowledge about the impact of the early years, cerebral and social development and windows of opportunity for the creation of intelligence (Perkins 1998).

The ISEP approach and ISEP tools have been put to good service in the national evaluation of out-of-school learning. It has proved challenging because of the voluntary nature of study support, the intermittent attendance patterns of students and the transitory nature of many of the clientele. Nonetheless, the national evaluation study (Myers and MacBeath 1998) is breaking new ground in tracking a cohort of 7000 secondary students over three years, measuring achievement and attitudes against the type of provision attended, using as a control group those who never attended any out-of-hours activity. The implications for where and how we engage young people in their learning are likely to be significant and far-reaching.

Listen to the pupil's voice

As access to learning changes, so does the relationship between teacher and learner. If knowledge is power, the mediation of knowledge by the teacher increases his or her power while diminishing that of the pupil. When pupils become as knowledgeable as their teachers, or more so, the balance of power shifts and with it the nature of the relationship. The most obvious example of this is in respect to information and communications technology (ICT), where pupils are often more skilled and knowledgeable than their teachers and can play a tutoring or even a staff development role. It will become increasingly commonplace for pupils to advise, manage and consult on ICT resources, to design and construct the school website, or to run workshops for their peers, parents, teachers or school management. Primary age as well as secondary age children will have their own personal website and, through access to the World Wide Web, journey well beyond the geographical and intellectual boundaries of the classroom.

In the future there will have to be greater respect for the pupil voice. Respect does not imply deference by, or disempowerment of, the teacher. Indeed, if the teacher is also viewed as a learner, this is likely to increase respect and strengthen the teacher's credibility. It was not uncommon in interviews with pupils in the ISE project for them to describe their teachers as omniscient or, in their terminology, 'she has the information', 'is really clever', 'knows a lot about everything'. While it is undisputed that there are benefits to having knowledgeable teachers, and these comments sometimes carried with them a sense of awe, significantly they were not always accompanied by respect for the person. Respect was more likely to be reserved for teachers who listened, and who 'let you have your say'.

Wylie (1999) describes pupils as coproducers and cocreators of their own learning: 'This is not to be promiscuous in pedagogy; rather it is to deploy the authority of the teacher in stimulating and sustaining responsible learning, a task so much more demanding than didacticism' (p. 186). Indeed, researchers at the forefront of explorations into the learning process (Dweck 1985; Rudduck *et al.* 1996; Perkins 1998) see the primary role of the teacher as helping pupils to think and to articulate their thinking effectively.

This presents a challenge of considerable magnitude to the classroom teacher. He or she may rightly respond that it is good theory, typical of researchers such as us who are insufficiently alive to the exigencies and pressures of the classroom. Given the rapidity and multiplicity of policy initiatives, it requires an exceptional teacher to cater to the intellectual, social and emotional needs of thirty or more pupils. Nor is the classroom, with its logistical and time constraints, the ideal environment for learning to take place. Hence the growth of out-of-hours learning – homework clubs, study support classes, curriculum enrichment activities, etc. – offering a complement to what happens in the classroom. These have increased the scope for young people to take charge. It is not new for pupils to start and run their own clubs, to form their own jazz bands or rock groups, but opportunities to exercise those entrepreneurial, leadership and team-working skills are now being extended to encompass more mainstream subjects of the curriculum. So young people themselves play an active role in the management and evaluation of their learning both in and out of the classroom.

These existed in a number of our ISEP schools, providing a forum in which teachers and pupils could experiment with different kinds of relationships and innovative approaches to learning. In a voluntary informal setting, teachers were able to relinquish the need for control and discipline. They could abandon the need to create distance and status; they could relax and be themselves. One teacher compared it to his role as a parent, able to listen to and learn from his children with genuine openness and unfeigned interest.

One of the most unhappy of findings from the ISEP teacher questionnaire was in response to the statement 'Pupils have some say in the school development plan'. Only 6 per cent of primary teachers and 11 per cent of their secondary peers said this was happening in their schools and only 23 per cent (in both phases) saw it as important. This may less be a reflection of how teachers perceive pupil voice than how teachers see development planning. Evidence from some case study schools in the project suggests the latter – that is, that development planning occupies a separate conceptual vocabulary in teachers', or headteachers', thinking, no matter how much they might value pupils' contribution to school life. It is also perhaps a reflection of the way in which policy makers saw and advocated development planning and how inspectors rated it during their visits to schools (MacGilchrist *et al.* 1995).

As schools mature and extend their boundaries into new learning networks, development planning, in its mechanistic form, will fade away, to be replaced by renewal processes involving all stakeholders.

Facilitate 'deep learning' of teachers

School improvement researchers have consistently stressed the importance of teachers' commitment to change, and a form of professional development that enhances their capacity to deal with it. Teachers' beliefs and values underpin what they do (Borko and Putnam 1995; Hill and Crevola 1997), and their preparedness to engage in change flows from their belief system (Joyce *et al.* 1992). Changing one's practice is notoriously difficult, requires considerable effort, and for teachers to invest the time and energy, they have to see a good reason for doing so. That is not to say that change cannot occur because of fear, but as the business management theorists argue, fear affects an organization's strength and success because it erodes trust and causes people to lie (Chowdhury 2000).

Distinctions have been made between deep and shallow learning of students (Entwistle 1987). The same distinctions could be applied to teachers. Even by the end of the ISEP study, more than a quarter (28 per cent) of the primary and secondary teachers did not think it was particularly important that 'teachers as well as pupils learn in this school'. In changing times, as we have already argued, such perceptions are not tenable. If teachers, for whatever reason, believe that they have nothing more to learn, education is in grave difficulties. However, what teacher learning will mean in the future and the form that it will take are likely to be very different from the model currently practised in many schools and education systems. Increasingly, the workplace is being highlighted as the key location for learning (Rosenholtz 1989; Nias *et al.* 1992; Smylie 1995; Day 1999).

One of the most revealing and challenging of the findings from the ISEP study was teachers' response to the questionnaire item 'Teachers regularly observe each other in the classroom and give each other feedback' (33 per cent in both phases, although this represented a 14 per cent increase since 1995 in primary teachers' perceptions of its importance). It was a stark contrast to other aspects of their work that they rated highly, for example, 'New staff are well supported in this school' – 73 per cent agreement.

As Little (1990b) has pointed out, 'Serious collaboration, by which teachers engage in the rigorous mutual examination of teaching and learning, turns out to be rare' (p. 187). Recent studies in the USA, however, have described the benefits of developing school-based professional communities (Louis *et al.* 1995). In such communities, attention is paid to the structural conditions that inhibit progress and to the social forces that can so frequently constrain serious dialogue among teachers about their practice. Louis argues for a 'deprivatization' of practice, including mutual observation, and collective responsibility for student learning. In professional school communities benefits are seen both in student learning outcomes and in greater teacher satisfaction. Further work is necessary on understanding how deep and meaningful teacher learning can be promoted.

Promote self-evaluation

In Chapter 1 we described how the tools and strategies of researchers are being made more accessible to practitioners. One of the strengths of the ISE project was the feedback of data to schools and, through critical friends, encouragement to go deeper and explore further. It provides the basis for customizing and developing tools for more fine-grained investigation of learning and teaching, strengthening schools' internal capacity to be self-critical and self-improving. In one case study school, described in Chapter 9, a teacher worked together with the critical friend to develop a before-and-after assessment tool to measure the self-esteem of pupils in his class. He tested it on three different cohorts over a period of two years, in the second year bringing in other members of staff and, later on, using the instrument in other schools as well.

Many of the tools used in ISEP had a life beyond the end of the project. One of these instruments was the change profile. In ISEP it was used by management, teachers, researchers and critical friends to arrive at judgements about schools across ten different dimensions (see Chapter 9). It proved to be a powerful tool in focusing and generating dialogue and questioning sources of evidence, shining an exposing beam through the PHOG – prejudice, hunch, opinion and guesswork (Highett 1999). The change profile was adopted and adapted for the European project, Evaluating Quality in School Education, involving 101 schools in 18 countries (MacBeath *et al.* 2000), in which 12 dimensions were offered, most of them different from the original ISEP ten. Stakeholder involvement in the process of evaluation was extended to pupils, parents and school boards and governors.

The ISEP bipolar teacher questionnaire, developed from one used in the Halton Effective Schools project in Ontario (Stoll and Fink 1996), proved to be a valuable instrument in helping schools work through the issues hindering their attempts to bring about change. One of the challenges in the project was how to feed back all of the data in a user-friendly form. Various forms of reporting evolved, culminating in the development of a software package for teacher, pupil and parent questionnaires that promises to be a flexible self-evaluation tool for the future.

A third instrument was a rating scale that asked respondents to rate their school on 17 themes, each defined for them and then presented in two polar opposite statements, lying at either end of a continuum. The teachers, or other respondents, were asked to place their school somewhere on that continuum, (an example of this is contained in Chapter 7). The instrument was developed from issues emerging from the 24 case study schools and applied to the 56 schools not part of the case study sample (Toal and Robertson 1998). As a tool for self-evaluation it expands teachers' repertoire and enhances the capacity of the school for growth and change.

Self-evaluation is open to criticism as soft and lacking in rigour. Its very terminology seems to suggest this, and in many instances practice may serve to confirm that assumption. It can be complacent, defensive or self-congratulatory, but when implemented in the fullest and most inclusive sense, it can be more rigorous and searching than any external approach.

After a decade of self-evaluation in Scottish schools, we might categorize schools in the following way:

- exuberantly effective;
- dutifully diligent;
- mechanistically moribund;
- haphazardly hanging on.

There are few schools that fall completely and wholeheartedly into the first category. Those that do have matured over a period of many years. They are self-confident and risk-taking schools with courageous shared leadership.

More common are those dutifully diligent schools, following the guidelines and implementing the procedures earnestly and with good faith but rarely exceeding the boundaries of the national protocol or employing joined-up practice which unites self-evaluation, appraisal, staff development and development planning into one coherent ongoing dynamic process. Some, obliged by government or by the threat of inspection, go through the motions, mechanistically moribund, never touching the real heartbeat of the school, while others are haphazard and unsystematic in their approach to the issues.

A 1996 study sponsored by the National Union of Teachers (MacBeath 1999) demonstrated how self-evaluation can reach the epicentre of school life and what matters to pupils, teachers and parents. In collaboration with teachers it developed an approach whose first building block was *their* experience, *their* expectations and *their* needs. Its adoption by many schools and authorities has not been limited to the United Kingdom but many other countries of the world where it struck a resonant chord with teachers as well as administrators and policy makers. One reason for its adoption by English authorities has been as a response to what they saw as the narrowness and sterility of the Ofsted approach to self-evaluation.

We have really only somewhat timidly opened the door to the self-evaluating school. As a door to school improvement (Joyce 1991) it will have to be opened still wider.

Emphasize leadership and management

School effectiveness and school improvement research in the UK and many other countries has consistently emphasized the importance of leadership and management. Leadership and management have also become increasingly recognized within the policy arena, with the introduction of a National Professional Qualification for Headship and, most recently, a National College for School Leadership. In Scotland, the Scottish Executive Education Department (in their previous incarnation as the Scottish Office Education and Industry Department) have made leadership a keystone of policy development and a focal point of school inspection. They have put in place the Scottish Qualification for Headteachers and commissioned the development of a programme for practising heads.

While leadership was not one of the original themes of the ISE project, analysis of various of our initial data sets suggested that it was, indeed, an important issue in Scottish schools and one that merited inclusion as a main theme. High value-added attainment in the ISEP primary schools was associated with greater stakeholder satisfaction with leadership and management in their schools (Smith *et al.* 1998b), while case study evidence suggested that effective heads were those most in touch with the views of their staff, pupil and parent body and most open to reviewing their own preconceptions when challenged by alternative views of reality.

The evidence from questionnaires (Chapter 5) and the change profile

(Chapter 9) showed a clear and consistent trend for senior managers to hold quite different and more sanguine perceptions of their schools and to hold a more optimistic view than classroom teachers of policy and practice and of themselves. This was true of both primary and secondary schools (Stoll and Smith 1997). Deeper probing into heads' thinking and development planning did, as Chapter 7 illustrates, reveal a clear association between capacity building and shared leadership.

In a four-country study of leadership (MacBeath 1998) which examined the expectations of parents, pupils and teachers, the most consistent theme across national boundaries was the importance of listening and responsive leadership. Good heads, as judged by their respective groups of stakeholders, tuned in to the 'secret harmonies' (Nias *et al.* 1989) of the school. They cared about pupil voice and modelled a listening/learning stance.

One Scottish headteacher described being invited into a French class to engage in conversational French with the third year. When he objected that his French was execrable, the French teacher informed him that that was precisely why she wanted him in her class. She wanted her pupils to see that they knew more than their headteacher and that his power had its limitations. Brighouse and Woods (1999) describes a similar scenario in which native Urdu speakers help their teacher with the proper inflection, by doing so 'increasing the receptiveness of her own pupils' learning in the process' (p. 15).

The ability to listen, to read the situation, to recognize the value of intuition and emotional intelligence, will be at a higher and higher premium in this millennium. The greater the instability, the greater the need for sharp antennae, for leading from the thick of things rather than from the apex of the organizational pyramid (Murphy 1992). The trend will be for institutions to become less important as people-centred learning comes increasingly into its own. The skills for management of a single, self-contained, hierarchical, time-defined organization like a school will be less and less relevant. The skills of people management, already so important, will commensurately increase in significance.

Chowdhury (2000) argues that twenty-first-century business leaders will need to focus on 'peoplistic' communication and touch on the 'inseparable twins' of people's emotion and belief. They will need to be multiskilled and have a 'next mentality', such that they 'hunger for the next goal'. He argues that twenty-first-century leaders and managers will have to rethink twentieth-century processes and involve themselves in four essential processes:

- grass-roots education – training and support for all staff;
- fire prevention – preventing problems, rather than dealing with them;
- direct interaction with customers – 'Twenty-first century organizations will strive for customer enthusiasm instead of customer satisfaction' (p. 8);
- effective globalization – adapting products, services, and processes to local requirements.

Although these processes are propounded by Chowdhury in a business context, they have clear applications for schools and education beyond schooling. Customer enthusiasm is an ambitious goal for education in the future, but one which good leaders in the present do not view with scepticism or dismay.

Ensure high-quality critical friendship

While self-evaluation and self-improvement are hallmarks of effective organizations, and essential for schools in decentralized administrations, our own and other research (see for example Townsend 1994) argues forcibly that schools need friends. They need the external challenge, 'the visitor's-eye view', as it is known in Iceland.

ISEP found that outsiders offering schools critical friendship can be valuable external change agents. As Earl and Lee (1998) have also found, in their study of 22 schools involved in the Manitoba School Improvement program in Canada, 'Critical friends are both critical (challenging critics) and critical (essential)' (p. 76). The ISE project findings suggest that the ultimate objective', however, of critical friends is to help schools become more self-sufficient in their own improvement processes – in short, to become their own critical friends:

> There is one touchstone question for the critical friend, which is not too far away from what a teacher would, or should, ask in relation to the class or individual learner: 'Will this help to develop independence, the capacity to learn and to apply learning more effectively over time?'
>
> (MacBeath 1998: 131)

While many people may be attracted to the idea of offering, or 'selling', their services as critical friends, this study suggests that being a critical friend requires a range of skills, as well as good judgement, empathy and flexibility. Schools have different needs. Some do not even know what they need, or do not believe that they need to change (Stoll and Fink 1998). Moreover, as patterns of learning change, critical friends will be required to work with a wider range of learners in different contexts, in networks, clusters, zones, in community and other loci for learning.

Schools, like other organizations, go through different stages of change, as do the learners within them. In the process, their needs change, as does the relationship between them and their critical friend. The early stages are important times for building relationships, establishing ground rules for future collaboration, agreeing broad parameters within which the learners and critical friend will work and, particularly, creating a 'mutual comfort zone' (MacBeath 1998). Mitchell and Sackney (1998) have described this as the 'naming and framing' phase.

In the next stage, moving out of the 'comfort zone', critical friends need to clarify the neutrality and boundaries of their role. Data feedback, for example, can be a sensitive task, but the situation can be eased if critical friends are totally familiar with the data and comfortable with handling it and its interpretation, both generally as a research instrument and within the particular learning context involved.

A further stage can be characterized by the questions 'Where do we go from here?' and 'how do we set about it?' Most notably, this is the time when the critical friend begins the transition from the role of friend to that of critic. In the final stage of disengagement from the school, the critical friend helps people move to a reflective, dialogic approach that incorporates greater openness to questioning and a respect for evidence. 'The question "How do you know?" eventually ceases to be put by the critical friend and becomes a routine way of thinking' (MacBeath 1998: 129).

What critical friends in the ISE project learned was that there is no one pattern for working with all schools or with all learners, or a single path to take. It depends on comfort levels and readiness for change. Critical friends need to be able to take on a variety of roles, and offer a range of skills as diverse as data analysis and feedback and counselling as they work with learners and their agreed agendas. As Earl and Lee (1998) have found, 'It is not just quantity, or even quality, of support that matters, but access to the right type of intervention at the right time' (p. 66). This they have described as 'just in time delivery'.

Build communities, networks and partnerships

Educational improvement and effectiveness depend on people working collaboratively. They are not achievable individually. Certainly, an individual may decide to learn something new and choose to do this by reading a book, although we might argue that even then she is engaging with the author. But if we are thinking about improving learning processes and outcomes for significant numbers of people, this requires collaborative endeavour. Louis *et al.* (1995) have found that in schools with a genuine sense of community, such endeavour leads to increased sense of work-efficacy, which in turn results in heightened classroom motivation, more satisfaction at work, and greater collective responsibility for pupil learning. In such communities, teachers pursue a clear shared purpose, engage in professional dialogue and open up their classrooms to colleagues. The result of this process is improved pupil learning (Newmann and Wehlage 1995).

Clarke (2000) argues that as schools continue to improve, 'they will eventually come to a point where they need to communicate and examine what other schools are doing' (p. 16 in manuscript). He argues that it is easier for schools to establish working partnerships with other schools, to work cooperatively and share ideas, than to try to pursue individualistic agendas and then try to gain from the experiences of other schools. The ideal power arrangement for such a relationship, Clarke suggests, is a network. Networking of ISEP schools occurred, to some extent, in areas where the project focus was similar. The project brought all participating case study schools together to share experiences, leading to some exchange visits and staff development activities. One lesson from a bad experience was that a successful head in one school cannot easily inspire staff in a second school by way of success stories imported from a different context, from a different set of circumstances.

Networking involved a collegial meeting ground of shared interests, common problems and mutual concerns. Networking needs to find forums in which people with a variety of interests and backgrounds can meet, face-to-face, through telephone or video conferencing or via the Internet, to discuss experiences, and work together towards shared solutions (Stoll 1995). Access to the Internet is providing increasing opportunities for online 'chat', offering proximity to others in distant and disparate locations.

As Hargreaves and Fullan (1998) have argued, in times of turbulent social change it is crucial to redefine one's relationship to the environment, because 'what's out there' is 'in here'. They maintain, however, that this should not mean more work for schools but should be about changing *how* they work. The number of potential partners is considerable. With an ageing population the potential for grandparents, and even great-grandparents, to help children's learning is enormous, but, as we have already argued, this works both ways. Young people can help with their grandparents' learning and families and extended families can engage in intergenerational collaborative learning. Members of the community can also be a resource for young people's learning, in the process helping themselves and extending their own repertoire of skills. Companies are increasingly encouraging employees to have this kind of experience, not simply as a form of community service but as an integral part of continuing professional development and 'peoplistic' skills.

As we have found from national initiatives into study support, possibilities within the community offer an almost inexhaustible resource. In late 1999, a major initiative began in Glasgow to turn libraries into 'REAL centres', community learning resources for all ages, places for children and young people to do homework, study, learn together and learn across ages and generations. There are now study centres in schools, community centres, churches, mosques and football clubs. The 'Playing for Success' initiative (NFER 2000) defied those critics who saw study centres in Premiership Football Clubs as a gimmick, demonstrating that there are other sites for learning and that children can be motivated to learn out of hours.

As we argued in the opening chapter of this book, individual schools make a difference to the amount of successful learning achieved by an individual, but it would be foolish to imagine that the school can – by itself – overcome the effects of sustained disadvantage. This is the conclusion reached in a review of the evidence by Mortimore and Whitty (1997). Schools exist within a wider system that has an enhancing and constraining role on the capacity of schools to be all things to all children. If we wish to raise standards, as Coleman and Jencks concluded thirty years ago, we have to work on what happens outside school too and make demands on members of that wider system to play their part.

Take a 'connected' approach to improvement

When we started ISEP, our brief was to work with 80 schools, each of which was asked to select and develop one of three approaches to improvement – school development planning; teaching and learning; or ethos. These were three policy priorities emphasized by the (then) Scottish Office. While we thought that separating three important facets of schools' work appeared artificial, we followed this plan, although several schools immediately chose to focus on more than one approach. Our baseline interviews and teacher surveys suggested to us that a fourth theme – leadership and management – was significant to understanding how schools approached improvement.

As we reflect on this, our research findings, and more recent whole-school improvement 'designer' approaches, particularly those emanating from the United States (e.g. Stringfield *et al.* 1996; Bryk and Rollow 1999) and Australia (Hill and Crevola 1997; Hill and Russell 1999), it is increasingly clear that 'add-on' improvement programmes will not work. What is needed, to use Hill's words, are 'deliberate attempts to transform the entire ecology of schooling . . . [requiring] each of the critical elements of schools and of school systems . . . [to be] identified, those aspects that need to change in order for them to operate effectively and in alignment with all the other elements . . . [to be] attended to, and each element . . . [to be] redesigned accordingly'. In essence, such a holistic approach mirrors that of a holistic health practitioner, who looks at the whole person in order to try to understand the specific presenting problem, and focuses on prevention rather than cure.

We have discussed above most of the elements we would view as necessary to include in a design (for example self-evaluation, a focus on learning, leadership and management, assistance from critical friends). Nonetheless, if we look at the varied routes the more successful schools took to improvement, even if the right design elements are known, it is essential to understand how each element works in different kinds of schools. Our examples from St Leopold's, St Aubrey's and Glendale illustrate that the process of improvement, like the path to attrition (Fink 1999), follows a very different course according to the school's context and history. ISEP, in common with many other studies (for example Stoll and Fink 1996; Slavin, 1998; Gray *et al.* 1999), found that one size of improvement strategy does not fit all schools and that we cannot simply 'improve' without an understanding of how each element connects with others. With such knowledge and insight we can 'move into an understanding of integrated learning and away from the individualised simplistic, piece by piece approach to reform' (Clarke 2000: 19 in manuscript).

Strive for sustainability of improvement

We have argued for a holistic 'design' approach to improvement, one that requires that we pay close attention to conditions for learning, paralleling and mirroring conditions for improvement (van Velzen *et al.* 1985). We have also seen that schools embark on improvement from very different starting points, and some find it extremely difficult even to get started at all. This is because of differences in the internal capacity of schools to engage in and sustain the continuous learning necessary for improvement. In short, some schools are more 'ready' than others to deal with and work through the challenges that improvement efforts bring. They have the resources, the resilience and the will to engage in and sustain continuous learning of teachers, and they have a clear vision of its primary purpose as enhancing pupil learning (Stoll 1999). Influences on a school's internal capacity operate at the individual teacher level, the school level (and, in secondary schools, also at department or faculty level), and at the external contextual level. Determining the particular patterns of influences on a school's internal capacity is essential because they will influence the school's readiness for change as well as its ability to sustain the improvement process and enhance outcomes over time.

Sustaining improvement is particularly challenging. In a case study of the 25-year history of 'a new and purposefully innovative school' in Ontario, Fink (1999) found, in common with other similar studies, 'a very definite and definable cycle in [the school's] evolution. From its creative and experimental origins, it evolved through a phase of overreaching and entropy, to a third stage, survival and continuity' (p. 132). While this is the story of a new school, parallels might be drawn with the change process once a school gets involved in improvement. After the catalyst that promotes the decision to change, there is a surge of energy as people become actively involved in the early stages (Earl and Lee 1998). Initial 'excitement', however, wears off as teachers are faced with other demands, as well as inevitable difficulties presented by both the innovation and the school's internal capacity: for example, overload, complexity, internal power struggles, or an impending inspection. The school, or at least the intended improvement focus, faces turbulence (Huberman 1992) and without 'agency' – internal resources or access to appropriate and timely support (Earl and Lee 1998) – entropy can ensue.

Institutionalization is not without its problems. Schools, LEAs or national policy makers may implement poor quality innovations. Schools may also be organizationally rigid so that they are 'impermeable to improvement efforts. At their best, they may be good at getting and using "innovations" – but rarely bringing about serious changes in their overall structure and functioning' (Miles and Louis 1985: 42–3). It is a change in the deeper levels of a school's functioning that is necessary to provide the environment in which improvements can be sustained. This underpins the arguments for reculturing schools (Fullan 1993; Hargreaves 1994; Fink and Stoll 1998). There is, however, a further difficulty. As Miles and Louis point out, 'we should not ignore the fact that institutionalization in itself is not necessarily a good idea. In rapidly-changing areas of knowledge, for example, "light" institutionalization is undoubtedly a wise idea' (p. 42). More needs to be known about the processes and conditions necessary to support 'light institutionalization'.

ISEP had a significant impact on our thinking about school effectiveness and improvement. Although we were able to follow schools for two years, it was a short lifetime in which to see the effects of change or to measure the impact of what critical friends brought to that process. The project was entitled 'Improving School Effectiveness' and its purpose was to further our knowledge of that process. Hopefully this chapter and those that preceded it have shed some light on that process and shifted the paradigm from improving school effectiveness to 'effective school improvement' (Creemers and Hoeben 1998) and, as the next bold step, to the wider concept of regenerational learning.

● Conclusion

School effectiveness and school improvement research have played a signifi-cant role in the last two decades, validating the belief that schools make a difference, helping to discover many of the conditions and strategies that can lead to improved school effectiveness. They have also sharpened the debate on the importance of the outcomes of schooling as well as its processes. The ISE project has continued to break new ground, drawing on mixed methodologies from both school effectiveness and school improvement, in particular in its rich and diverse sets of qualitative data designed to further understanding of the complex process of change, people's perceptions towards it, its manage-ment and schools' capacity for change. We are, however, now moving into a new era when what is currently considered effective, and the processes for achieving and sustaining it, may not serve learners well as they live in an increasingly complex and fast-changing world. It is now time for schools and everyone with a stake in education to shift focus to individual learners and the range of learning opportunities that might be created and sustained to help all learners realize their potential.

Bibliography

Adler, M. (1993) Parental choice and the enhancement of children's interests, in P. Munn (ed.) *Parents and School*. London: Routledge.

Ainley, J. (1994) Multiple indicators of high school effectiveness. Paper presented to the Annual Conference of the American Educational Research Association, New Orleans, April.

Argyris, C. and Schön, D. (1978) Organisational Learning: A Theory of Action Perspective. Reading, MA: Addison Wesley.

Aronowitz, S. and De Fazio, W. (1994) The new knowledge work, in A. H. Halsey, H. Lauder, P. Brown and A. S. Wells (eds) *Education: Culture, Economy, Society*. Oxford: Oxford University Press.

Ball, S. J. (1987) *The Micro-Politics of the School: Towards a Theory of School Organization*. London: Methuen.

Ball, S. (1996) ESRC Culture and Values Project Paper No. 1: Good School, Bad School. British Educational Research Association Conference, University of Lancaster.

Bandura, A. (1982) Self-efficacy mechanism in human agency, *American Psychologist*, 37: 122–48.

Barber, M. (1994) *Young People and Their Attitudes to School: An Interim Report of a Research Project in the Centre for Successful Schools*. Keele: Keele University.

Barber, M. (1999) Department for Education and Employment press release, 15 October.

Bastiani, J. (1997) *Exploring Educational Issues: Block 2 Family and School: Linking Home and School*. Milton Keynes: Open University Educational Enterprises.

Bayliss, S. (1999) *Opening Minds: Education for the 21st Century*. London: Royal Society of the Arts.

Benn, C. and Chitty, C. (1996) *Thirty Years On Is Comprehensive Education Alive and Well or Struggling to Survive?* London: David Fulton.

Bentley, T. (1998) *Learning Beyond the Classroom: Education for a Changing World*. London: Routledge and Demos.

Bloomer, K. (1999) The local governance of education: an operational perspective, in T. G. K. Bryce and W. M. Humes (eds) *Scottish Education*. Edinburgh: Edinburgh University Press.

Borko, H. and Putnam, R. T. (1995) Expanding a teacher's knowledge base: a cognitive perspective on professional development, in T. R. Guskey and M. Huberman (eds) *Professional Development in Education: New Paradigms and Practices*. New York: Teachers College Press.

Boyle, E. and Crosland, A. (1971) *The Politics of Education*. Harmondsworth: Penguin.

Brandsma, H. P. and Dollard, S. (1996) The effects of between-school differences in effectiveness on advice for secondary education for individual pupils, *School Effectiveness and Improvement*, as yet unpublished.

Brandsma, H. and Knuver, J. (1989) Effects of school and classroom characteristics on pupil progress in language and arithmetic, *International Journal of Educational Research*, 13: 777–88.

Brighouse, T. and Woods, D. (1999) *How to Improve Your School*. London: Routledge.

Brookover, W. *et al.* (1979) *School Social Systems and Student Achievement; Schools Can Make a Difference*. New York, NY: Praeger.

Brown, P. (1997) The third wave: education and the ideology of parentocracy, in A. H. Halsey, H. Lauder, P. Brown and A. S. Wells (eds) *Education: Culture, Economy, and Society*: Oxford University Press.

Brown, S. and Riddell, S. (eds) (1992) *Class, Race and Gender in Schools: A New Agenda for Policy and Practice in Scottish Education*. Glasgow: Scottish Council for Research in Education.

Brown, S. and Riddell, S. (1996) Paper delivered to the CES Conference on School Effectiveness and School Improvement: The Ways Forward, Department of Education, University of Stirling, 5 February.

Brown, S., Duffield, J. and Riddell, S. (1995) School effectiveness research: the policy makers' tool for school improvement, *European Educational Research Association Bulletin*, 1 (1) : 6–15.

Bryce, T. G. K. and Humes, W. M. (1999) Scottish secondary education: philosophy and practice, in T. G. K. Bryce and W. M. Humes (eds) *Scottish Education*. Edinburgh: Edinburgh University Press.

Bryk, A. and Rollow, S. (1999) *A Social History of the Center for School Improvement*. Paper presented at the Annual Meeting of the American Educational Research Association, Montreal, Canada, April.

Caldwell, B. and Spinks, J. M. (1992) *Leading the Self-managing School*. London: The Falmer Press.

Cheng, Y. C. (1994) Principals' leadership as a cultural factor for school performance, *School Effectiveness and School Improvement*, 5(3): 299–317.

Chowdhury, S. (2000) Towards the future of management, in S. Chowdhury (ed.) *Management 21C: Someday We'll All Manage This Way*. Harlow, Financial Times and Prentice Hall.

Chubb, J. and Moe, Y. (1992) *A Lesson in Reform from Great Britain*. Washington, DC: Brookings Institute.

Clarke, P. (2000) *Learning Schools, Learning Systems*. London: Cassell.

Coleman, J. S. (1995) Families and Schools, *Zeitschrift fur Socialisationsforschung und Erziehungssuziologie*, 4 P1545: 362–75.

Coleman, J. S., Campbell, E. Q., Hobson, C. J. *et al.* (1966) *Equality of Educational Opportunity*. Washington, DC: Office of Education.

Coleman, P. (1998) *Parent, Student and Teacher Collaboration: The Power of Three*. London: Paul Chapman.

Coleman, P. and Collinge, J. (1995) An inside-out approach to school improvement. Paper presented to the International Congress for School Effectiveness and Improvement, Leeuwarden, January.

Costa, A. L. and Kallick, B. (1993) Through the lens of a critical friend, *Educational Leadership*, 51(2): 49–51.

Cousin, O. and Guillemet, J. P. (1992) Variations des performances scolaires et effets d'établissement, *Education et Formations*, No. 31.

Cox, C. B. and Dyson, A. E. (1968) (eds) Fight for Education, *London Critical Quarterly*.

Creemers, B. P. M. and Hoeben, W. T. I. G. (1998) Capacity for change and adaptation of schools: the case of effective school improvement (ESI), in W. T. I. G. Hoeben (ed.) *Effective School Improvement: State of the Art Contribution to a Discussion*. University of Groningen, the Netherlands: GION.

Croxford, L. and Cowie, M. (1996) *The Effectiveness of Grampian Secondary Schools*. Grampian Regional Council. Edinburgh: Centre for Educational Sociology.

Cuttance, P. (1987) *Modelling Variation in the Effectiveness of Schooling*. Edinburgh: Centre for Educational Sociology.

Cuttance, P. (1988) Intra-system variation in the effectiveness of schooling, *Research Papers in Education*, 3: 183–219.

Dalin, P. and Rust, V. D. (1996) *Towards Schooling for the Twenty-First Century*. London: Cassell.

Dalin, P. with Rolff, H.-G. in cooperation with Kleekamp, B. (1993) *Changing the School Culture*. London: Cassell.

Datnow, A. (1998) The relationship between informed choices and early implementation success in schools attempting diverse restructuring designs. Paper presented at the Annual Conference of the American Educational Research Association, San Diego, April.

Delors, J., Al Mufti, I., Amagi, A. *et al.* (1996) *Learning: The Treasure Within. Report to UNESCO of the International Commission on Education for the Twenty-First Century*. Paris: UNESCO.

Davies, N. (1999) Political coup bred educational disaster, *Guardian*, 16 September.

Day, C. (1999) *Developing Teachers: The Challenges of Lifelong Learning*. London: Falmer Press.

Department for Education and Employment (1998) *School Evaluation Matters*. London: Ofsted.

Department for Education and Science (1988) Education Reform Act. London: HMSO.

DuBrin, A. J. (1995) *Leadership: Research Findings, Practice and Skills*. Boston, MA: Haughton Mifflin Co.

Dweck, C. S. (1985) Intrinsic motivation, perceived control and self-evaluation maintenance; an achievement goal analysis, in C. Ames and R. E. Ames (eds) *Research on Motivation in Education, Vol. 2: The Classroom Milieu*. London: Academic Press.

Dweck, C. S. (1986) Motivational processes affecting learning, *American Psychologist*, 41: 1040–8.

Dweck, C. S. and Licht, B. G. (1980) Learned helplessness and intellectual achievement, in J. Garbar and M. Seligman (eds) *Human Helplessness*. New York, NY: Academic Press.

Earl, L. and Lee, L. (1998) *Evaluation of the Manitoba School Improvement Program*. Toronto: Walter and Duncan Gordan Foundation.

Elliott, M. (1989) *Kidscape*. London: Kidscape.

Entwistle, N. (1987) *Understanding Classroom Learning*. London: Hodder and Stoughton.

Evans, R. L. (1998) Teachers' perceptions of principals' facilitator styles in schools that differ according to effectiveness and socio-economic context. Unpublished doctoral dissertation, University of New Orleans.

Fielding, M. (1997) Beyond school effectiveness and school improvement: lighting the slow fuse of possibility, in J. White and M. Barber (eds) *Perspectives on School Effectiveness and School Improvement*. London: Institute of Education.

Fielding, M. (1999) Students as radical agents of change: a three year case study. Paper presented at the British Educational Research Association, University of Sussex, September.

Fink, D. (1999) The attrition of change, *School Effectiveness and School Improvement*, 10(3): 269–95.

Fink, D. and Stoll, L. (1998) Educational change: easier said than done, in A. Hargreaves (ed.) *International Handbook on Educational Change: Part 1*. Leuven: Kluwer.

Freedland, J. (1998) *Bring Home the Revolution*. London: Fourth Estate.

Fullan, M. G. (1993) *Change Forces: Probing the Depths of Educational Reform*. London: Falmer Press.

Fullan, M. G. (1995) *Successful School Improvement*, 2nd edn. Buckingham: Open University Press.

Fullan, M. G. with Stiegebauer, S. D. (1991) *The New Meaning of Educational Change*. London: Cassell.

Fullan, M. and Watson, N. (1997) *Building Infrastructures for Professional Development: An Assessment of Early Progress*. New York: Rockefeller Foundation.

Gardner, H. (1983) *Frames of Mind*. New York, NY: Basic Books.

Goldstein, H. (1995) *Multilevel Statistical Models*, 2nd edition. London: Edward Arnold and New York, NY: Halsted Press.

Goleman, D. (1996) *Emotional Intelligence: Why It Can Matter More Than IQ*. London: Bloomsbury.

Gow, L. and McPherson, A. (eds) (1980) *Tell Them From Me*. Aberdeen: Aberdeen University Press.

Grace, G. (1997) Politics, markets and democratic schools: on the transformation of school leadership, in A. H. Halsey, H. Lauder, P. Brown and A. S. Wells (eds) *Education: Culture, Economy and Society*. Oxford: Oxford University Press.

Gray, J. and Wilcox, B. (1994) *The Challenge of Turning Round Ineffective Schools*. Buckingham: Open University Press.

Gray, J. and Wilcox, B. (1995) *Good Schools, Bad Schools*. Buckingham: Open University Press.

Gray, J., McPherson, A. and Raffe, D. (1983) *Reconstructions of Secondary Education*. London: Routledge and Kegan Paul.

Gray, J., Goldstein, H. and Jesson, D. (1996) Changes and improvements in schools' effectiveness: trends over five years, *Research Papers in Education*, 11(1): 35–51.

Gray, J., Hopkins, D., Reynolds, D. *et al.* (1999a) *Improving Schools: Performance and Potential*. Buckingham: Open University Press.

Gray, J., Reynolds, D., Fitzgibbon, C. T. and Jesson, D. (eds) (1999b) *Merging Traditions: The Future of Research on School Effectiveness and School Improvement*. London: Cassell.

Grisay, A. (1997) Evolution des acquis cognitifs et socio affectifs au collège. Dossiers Education et Formation, 32, Ministère de l'éducation nationale.

Groundwater-Smith, S. (1991) Students as researchers: two Australian case studies. Paper presented at the British Education Research Association, University of Sussex, September.

Hallinger, P. and Heck, R. H. (1996) Reassessing the principal's role in school effectiveness: A review of the empirical research, 1980–95, *Educational Administration Quarterly*, 32(1): 5–44.

Hallinger, P. and Murphy, J. F. (1986) The social context of effective schools, *American Journal of Education*, 94(3): 328–55.

Hampden-Turner, C. and Trompenaars, L. (1993) *The Seven Cultures of Capitalism*. New York, NY: Doubleday.

Handy, C. and Aitken, R. (1986) *Understanding Schools as Organisations*. Harmondsworth: Penguin.

Haq, K. and Kirdar, M. (eds) (1986) *Human Development: The Neglected Dimension*. Islamabad: North South Roundtable.

Hargreaves, A. (1994) *Changing Teachers, Changing Times: Teachers' Work and Culture in the Post-Modern Age*. London: Cassell.

Hargreaves, A. and Fullan, M. (1998) *What's Worth Fighing for Out There?* Mississauga, Ontario: Ontario Public School Teachers' Federation.

Hargreaves, D. H. (1999) *Creative Professionalism: The Role of Teachers in the Knowledge Society*. London: DEMOS.

Hargreaves, D. H. (1967) *Social Relations in A Secondary School*. London: Routledge and Kegan Paul.

Harlen, W., MacBeath, J., Simpson, M. and Thomson, G. (1994) Implementing 5–14 – A Progress Report, Interchange. Scottish Office Education Department, SCRE.

Harris, J. R. (1998) *The Nurture Assumption*. London: Bloomsbury.

Hatch, M. J. (1997) *Organisation Theory: Modern, Symbolic and Postmodern Perspectives*. Oxford: Oxford University Press.

Hellriegel, D., Slocum, J. W. and Woodman, R. W. (1989) *Organisational Behaviour*, 5th ed. St Paul: West Publishing Company.

Helsby, G. and McCulloch, G. (1996) Teacher professionalism and curriculum control, in I. F. Goodson and A. Hargreaves (eds) *Teachers' Professional Lives*. London: Falmer Press.

Highett, N. (1999) Students evaluating schools. Paper presented at Queensland Conference for Principals, Surfers' Paradise, July.

Hill, P. and Crevola, C. (1997) *The Literacy Challenge in Australian Primary Schools*. Jolimont, Victoria: IARTV.

Hill, P. W., Rowe, K. J. and Holmes-Smith, P. (1995) Factors affecting students' educational progress. Paper delivered at the 8th International Congress of School Effectiveness and School Improvement, Leeuwarden, 3–6 January.

Hill, P. W. and Russell, V. J. (1999) *Systemic, whole-school reform of the middle years of schooling*. Unpublished paper, Victoria: Centre for Applied Educational Research, University of Melbourne.

Hodgkinson, C. (1983) *The Philosophy of Leadership*. Oxford: Blackwell.

Hopkins, D. (1994) Towards a theory for school improvement. Paper presented to ESRC Seminar Series on School Effectiveness and School Improvement, University of Newcastle Upon Tyne, October.

Hopkins, D. and Harris, A. (1997) Understanding the school's capacity for development: growth states and strategies, *School Leadership and Management*, 17 (3): 401–11.

House, E. (1973) *School Evaluation: The Politics and Process*. San Francisco: McCutcheon Publishing Corporation.

Huberman, M. (1992) Critical Introduction, in M. Fullan (ed.) *Successful School Improvement*. Buckingham: Open University Press.

Institute of Fiscal Studies (1998) in J. Freedland (ed.) *Bring Home the Revolution*. London: Fourth Estate.

International Essesement for the Evaluation of Education (IEA) (1998) *Third International Mathematics and Science Study, Volume 3: Implementation and Analysis*. Boston: Boston College.

Jencks, C. *et al.* (1972) *Inequality: A Reassessment of the Effect of Family and Schooling in America*. New York, NY: Basic Books.

Jirasinghe, D. and Lyons, G. (1996) *The Competent Head: A Job Analysis of Heads' Tasks and Personality Factors*. Lewes: Falmer Press.

Joyce, B. R. (1991) The doors to school improvement, *Educational Leadership*, 48(8): 59–62.

Joyce, B. R., Showers, B. and Weil, M. (1992) *Models of Teaching*. Englewood Cliffs, NJ: Prentice-Hall.

Keys, W. and Fernandes, C. (1993) *What Do Students Think about School? Research into Positive and Negative Attitudes towards School and Education*. Slough: NFER.

Koch, R. (1998) *The 80:20 Principle*. London: Nicholas Brealey.

Le Doux, J. (1997) *The Emotional Brain*. Allendale, PA: Touchstone Books.

Leithwood, K., Edge, K. and Jantzi, D. (1999) *Educational Accountability: The State of the Art*. Gutersloh: Bertelsmann Foundation Publishers.

Leitner, D. (1994) Do principals affect student outcomes? An organisational perspective, *School Effectiveness and School Improvement*, 5(3): 219–38.

Lindell, P., Melin, L., Gahmberg, H. J., Hellqvist, A. and Melander, A. (1998) Stability and change in a strategist's thinking, in C. Eden and J. C. Spender (eds) *Managerial and Organisational Cognition: Theory, Methods and Research*. London: Sage Publications.

Little, J. W. (1990a) The persistence of privacy: autonomy and initiative in teachers' professional relations, *Teachers College Record*, 91(4): 509–36.

Little, J. W. (1990b) Teachers as colleagues, in A. Lieberman (ed.) *Schools as Collaborative Cultures: Creating the Future Now*. Basingstoke: Falmer Press.

Louis, K. S. and Miles, M. B. (1990) Improving the Urban High School: what works and why. New York: Teachers College Press.

Louis, K. S., Kruse, S. D. and associates (1995) *Professionalism and Community: Perspectives on Reforming Urban Schools*. Thousand Oak, CA: Corwin.

Luyten, H. (1994) *School Effects: Stability and Malleability*. Enschede, the Netherlands: University of Twente.

Luyten, J. W. and Snidjers, T. A. B. (1996) School effects and teacher effects in Dutch elementary education, *Educational Research and Evaluation*, 2, 1–24.

MacBeath, J. (1993) The threefold path to enlightenment, *Times Educational Supplement*, 15 September.

MacBeath, J. (1998) 'I didn't know he was ill': the role and value of the critical friend, in L. Stoll and K. Myers (eds) (1998) *No Quick Fixes: Perspectives on Schools in Difficulty*. London: Falmer Press.

MacBeath, J. (1999) *Schools Must Speak for Themselves*. London: Routledge.

MacBeath, J. (ed.) (1998) *Effective Leadership: Responding to Change*. London: Paul Chapman.

MacBeath, J. and Dobie, T. (1995) *Devolved School Management in Fife*. Glenrothes: Fife Regional Council.

MacBeath, J. and Mortimore, P. (1995) *Improving School Effectiveness*, Proposal for a Research Project for the Scottish Office Education Department. Glasgow: Quality in Education Centre, University of Strathclyde.

MacBeath, J. and Mortimore, P. (1994) *Improving School Effectiveness – A Scottish Approach*. Paper presented at the British Educational Research Association Twentieth Annual Conference, St Anne's College, Oxford, September.

MacBeath, J. and Weir, D. (1991) *Attitudes to Schools*, occasional paper. Glasgow: Jordanhill College.

MacBeath, J., Mearns, D. and Smith, I. (1986) *Home from School*. Glasgow: Scottish Education Department, Jordanhill College.

MacBeath, J., Mortimore, P., Robertson, P., Sammons, P. and Thomas, S. (1998) The Improving School Effectiveness Project: issues for policy and practice. Paper presented at the Annual Meeting of the International Congress for School Effectiveness and School Improvement, San Antonio, Texas: January 3–6.

MacBeath, J., Jakobsen, L., Meuret, D. and Schratz, M. (2000) *Self-evaluation in European Schools: A Story of Change.* London: Routledge/Falmer.

McCall, J., Toal, D. and McKay, E. (2000) *Factors Affecting School Effectiveness: An Extension of the Improving School Effectiveness Project.* Glasgow: QIE Centre, University of Strathclyde.

McCombs, B. J. and Whisler, J. S. (1997) *The Learner Centered Classroom and School: Strategies for Enhancing Student Motivation and Achievement.* San Francisco: Jossey-Bass.

MacGilchrist, B., Mortimore, P., Savage, J. and Beresford, C. (1995) *Planning Matters: The Impact of Development Planning in Primary Schools.* London: Paul Chapman.

MacGilchrist, B., Myers, K. and Reed, J. (1997) *The Intelligent School.* London: Paul Chapman Publishing.

McGlynn, A. S. and MacBeath, J. (1995) *Public Expectations of the Final Stage of Compulsory Schooling.* Paris: OECD.

McKay, E. (1999) *Class Size – What Counts? Evaluation of the Reduced Pupil–teacher Ratio in Primary 1–3 Classes.* Quality in Education Centre, University of Strathclyde: East Dunbartonshire Council.

McLaughlin, M. (1990) The Rand Change Agent Study revisited: macro perspectives, micro realities, *Educational Researcher*, 19(9): 11–16.

McLaughlin, M. and Talbert, J. E. (1993) *Contexts that Matter for Teaching and Learning: Strategic Opportunities for Meeting the Nation's Educational Goals.* Stanford, CA: Center for Research on the Context of Secondary School Teaching, Stanford University.

McNay, I. (1995) Constructing the vision: changing the culture, in J. Bell and B. T. Harrison (eds) *Vision and Values in Managing Education: Successful Leadership Principles and Practice.* London: David Fulton Publishers.

McNeil, F. (1999) *Brain Research and Learning: An Introduction.* Research Matters No. 10. School Improvement Network. London: Institute of Education.

McPherson, A. (1992) *Measuring Added Value in Schools*, briefing no. 1. London: National Commission on Education.

Mann, D. (1997) *Using New Technologies to Promote Successful Learning.* Paper presented at the Successful Schools Conference, University of Melbourne and Victoria Ministry of Education, June.

Martin, P. (1997) *The Sickening Mind.* London: Flamingo.

Miles, M. B. and Huberman, A. M. (1994) *Qualitative Data Analysis.* London: Sage.

Miles, M. B. and Louis, K. S. (1985) Research on institutionalization: a reflective review, in M. B. Miles, M. Ekholm and R. Vandenberghe (eds) *Lasting School Improvement: Exploring the Process of Institutionalization.* Leuven: ACCO, in association with OECD.

Mintzberg, H. (1979) *The Nature of Managerial Work*, 2nd ed. New Jersey, NJ: Prentice Hall.

Mitchell, C. and Sackney, L. (1998) Learning about organizational learning, in K. Leithwood and K. S. Louis (eds) *Organizational Learning in Schools.* Lisse, the Netherlands: Swets and Zeitlinger.

Moorman, C. and Miner, A. S. (1998) Organisational improvisation and organisational memory, *The Academy of Management Review*, 23(4) : 698–723.

Morgan, J. (1996) A defence of autonomy as an educational ideal, *Journal of Philosophy of Education*, 30(2): 239–52.

Morrison, K. (1998) *Management Theories for Educational Change.* London: Paul Chapman Publishing.

Mortimore, P. (1998) *The Road to Improvement: Reflections on School Effectiveness.* Lisse, the Netherlands: Swets and Zeitlinger.

Mortimore, P. (2000) Address to school governors, London Borough of Richmond upon Thames, 5 April.

Mortimore, P. and Blackstone, T. (1982) *Disadvantage and Education*. London: Heinemann.

Mortimore, P. and Mortimore, J. (1991) *The Primary Head: Roles, Responsibilities and Reflections*. London: Paul Chapman.

Mortimore, P. and Mortimore, J. (1999) Improving educational performance of at-risk youth, in *Preparing Youth for the 21st Century*. Paris: OECD.

Mortimore, P. and Whitty, G. (1997) *Can School Improvement Overcome the Effects of Disadvantage?* Institute of Education: University of London.

Mortimore, P., Sammons, P., Stoll, L., Lewis, D. and Ecob, R. (1986) *The Junior School Project: Technical Appendices*. London: ILEA Research and Statistics Branch.

Mortimore, P., Sammons, P., Stoll, L., Lewis, D. and Ecob, R. (1988) *School Matters: The Junior Years*. Somerset: Open Books (reprinted in 1994 by Paul Chapman, London).

Mortimore, P., Gopinathan, S., Leo, E. *et al.* (2000) *The Culture of Change: Case Studies of Improving Schools in Singapore and London*. London: Institute of Education.

MVA Consultancy and MacBeath, J. (1989) *Talking about Schools*. Edinburgh: Scottish Education Department, HMSO.

Murphy, J. (1992) School effectiveness and school restructuring: contributions to educational improvement, *School Effectiveness and School Improvement*, 3(2): 90–109.

Myers, K. (1994) Why schools in difficulty may find the research on school effectiveness and school improvement inappropriate for their needs. Unpublished paper for doctoral thesis. London: Institute of Education.

Myers, K. (1996) *School Improvement in Practice: Accounts from the Schools Make a Difference Project*. London: Falmer Press.

Myers, K. and MacBeath, J. (1998) Changing your life through study support: how can we know it makes a difference? Paper delivered at the American Educational Research Association, San Diego, April.

NFER (National Foundation for Education Research) (2000) *Playing For Success: An Evaluation of the First Year*. DfEE.

Newmann, E. M. and Wehlage, G. G. (1995) *Successful School Restructuring: A Report to the Public and Educators by the Center on Organization and Restructuring of Schools*. Madison: Board of Regents of the University of Wisconsin System.

Nias, J., Southwaite, G. and Yeomans, R. (1989) *Staff Relationships in a Primary School: A Study of Organisational Cultures*. London: Cassell.

Nias, J., Southworth, G. and Campbell, P. (1992) *Whole School Curriculum Development in the Primary School*. London: Falmer Press.

NREL (Northwest Regional Educational Laboratory) (1989) *Effective Schooling Practices: A Research Synthesis*. Portland, OR: Northwest Regional Educational Laboratory.

Ornstein, R. (1993) *The Roots of the Self*. San Francisco: Harper & Row.

OECD (1992) *New Technology and its Impact on Educational Buildings*. Paris: OECD.

OECD (1995) *Education at a Glance*. Paris: OECD.

Paterson, L. (1992) Social class in Scottish education, in S. Brown and S. Riddell (eds) *Class, Race and Gender in Schools: A New Agenda for Policy and Practice in Scottish Education*. Glasgow: Scottish Council for Research in Education.

Paterson, L. and Goldstein, H. (1991) New statistical methods of analysing social structures: an introduction to multilevel models, *British Educational Research Journal*, 17 (4): 387–93.

Perkins, D. (1995) *Smart Schools*. New York: The Free Press.

Perkins, D. (1998) Learning for understanding. Paper presented at West Lothian/Quality in Education Seminar, September.

Phillips, M. (1996) *All Must Have Prizes*. London: Warner.

Pickering, J. (1997) *Involving Pupils*, School Improvement Network Research Matters no. 6. London: Institute of Education.

Postlethwaite, T. N. and Ross, K. N. (1992) *Effective Schools in Reading: Implications for Educational Planners*. The Hague: IEA.

Raffe, D. (1999) CES findings on participation and attainment in Scottish education, in T. G. K. Bryce and W. M. Humes (eds) *Scottish Education*. Edinburgh: Edinburgh University Press.

Raudenbush, S. W. and Willms, J. D. (1988) Procedures for reducing bias in the simulation of school effects. Paper presented at the American Educational Research Association, New Orleans, April.

Reeves, J. (1999) Development planning: tracking the complexities of change in Scottish schools. Unpublished PhD thesis, University of Strathclyde.

Reeves, J. (2000) Tracking the links between pupil attainment and development planning, *School Leadership and Management*, forthcoming.

Reeves, J. and MacGilchrist, B. (1997) Gauging the impact of improvement strategies. Paper presented at the British Educational Research Association Annual Conference, University of York, 11–14 September.

Reynolds, D. (1991) Changing ineffective schools, in M. Ainscow (ed.) *Effective Schools for All*. London: Fulton.

Reynolds, D. (1992) School effectiveness and school improvement: an updated review of the British literature, in D. Reynolds and P. Cuttance (eds) *School Effectiveness: Research, Policy and Practice*. London: Cassell.

Reynolds, D. (1995) The effective school: an inaugural lecture, *Evaluation and Research in Education*, 9 (2): 57–73.

Reynolds, D. and Farrell, S. (1996) *Worlds Apart? A Review of International Surveys of - Educational Achievement involving England (OFSTED Reviews of Research)*. London: HMSO.

Reynolds, D. and Stringfield, S. (1996) Failure free schooling is ready for take off, *Times Educational Supplement*, 19 January.

Riddell, S. and Brown, S. (eds) (1991) *School Effectiveness Research: Its Messages for School Improvement*. London: HMSO.

Riley, J. and Reedy, D. (2000) *Writing for Different Purposes: Teaching Young People about Genre*. London: Paul Chapman.

Riley, J. and MacBeath, J. (1999) Effective Leaders and Effective Schools, in J. MacBeath (ed.) *Effective School Leadership: Responding to Change*. London: Paul Chapman.

Riley, K. (1999) *Whose School is it Anyway?* London: Falmer.

Robertson, P. (1998a) Improving school effectiveness. Summary paper presented to the Scottish Office Education and Industry Department, February.

Robertson, P. (1998b) Teaching and learning: teachers' views as indicators of school quality. Paper presented at the British Educational Research Association Annual Conference, University of Belfast, 26–9 August.

Robertson, P. and Sammons, P. (1997) The Improving School Effectiveness project: understanding change in schools. Paper presented at the British Educational Research Association Annual Conference, University of York, 11–14 September.

Robertson, P., Toal, D., MacGilchrist, B. and Stoll, L. (1998) Quality counts: evaluating evidence from school improvement. Paper presented at the International Congress for School Effectiveness and Improvement, University of Manchester, January.

Rodrik, D. (1997) *Has Globalization Gone Too Far?* Washington: Institute for International Economics.

Rosenholtz, S. J. (1989) *Teachers' Workplace: The Social Organization of the School*. New York, NY: Longman.

Rudduck, J. (1995) Transitions in the secondary school and their significance for students' commitment to learning, *Education Section Review*, 19(2): 69–74.

Rudduck, J., Chaplain, R. and Wallace, G. (1996) *School Improvement: What Can Pupils Tell Us?* London: Fulton.

Rutter, M. and Madge, N. (1976) *Cycles of Disadvantage*. London: Heinemann.

Rutter, M., Maugham, B., Mortimore, P. and Ouston, P. with Smith, A. (1979) *Fifteen Thousand Hours: Secondary Schools and their Effects on Children*. London: Open Books.

Sacks, P. (1999) *The Sickening Mind: Mind, Brain, Immunity and Disease*. London: Harper-Collins.

Salovey, P. and Mayer, J. D. (1990) Emotional intelligence, *Imagination, Cognition and Personality*, 9: 185–211.

Sammons, P. (1993) *Measuring and Resourcing Educational Need: Variations in LEAs LMS Policies in Inner London*. Clare Market Paper no. 6. London: Centre for Educational Research, LSE University of London.

Sammons, P. (1995) Gender, ethnic and socio-economic differences in attainment and progress: a longitudinal analysis of student achievement over nine years. *British Educational Research Journal*, 21 (4): 465–85.

Sammons, P. (1998) Diversity in Classrooms: Effects on educational outcomes, in D. Sharrocks-Taylor (ed.) *Directions in Educational Psychology*. London: Whurr Publishers Ltd.

Sammons, P. (1999) *School Effectiveness: Coming of Age in the Twenty-first Century*. Lisse, the Netherlands: Swets and Zeitlinger.

Sammons, P. and Smees, R. (1998a) Measuring pupil progress at Key Stage 1, *School Leadership and Management*, 18 (3): 389–407.

Sammons, P. and Smees, R. (1998b) *Parents' Views of their Child's School*, Policy Paper no. 4 of the Improving School Effectiveness project. London: unpublished.

Sammons, P., Nuttall, D. and Cuttance, P. (1993) Differential school effectiveness: results from a reanalysis of the Inner London Education Authority's Junior School project data, *British Educational Research Journal*, 19 (4): 381–405.

Sammons, P., Hillman, J. and Mortimore, P. (1994) *Key Characteristics of Effective Schools: A Review of School Effectiveness Research*. London: Office of Standards in Education.

Sammons, P., Hillman, J. and Mortimore, P. (1995) Accounting for variations in academic effectiveness between schools and departments: results from the 'Differential Secondary School Effectiveness' project – a three-year study of GCSE performance. Paper presented at the European Conference on Educational Research/BERA Annual Conference, Bath, September.

Sammons, P., Mortimore, P. and Thomas, S. (1996) Do schools perform consistently across outcomes and areas? in J. Gray, D. Reynolds, C. Fitz-Gibbon and D. Jesson (eds) *Merging Traditions: The Future of Research on School Effectiveness and School Improvement*. London: Cassells.

Sammons, P., Smees, R., Thomas, S., Robertson, P., McCall, J. and Mortimore, P. (1998) The impact of background factors on pupil attainment and progress in Scottish Schools: A summary of findings. Paper presented at the International Congress for School Effectiveness and Improvement, University of Manchester, January.

Sammons, P., Thomas, S. and Mortimore, P. (1997) *Forging Links: Effectiveness Schools and Effective Departments*. London: Paul Chapman.

Scheerens, J. (1997) Theories on effective schooling, *School Effectiveness and School Improvement*, 8(3): 220–42 .

Scheerens, J. and Bosker, R. (1997) *The Foundations of Educational Effectiveness*. London: Pergamon.

Scheerens, J., Vermeulen, C. and Pelgrum, W. (1989) Generalisability of instructional and school effectiveness indicators across nations, *International Journal of Educational Research*, 13 (7): 789–99.

Schein, E. H. (1985) *Organizational Culture and Leadership*. San Francisco: Jossey-Bass.

Scottish Consultative Council on the Curriculum (1997) *Teaching for Effective Learning*. Dundee: SCCC.

Scottish Executive Education Department (1999) *Improving Our Schools: Consultation on the Improvement in Scottish Education Bill*. Edinburgh: The Stationery Office Ltd.

Scottish Executive Education Department (2000) *Standards in Scotland's Schools*, Bill introduced to the Scottish Executive. Edinburgh: The Stationery Office Ltd.

Scottish Office Education Department (1988) *Effective Secondary Schools: A Report by HM Inspectors of Schools*. Edinburgh: HMSO.

Scottish Office Education Department (1989) *Effective Primary Schools: A Report by HM Inspectors of Schools*. Edinburgh: HMSO.

Scottish Office Education Department (1990) *The Role of School Development Plans in Managing School Effectiveness*. Edinburgh: HMSO.

Scottish Office Education Department (1992a) *Using Ethos Indicators in Secondary School Self-Evaluation: Taking Account of the Views of Pupils, Parents and Teachers*. HM Inspectors of Schools. Edinburgh: HMSO.

Scottish Office Education Department, Research and Intelligence Unit (1992b) Performance indicators and examination results, *Interchange*, no. 11. Edinburgh: HMSO.

Scottish Office Education and Industry Department (1996) *How Good is our School? Self-evaluation Using Performance Indicators*. Edinburgh: Audit Unit, SOEID.

Scottish Office Education and Industry Department (1998) *Setting Targets – Raising Standards in Schools*. Edinburgh: The Scottish Office.

Senge, P. (1990) *The Fifth Discipline: The Art and Practice of the Learning Organisation*. New York, NY: Doubleday.

Senge, P. (1996) The leader's new work, in K. Starkey (ed.) *How Organisations Learn*. London: International Thomson Business Press.

Sexton, S. (1987) *Our Schools: A Radical Policy*. London: Institute of Economic Affairs.

Silins, H. C. (1994) Leadership characteristics and school improvement, *Australian Journal of Education*, 38(3): 266–81.

Slavin, R. (1995) Success for all: restructuring elementary schools. Paper presented at the International Congress for School Effectiveness and Improvement, Leeuwarden, January.

Slavin, R. (1998) Sands, bricks, and seeds: school change strategies and readiness for reform, in A. Hargreaves, M. Fullan, A. Lieberman and D. Hopkins (eds) *International Handbook of Educational Change*, Part Two. Dordrecht: Kluwer.

Slee, R. and Weiner, G. with Tomlinson, S. (1998) *School Effectiveness for Whom? Challenges to the School Effectiveness and School Improvement Movements*. London: Falmer Press.

Smees, R. and Thomas, S. (1998) Interpreting pupil attitude data in Lancashire. Paper submitted to *Improving Schools*, as yet unpublished.

Smith, D. and Tomlinson, S. (1989) *The School Effect: A Study of Multi-racial Comprehensives*. London: Policy Studies Institute.

Smith, I. and Stoll, L. (1998) *Teacher Questionnaires 1995–1997*, Policy Paper no. 6 of the Improving School Effectiveness project. University of Strathclyde: unpublished.

Smith, I., Stoll, L., McCall, J. and MacGilchrist, B. (1998) *Improving School Effectiveness*

Project Final Report April 1998: Teacher Questionnaires 1995/97. Glasgow: Quality in Education Centre and London: Institute of Education.

Smylie, M. (1995) Teacher learning in the workplace: implications for school reform, in T. R. Guskey and M. Huberman (eds) *Professional Development in Education: New Paradigms and Practices*. New York: Teachers College Press.

SooHoo, S. (1993) Students as partners in research and restructuring schools, *The Educational Forum*, 57: 386–92.

Sternberg, R. J. (1985) *Beyond IQ*. New York: Cambridge University Press.

Stoll, L. (1992) Making schools matter: a study of improvement in a Canadian school district. Unpublished doctoral dissertation, University of London.

Stoll, L. (1995) Asking the right questions, *Managing Schools Today*, September, March, 5(6): 13–17.

Stoll, L. (1999) Realising our potential: understanding and developing capacity for lasting improvement, *School Effectiveness and School Improvement*, 10 (4): 503–32.

Stoll, L. and Fink, D. (1996) *Changing Our Schools: Linking School Effectiveness and School Improvement*. Buckingham: Open University Press.

Stoll, L. and Fink, D. (1998) The cruising school: the unidentified ineffective school, in L. Stoll and K. Myers (eds) *No Quick Fixes: Perspectives on Schools in Difficulty*. London: Falmer Press.

Stoll, L. and Myers, K. (eds) (1998) *No Quick Fixes: Perspectives on Schools in Difficulty*. London: Falmer Press.

Stoll, L. and Smith, I. (1997) Closing the gap: what teachers expect and what they get. Paper presented to the Tenth International Congress for School Effectiveness and Improvement, Memphis, Tennessee, January.

Strathclyde Regional Council (1984) *Social Strategy for the Eighties*. Glasgow: Strathclyde Regional Council Chief Executive's Department.

Strathclyde Regional Council (1994) *Social Strategy for the Nineties*. Glasgow: Strathclyde Regional Council Chief Executive's Department.

Stringfield, S., Ross, S. and Smith, L. (1996) *Bold Plans for Restructuring: New American School Designs*. New Jersey, NJ: Lawrence Erlbaum Associates.

Teddlie, C. and Stringfield, S. (1993) *Schools Make a Difference: Lessons Learned from a Ten-year Study of School Effects*. New York: Teachers College Press.

Thiessen, D. (1995) Whose voices? Whose perspectives? Some challenges in understanding the curriculum experiences of primary pupils. Paper presented at the European Conference in Educational Research, Seville, September.

Thomas, S. (1995a) *Considering Primary School Effectiveness: An Analysis of 1992 Key Stage 1*.

Thomas S. (1995b) Differential secondary school effectiveness. Paper presented at the Annual Conference of the British Educational Research Association, Bath, September.

Thomas, S. and Mortimore, P. (1996) Comparison of value-added models for secondary school effectiveness, *Research Papers in Education*, 11 (1): 5–33.

Thomas, S., Smees, R. and Boyd, B. (1998a) *Using Pupil Attitude Data in Scottish Schools: A Policy Paper*. London: University of London, Institute of Education.

Thomas, S., Smees, R. and Boyd, B. (1998b) *Valuing Pupils' Views in Scottish Schools: Policy Paper No. 3*. London: Institute of Education and Glasgow: University of Strathclyde.

Thomas, S., Sammons, P., Mortimore, P. and Smees, R. (1997a) Differential secondary school effectiveness: examining the size, extent and consistency of school and departmental effects on GCSE outcomes for different groups of students over three years, *British Educational Research Journal*, 23 (4): 451–69.

Thomas, S., Sammons, P., Mortimore, P. and Smees, R. (1997b) Stability and consistency in secondary schools' effects on students' GCSE outcomes over 3 years, *School Effectiveness and School Improvement*, 8 (2): 169–97.

Thomas, S., Smees, R., MacBeath, J., Sammons, P. and Robertson, P. (1998) *Creating a value-added framework for Scottish schools: a policy paper*. Paper presented at the International Congress for School Effectiveness and Improvement, University of Manchester, January.

Thrupp, M. (1999) *Schools Making a Difference: Let's Be Realistic*. Buckingham: Open University Press.

Tibbitt, J. D., Spencer, E. and Hutchinson, C. (1994) Improving school effectiveness: policy and research in Scotland, *Scottish Educational Review*, 26(2): 151–57.

Toal, D. (1998) Expanding the qualitative knowledge base of the Improving School Effectiveness project. Paper presented at the Annual Conference of the British Educational Research Association, Queen's University of Belfast, 27–30 August.

Toal, D. and Robertson, P. (1998) Expanding the qualitative knowledge base of ISEP: building profiles of Scottish schools from teacher views. Paper presented at the Annual Conference of the British Educational Research Association, Queen's University, Belfast, August.

Townsend, T. (1994) Goals for effective schools: the view from the field, *School Effectiveness and School Improvement*, 5(2): 127–48.

Townsend, T., Clarke, P. and Ainscow, M. (1998) Third millennium schools: prospects and problems for school effectiveness and school improvement, in T. Townsend, P. Clarke and M. Ainscow (eds) *Third Millennium Schools: A World of Difference in Effectiveness and Improvement*. Lisse, the Netherlands: Swets and Zeitlinger.

Tymms, P. (1999) *Baseline Assessment and Monitoring in Primary Schools*. London: David Fulton.

Vaill, P. B. (1996) The purposing of high performance systems, in K. Starkey (ed.) *How Organisations Learn*. London: International Thomson Business Press.

Van Velzen, W. G., Miles, M. B. and Ekholm, M. (1985) *Making School Improvement Work*. Leuven: ACCO.

Victoria Office of Review (1997) *Improving the Performance of Schools: A Framework for School Improvement and Renewal*. Victoria: Office of Review, Department of Education.

Watkins, C. and Mortimore, P. (1999) Pedagogy: what do we know? in P. Mortimore (ed.) *Understanding Pedagogy and its Impact on Learning*. London: Paul Chapman.

Watkins, C., Carnell, E., Lodge, C. and Whalley, C. (1996) *Effective Learning. School Improvement Network Research Matters No 5*. London: Institute of Education.

White, J. (1997) Philosophical perspectives on school effectiveness and school improvement, in *Perspectives on School Effectiveness and School Improvement*, Bedford Way Papers. London: Institute of Education.

Wikely, F. (1998) Dissemination of research as a tool for school improvement?, *School Leadership and Management*, 18 (10): 59–73.

Willms, D. (1996) Verbal report to conference, Centre for Educational Sociology, University of Edinburgh, May.

Willms, J. D. (1985) The balance thesis – contextual effects of ability on pupils' 'O' grade examination results, *Oxford Review of Education*, 11 (1): 33–41.

Willms, J. D. (1986) Social class segregation and its relationship to pupils' examination results in Scotland, *American Sociological Review*, 51: 224–41.

Willms, J. D. (1997) Parental choice and education policy, *CES Briefing*, 12, August.

Willms, D. and Echols, F. (1992) Alert and inert clients: the Scottish experience of parental choice of schools, *Economics of Education Review*, 1: 339–50.

Willms, J. D. and Kerr, M. (1987) Changes in sex differences in school examination results since 1975, *Journal of Early Adolescence*, June.

Willms, J. D. and Raudenbusch, S. W. (1989) A longitudinal hierarchical linear model for estimating school effects and their stability, *Journal of Educational Measurement*, 26 (3): 209–32.

Winch, C. (1997) Accountability, controversy and school effectiveness research, in *Perspectives on School Effectiveness and School Improvement*, Bedford Way Papers. London: Institute of Education.

Woodhead, C. (1998) What makes a good teacher? *Parliamentary Brief*, 31.

Woods, P., Jeffrey, B., Troman, G. and Boyle, M. (1997) *Restructuring Schools, Reconstructing Teachers*. Buckingham: Open University Press.

Wright, P. L. and Taylor, D. S. (1994) *Improving Leadership Performance: Interpersonal Skills for Effective Leadership*, 2nd ed. Hemel Hempstead: Prentice Hall International Ltd.

Wylie, T. (1999) School and beyond, in B. O'Hagan (ed.) *Modern Educational Myths*. London: Kogan Page.

Index